Promoting the Success of Individual Learners

Promoting the Success of Individual Learners

Teachers Applying Their Craft at the Undergraduate Level

Edited by Jeffrey E. Porter

BERGIN & GARVEY
Westport, Connecticut • London

Library of Congress Cataloging-in-Publication Data

Promoting the success of individual learners : teachers applying their craft at the undergraduate level / edited by Jeffrey E. Porter.
   p. cm.
Includes bibliographical references and index.
ISBN 0–89789–840–0 (alk. paper)
  1. Individualized instruction. 2. College teaching. 3. Education, Higher—Curricula.
1. Porter, Jeffrey Edward.
LB1031.P78 2002
  378.1'2—dc21   2002016484

British Library Cataloguing in Publication Data is available.

Library of Congress Catalog Card Number: 2002016484
ISBN: 0–89789–840–0

First published in 2002

Bergin & Garvey, 88 Post Road West, Westport, CT 06881
An imprint of Greenwood Publishing Group, Inc.
www.greenwood.com

Printed in the United States of America

∞™

The paper used in this book complies with the
Permanent Paper Standard issued by the National
Information Standards Organization (Z39.48–1984).

10 9 8 7 6 5 4 3 2 1

Copyright Acknowledgments

The editor and publisher gratefully acknowledge permission for use of the following material:

From *Selected Poems* by Mark Strand, copyright © 1979, 1980 by Mark Strand. Used by permission of Alfred A. Knopf, a division of Random House, Inc.

Excerpts from Gwendolyn Brooks. "The Boy Died in My Alley." In R. Ellman and R. O'Clair (Eds.), *The Norton Anthology of Modern Poetry* (2d ed., pp. 49–50). New York: W.W. Norton, 1988. Reprinted by permission of the Estate of Gwendolyn Brooks.

To Jim, Ev, Glenn, and Alissa for reminding me without fail, without knowing it, the person I aspire to be.

To Rosie, for the minutes and years of loving support, steadying balance, sustaining joy, and unearthly patience.

Contents

Preface

Undergraduate education wrestles with a growing challenge: how to support an increasingly diverse range of learners realize curricular goals and standards that in turn are tied to the ever-increasing demands of a rapidly changing world?

How do we, at the classroom level of teachers working with individual students, respond to this challenge? In the words of K. Patricia Cross, how do we simultaneously serve *all* students, as well as *each and every* student? This book explores the thoughts and actions of a sampling of skilled undergraduate teachers who are taking up this challenge. In doing so, it is intended to serve as a "practitioner resource" for undergraduate teachers in two ways. First, both general and specific teaching and assessment strategies for supporting individual learners within a variety of discipline contexts are offered. The book's goal, however, is more than providing a collection of pedagogical techniques. Just as important, contributing authors highlight those particular guiding assumptions about learning, the role and responsibilities of students, and their aims and responsibilities as teachers that give rise to and frame their instructional strategies. This is the second way the book serves as a resource. Readers are encouraged to engage the book not only for considering and perhaps adding to their repertoire of instructional strategies, but also for reviewing and reevaluating their own "theories-in-practice" regarding the challenge of supporting individual learners.

Chapters 1 to 4 serve as an introduction. Chapter 1 establishes three guiding premises: (1) the most meaningful criterion of excellence for undergraduate education is the "difference made" with individual students in realizing graduation goals and standards (i.e., the talent development model); (2) student diversity at the pragmatic level of teacher/student interaction means nothing less than the reality of learning differences among each and every student (beyond demographic categories and learning-style taxonomies); and (3) the intersection of the "difference made" criterion of educational excellence with the reality of individual differences underscores the importance of undergraduate teachers "individualizing" instructional approaches within their disciplines. These premises lead the way for the next three chapters.

Chapter 2 considers the nature of student learning in a classroom context. The active, constructive, and personal dimensions of learning are emphasized, as is the reality of individual differences and the importance of student engagement for productive learning. Chapter 3 takes up the meaning and implications of individualizing instruction, establishing individualizing instruction as the basis of effective instruction, beyond representing one instructional approach among many. A framework for individualizing instruction is presented, highlighting key variables and processes. Within this framework, Chapter 4 delineates some cross-disciplinary guidelines for individualizing instruction, based on research and skilled practice.

Chapters 5 to 12 provide discipline-based approaches to individualizing instruction. Within this introductory context, eight teachers, through their own voices and representing diverse disciplines and undergraduate institutions, contribute their ways of thinking and acting related to the challenge of individualizing instruction. The teachers were recruited and chosen based on their experience, skill, and passion in supporting the learning of individual students. The tone of their chapters is personal and informal, one of "teachers talking to teachers." No one model for conceptualizing learning differences or instructional approaches was imposed. To realize a measure of coherence among the individual chapters, yet capitalize on the richness of their diversity, contributing authors were asked to address a common set of issues. These issues relate both to their guiding assumptions and the instructional strategies that flow from them in supporting the success of individual learners: (1) how they view the roles of teacher and student, as shaped by their conceptions of learning and the intellectual demands of their disciplines; (2) implications of these views for supporting the academic success of individual learners, both in terms of general classroom approach and specific instructional techniques; (3) their processes of instructional problem-solving in supporting the learning of individual students; (4) strategies for helping students become more proficient learners and accepting responsibility for their own learning; and (5) strategies for using instructional technologies in individualizing instruction. Each chapter has sections on setting and personal background, guiding assumptions about learning and teaching, and approaches and techniques for individualizing instruction.

The culminating chapter provides a recapitulation of the book's introductory framework. It synthesizes the salient, cross-discipline insights on individualizing instruction generated by the contributing authors, providing some sample practices where appropriate. The significance of these insights for needed changes in undergraduate education's current culture in better supporting efforts to individualize instruction is analyzed.

Teaching is a difficult, humbling endeavor. Teachers typically conclude their work with students at the end of a course with as many (if not more) feelings of "missed connections" and "failed opportunities" as "successful partnerships" and "potentials realized." We need to unburden ourselves a bit by appreciating what we can and cannot control. We too easily view ourselves as somehow directly responsible for student learning. From this premise, it is a short step to viewing ourselves as responsible for the learning successes and failures of students. We are not, and the premise is warped to start with.

Learning, like any other human action, has its source in the agent, the learner. As the source of learning, the learner also has the responsibility for whether or not, and how, learning ultimately happens. We each are responsible for our own learning. The special, timeless relationship between teachers and students does not locate responsibility for learning with the teacher, nor should we presumptuously claim it. Our responsibility as teachers within this relationship is nothing more, and nothing less, than doing whatever it takes to *support* students in learning optimally for themselves.

A reality underlying the teacher–student relationship, too often denied within an undergraduate culture that makes too many competing demands on teachers, is that different students learn differently. An instructional approach effectively supporting and extending one student's learning will not do so for another. Acknowledging this reality, and suggesting some philosophical and practical approaches for making peace with it, is the purpose of this book.

So, if our nature as teachers dooms us to kick ourselves at course's end as we tally final grades, let it not be for failed learning. That is an outcome for students to contemplate. Let it be instead for instructional problem solving not yet quite up to the task (as if it ever will be) of finding enough different ways of supporting enough different students in realizing their own more effective ways of learning. And let such self-castigation channel itself into more inspired, reflective, and effective instructional problem solving next time around.

Efforts to individualize instruction, to support and extend the academic success of each individual student, claim enormous focus, time, and energy on the part of undergraduate teachers; personal investments that may be out of step with one's particular campus culture of priorities and incentives. Further, given the complexity of the learning/teaching enterprise and, ultimately, the lack of control one person has over another's learning, these efforts are guaranteed *not* to be successful all the time (on some days, most of the time). Against these cold realities, the competing rationale for proposing individualizing instruction as the basis of effective instruction is this: The appropriate perspective for judging the worth of individualizing instruction is not one grounded in day-to-day realities of success and failure. Instead, individualizing instruction is best judged as an educational ideal, one defining what learning means, what we as educators and educational programs should be about, and how we should regard excellence.

This book would not exist without the investments of the contributing authors. It is their assumptions about the meaning of learning and teaching, their passion about the promise of their students, and their skills in recreating learning/teaching transactions to better support and extend the success of individual students that this book attempts to capture for the rest of us to consider.

I am deeply grateful for the overall support of my college, the National Technical Institute for the Deaf within the Rochester Institute of Technology, and of my colleagues in pursuing this project. Specific thanks go to Susan Ciriello, Katrina Evringham, Alan Hurwitz, Mary Jo Ingraham, Jonathan Millis and Rosemarie Seewagen. Geof Garvey as copy editor showed the way with careful reading and clear thinking. Finally, I thank Jon Fife for his initial encouragement in seeing the value of this project and urging me to make it happen.

PART I

INTRODUCTION

Chapter 1

Developing Talent Through Individualizing Instruction

Jeffrey E. Porter

Like a "last stop for gas" before entering the socioeconomic superhighway, the role of undergraduate education in this country has become that of fueling individuals with the competencies and certification necessary for productive citizenship. At the same time, the number of individuals seeking access to this crucial resource and the diversity of their personal backgrounds, life circumstances, and educational goals is without precedent. Undergraduate education strains to fulfill its pivotal role in the face of this increasing diversity.

Reflecting this strain, a familiar issue haunts undergraduate education and ultimately our nation. Can undergraduate education more fully transcend its historical function of filter, a function serving to exacerbate the ever-widening socioeconomic gap between the haves and the have nots? Can it instead more fully realize the function of bridge, providing access and effective support for individuals who in the past would have been cut off from the socioeconomic mainstream?

A big part of the answer in realizing the transformation from filter to bridge lies in the realm of social policy and political consensus. Will affirmative action efforts to broaden access to undergraduate education for individuals historically excluded based on race be maintained, altered to focus on characteristics other than race, or abandoned completely? Will the role of standardized tests in admission decisions, even with their documented bias against certain demographic groups, become more or less dominant? Will the costs of undergraduate education become the determining factor in who goes to college and who doesn't? In today's political climate, the outcome of such issues remains unclear.

An equally big part in meeting this transformation lies in the realm of educational values and practice, beyond social policy and politics. It has to do with the basic issue of institutional commitment and daily practices in the undergraduate community for supporting individual students in realizing academic success. While maintaining common curricular outcomes and standards for all, can we in undergraduate education move beyond our traditional approach of defining narrowly the acceptable ways of learning and teaching? Can we instead create a more inclusive approach, one supporting academic success for all kinds of learners through crafting alternative learning/teaching paths leading to common outcomes and standards?

Within this realm of educational values and practice, what are some of the needed changes that will enable undergraduate education to become more a bridge and less a filter? This chapter takes up this question. It endorses a well-known model of educational excellence for guiding undergraduate education into the future. Further, it points to an attitude of reflective teaching and an approach of individualizing instruction for responding simultaneously to the endless diversity among individual learners and the common curricular goals and standards defining graduation requirements.

THE ROLE AND CHALLENGE OF UNDERGRADUATE EDUCATION

Soaring hopes and heavy expectations historically have confronted undergraduate education. The defining purposes of undergraduate education underlying this confrontation are an interesting mix of idealism and pragmatism (Bowen, 1977; Boyer, 1987; Knox, Lindsay, & Kolb, 1993). On the one hand undergraduate education aims at nothing less than facilitating lifelong learning and the pursuit of intellectual, moral, and aesthetic fulfillment. On the other, it focuses on the short-term development and certification of skills and knowledge needed for entry into the technical/professional work force and socioeconomic mainstream. Undergraduate education's mission encompasses both the promise of human fulfillment and the necessity of economic utility. It is both a liberating vehicle for personal development and one of the few institutional means available for narrowing our growing socioeconomic gap between the haves and have nots (Gardner, 1999).

Graduating from college long has been recognized as conferring special socioeconomic status (Riesman and Jencks, 1968). Over a decade ago, Pascarella and Terenzini (1991) characterized the baccalaureate degree as "typically the single most important educational rung on the socioeconomic attainment ladder" (p. 575). This characterization is even truer today (Challenger, 2000; Gumport, Iannozzi, Sharman, & Zemsky, 1997; Knox et al., 1993). It certifies the graduate as ready to become a player in our highly dynamic socioeconomic system. In today's sharply divided socioeconomic landscape, there are viable jobs and careers for individuals who are highly skilled and well educated and little demand for those who are not (Wadsworth, 1995). Most every sector of our economy requires workers with competencies beyond those acquired in high school (Kuh, 2001). Being a college graduate means you are poised to merge with the high-speed traffic zooming along the socioeconomic superhighway. Not being one means you cannot even find the on ramp.

This importance of an undergraduate degree as a socioeconomic passport is widely recognized. A 1993 poll (Edgerton, 1993a) showed that 88% of Americans no longer believed a high school diploma was enough to qualify for well-paying jobs, with 73% believing a college degree was instrumental for career advancement.

From today's perspective, such beliefs are well grounded. As chronicled by Carnevale and Desrochers (2001), today's employers typically apply a college degree as a critical standard in screening job applicants. Attaining more formal education not only means greater access to jobs that provide more opportunities for ongoing training and development but greater access to jobs that use technological applications to enhance rather than replace employee skills. Employees with postsecondary education, even when working in fields outside their baccalaureate majors, demonstrate general skills (such as communication, problem solving, and interpersonal skills) that make them more productive than coworkers in the same jobs with less formal education. Further, research shows that, other things being equal, an associate degree adds 20 to 30% to the wages earned with a high school degree. A baccalaureate degree adds another 10–20% boost in wages over an associate degree. The earnings advantage of college-educated employees over high school graduates in 1979 was 36% for men and 34% for women. In 1997, this advantage was 67% for men and 72 % for women. Clearly, the earnings gap between individuals with a high school education only and those who graduate from college is growing (Reich, 2000).

As the demands of our increasingly technological, knowledge-based economy have increased, so too have the educational attainments of workers. In 1973 only 16% of workers between the ages of 30 and 59 had baccalaureate or advanced degrees. In 1998 that percentage was 30% (Carnevale & Desrochers, 2001). Further, those sectors of the economy requiring the most educated employees are growing the fastest (Blandin, 1994; Carnevale & Desrochers; Hughes, Frances, & Lombardo, 1991).

Our inexorable press towards improving the material quality of life, part of our social fabric, has spurred an economic vitality requiring continually up-grading skills and certification in response to an ever-changing world. Re-sponding to this pressure, a massive system of higher education has evolved through state, federal, and private funding (Orfield, 1993), now comprising more than 3,800 institutions ranging from community colleges to research in-stitutions and representing a $225 billion enterprise (Landscape, 2001). Trow (1989) proposes two related elements as shaping this evolution, diversity and market forces. Institutions of higher education are tremendously diverse in their missions, constituency base, and services provided to the greater commu-nity. At the same time, reflecting and feeding off this diversity, higher educa-tion institutions are driven by market forces, dependent on enrollment levels for fiscal solvency and competing with one another to identify and establish those programs and services most desirable in the eyes of students, employers of graduates, and donors.

The overall success of our system of undergraduate education is remark-able. Other countries send their best students to the U.S. for a university edu-cation. The incredible diversity of our institutions, responding to distinctive missions serving diverse constituencies, is unique in the world.

A third element also has guided higher education's evolution. This is the principle, reflecting the push of democratic ideals and the pull of market forces and global competition, that a college education should be as accessible as pos-sible for as many citizens as possible (Bowen, 1977). The principle of universal access has become a powerful symbol of our nation's commitment to enlight-ened democratic participation and equal socioeconomic opportunity for all (McPherson & Schapiro, 1995).

We have made significant progress in realizing this ideal (Bok, 1992). Be-fore World War II, only a small minority of U.S. citizens (mostly male and white) attended college. Triggered by the G.I. Bill of Rights, higher education experienced unprecedented growth in the number of enrolled students, a phe-nomenon termed "massification" by Gumport et al. (1997). Since World War II, undergraduate education has become a socioeconomic gatekeeper for all manner of skilled jobs and professional occupations. In 1940, 1.5 million peo-ple were enrolled in some sector of higher education; by 1990 the number was 14 million (Kerr, 1994). The number is projected to be almost 18 million by 2011 (National Center for Education Statistics, 2001). Over the last fifty years, higher education has transformed itself dramatically, from a social insti-tution founded to educate the elite to one endeavoring to educate the masses.

As part of higher education's massification, not only did the number of people attending college increase, but their diversity did as well. As traced by Gumport et al. (1997) the growing diversity was generated by governmental student financial aid programs in the 1960s and early 1970s, coupled with the civil-rights movement during the late 1960s. In 1964, for example, less than 10% of African Americans attended college; by 1976 their attendance rate had increased to just over 20%.

From the mid-1970s into the 1990s, even as rapid growth in the number of people enrolled in higher education slowed somewhat, the diversity of those entering continued to increase (Gumport et al., 1997). The age and enrollment status of the "typical" college student shifted throughout this time. By 1990 the majority of students in higher education were 22 years old and older, with an increasing proportion of students (close to 40%) enrolled part-time (although these trends in age and enrollment status are expected to reverse in the coming decade) (National Center for Education Statistics, 2000a; National Center for Education Statistics, 2000b). Likewise, enrollment of students from minority backgrounds (African-Americans, Hispanics, Asians/Pacific Islanders, American Indians/Alaskan Native) increased from 17% of all undergraduate students in 1976 to 26% in the fall of 1995 (National Center for Education Statistics, 2000a). According to McPherson and Schapiro (1999), current rates of high school graduates who enroll in college are at record levels for whites, African-American, Hispanics, and Asian/Pacific Islanders. More women attend undergraduate education than men, with the enrollment rate for women over the next decade projected to increase faster than for men (National Center on Education Statistics, 2000a). True to the ideal of universal access, undergraduate education's doors are opening wider and wider. Even though enrollment rates for groups of individuals throughout society are at record levels, however, have they increased in equal proportion across the societal spectrum? Then, beyond merely entering college, what about graduating?

BRIDGE OR FILTER

As noted earlier, ongoing technological innovation and the expansion of our knowledge-based economy continually generate demand for more highly educated workers. New jobs require increasingly advanced math, science, and literacy skills (Justiz, 1994), with a premium placed on problem solving and adapting to unforeseen problems rather than reproducing inert facts and applying practiced procedures no longer relevant to changing conditions (Halpern & Associates, 1994; McPherson & Schapiro, 1995; Reich, 2001).

Moreover, as Hughes et al. (1991) show, dynamics within our evolving economy influence long-term career fluidity beyond entry-level jobs. Constant workforce dislocations, reflecting such now-familiar workplace terms as downsizing and rightsizing, result in increased worker mobility and multiple career changes. This in turn leads to a growing need for continuing education by displaced workers, with higher education more and more expected to fill this need. In today's world, higher education is called upon to replace its historic function of providing a culminating education for young people on the brink of adulthood with the extended function of providing lifelong education for individuals of all ages navigating the turbulent waters of changing economies and discontinuous careers.

Clearly, undergraduate education, beyond fostering those skills and sensibilities important for lifelong learning and fulfillment, plays a vital role in equipping individuals with the competencies and certification necessary for joining the socioeconomic mainstream and prospering within it. There is growing concern, however, about undergraduate education's ability to satisfy this role equally well across the societal spectrum of individual and group differences (Astin, 1985; Knox et al., 1993). Far from bridging our national gap between the haves and have nots, undergraduate education may be serving to perpetuate, even widen, it.

In this context, several emerging realities loom large. The first, referenced earlier, is the growing earnings gap between those with only a high school education and those who go on to graduate from college. The second is the decline of those sectors of the economy requiring only a high school education and the increase of those sectors requiring a college education or more (Gumport et al., 1977; McPherson & Schapiro, 1995). Against these disturbing trends, a third is taking place. As noted earlier (McPherson & Shapiro, 1999), college enrollment rates for whites and various minority groups are at all-time highs. It is important to acknowledge, however, the longstanding discrepancies among these rates that continue to grow. During the 1970s, the enrollment rate for whites in higher education was roughly 5 percentage points higher than the rate for African-Americans and 3 percentage points higher than that for Hispanics. These discrepancies continued to widen through the 1980s. By late 1990s, the enrollment rate for whites was 10 percentage points higher than for African-Americans and 8 percentage points higher than for Hispanics.

Further, only 55 to 60% of all first-time entrants to two-year and four-year college programs eventually earn a degree of any sort (Gumport et al., 1997; Tinto, 1987). The filter metaphor is disturbingly real; worse, it is selective. In 1971 the percentage of whites between the ages of 25 and 29 who had completed high school and had earned with a bachelor's degree or above was roughly 11 percentage points higher than that for African-Americans and roughly 12 percentage points higher that for Hispanics. By 1999 the discrepancy between white and African-Americans was roughly 19 percentage points and roughly 22 percentage points between whites and Hispanics. These gaps widened even as the parallel discrepancy in high school completion rates closed dramatically (at least between whites and African-Americans) (National Center for Education Statistics, 2000a).

Capturing this same reality from a different perspective, 53% of all students who enrolled in four-year institutions in the fall of 1989 had achieved their baccalaureate degree by the spring of 1994. For whites, the percentage was 54%; for African-Americans, Hispanics, and Asian/Pacific Islanders, it was 42%, 47%, and 63% respectively. For this same pool of students, 24% of all students had achieved no degree by the spring of 1994 and were no longer enrolled. For whites, the percentage was 24%; for African-Americans, Hispanics, and Asian/Pacific Islanders, it was 28%, 28%, and 14% respectively (National Center for Education Statistics, 2000b). Further, selective filtering occurs not just in terms of racial/ethnic categories. For this same student pool, 49% of students from the lowest SES level, 33% who were first-generation college students, and 53% percent who had started college between the ages of 20 and 29 failed to earn the baccalaureate degree and were no longer enrolled in the spring of 1994. In comparison, the rates were 19% for students from the highest SES level, 17% for those whose parents held baccalaureate degrees or higher, and 20% for those who started college at age 18 (National Center for Education Statistics, 2000b).

With regard to current status, using U.S. Census Bureau data from March 2000, 17% of all adults age 25 and older hold a baccalaureate degree. For whites, African-Americans, Hispanics, and Asian/Pacific Islanders, the figures are approximately 19%, 12%, 7%, and 29% respectively (Chronicle of Higher Education, 2001).

From such data, it is clear that undergraduate education is a long way from transforming itself into a bridge, effectively supporting individuals from diverse backgrounds. Instead, it appears to serve more as a filter, particularly for those deviating from traditional norms. Strong consensus has existed for some time that finding ways to support the successful graduation of more students, both in general and for specific subgroups, remains a critical challenge for undergraduate education (Smith, 1989). Yes, undergraduate education's doors have been opening wider. For many students, however, they are revolving doors (Gumport et al., 1997), with the width of the opening varying with the characteristics of individual students.

Undergraduate education has an unenviable record of failing to engage and support effectively students from nontraditional backgrounds. In accounting for this failure, it too easily has relied on student shortcomings rather than the limitations of its own traditions (Gordon, 1999). Undergraduate education's emphasis over the last fifty years on access for diverse members of society needs serious rebalancing with equal emphasis on supporting the academic success of students once enrolled (Bok, 1992; Edgerton, 1993b).

Traditional instructional approaches applied as if students are the same and learn in the same way cannot be widely successful. In instructional approach, I include both teaching (i.e., establishing curricular goals and analyzing the short-term learning outcomes leading to these goals; designing and sequencing learning tasks in light of expected learning outcomes; and implementing learning tasks through teaching strategies that foster student engagement), and assessment as embedded in teaching (i.e., assessing those pertinent learning characteristics and strategies of individual students that have implications for teaching, monitoring the nature and quality of ongoing learning, and evaluating the degree to which students realize target goals). Academic success is fostered when skilled teachers focus on the learning characteristics and strategies of individual learners, adapting their instructional approaches to support student accomplishment of curricular objectives and standards. Academic success can suffer when there is incongruity between the learning characteristics and strategies of students and the instructional approaches chosen by teachers (Noel, 1987; Tinto, 1987).

Unfortunately, the culture of undergraduate education often devalues efforts to support the academic success of individual students (Gardner, 1999). Rewards and perquisites tend to flow to faculty who spend time and get results with scholarship and grants (rather than with students) and demonstrate outstanding skills in publication (rather than in supporting student learning) (Bok, 1992; Fairweather, 1993). According to data from the fall of 1992, at both higher education institutions granting doctorates and those that do not, the percentages of full-time instructional faculty who taught any undergraduate classes and those who taught such classes exclusively declined as their academic rank increased (National Center on Education Statistics, 2000a).

Such a culture has contributed in recent years to an erosion of public trust in undergraduate education. Since the early 1990s, the calls for greater accountability regarding institutional and faculty efforts in supporting student success and the questions about the overall costs and benefits of the undergraduate experience have been increasing (Bok, 1992; Edgerton, 1993c; Ewell, 1991; Fram & Camp, 1995; Gardner, 1999; Gumport & Pusser, 1997; Lazerson, Wagener, & Shumanis, 1999; Pascarella & Terenzini, 1991; Plater, 1995). Undergraduate educators reply with wide-ranging explanations of inadequate funding leading to overcrowded or unavailable courses, outdated facilities, and too little investment in innovative teaching/learning technologies. Students who are academically underprepared and educationally unmotivated are often cited as other factors, as are faculty who have a diminished focus on effective teaching because of the competing demands of research and service and a society that preaches the importance of education for fulfilling our collective destiny while bestowing its rewards on athletes, entertainers, and lottery winners.

These explanations possess kernels of truth, but they overlook a more fundamental issue; the definition of educational excellence that undergraduate education holds itself to and to which it is held by others. How does undergraduate education, or any enterprise, move toward excellence and gauge its progress if what it means to be excellent is vaguely or variously defined? When consensus about the meaning of excellence is elusive, agreement over what the obstacles are, how to overcome them, and which benchmarks to use in assessing progress likewise remains elusive. For undergraduate education to gain public trust, an agreed-upon model of excellence must exist. Unfortunately, it does not.

ALTERNATIVE MODELS OF EDUCATIONAL EXCELLENCE

No single model of excellence commands widespread endorsement throughout contemporary undergraduate education. Almost twenty years ago, Astin (1985) identified alternative models for defining excellence at the undergraduate level, each with its own supporting assumptions and criteria for judging relative effectiveness. Astin's analysis still fits today's landscape. The ongoing relevance of Astin's models is testimony to the fundamental and enduring differences within undergraduate education's various stakeholders (students, faculty, trustees, parents, taxpayers, legislatures) in how each interprets educational excellence. These differences guarantee divergent conclusions about how well the job is being done and what, if any, improvements are necessary.

Astin's analysis identifies four traditional models of undergraduate excellence:

1. Resource-based. When ample amounts of the right kinds of educational resources (e.g., highly paid faculty, academically talented students, well-equipped labs and libraries, modern buildings) come together, excellent education for students occurs. Educational excellence boils down to having a lot of the right kind of resources. Moving toward excellence therefore requires acquiring more resources, whether through recruiting faculty "stars," raising admission standards to screen out less talented students, or increasing the endowment. Institutions having more of the right kind of resources are closer to achieving excellence than those that do not.

2. Content-based. Educational excellence consists of student exposure to the correct subject matter. Undergraduate institutions possessing comprehensive, state-of-the-art curricula (or depending on your view, curricula rooted in the classics) are institutions best approximating excellence. This is particularly true for institutions that focus on curricula representing more prestigious disciplines (sciences and engineering, for example). Approaching excellence requires improving the quality of the institution's curriculum (and perhaps replacing majors in education and business management with majors in information technology).

3. Outcome-based. The educational excellence of an undergraduate program is determined by the success of its graduates, as represented by such measures as the percentage of students continuing to graduate school, average scores of graduating seniors on standardized tests, or the career achievements of alumni. Those programs with graduates scoring higher on such measures are closer to excellence than those with graduates scoring lower. The most direct means of improvement is to restrict admissions to more talented students from well-connected backgrounds.

4. Reputation-based. Everyone knows which undergraduate institutions are excellent and which are not, because everyone taps into the same sources of conventional wisdom: high school guidance offices, faculty clubs, family gatherings, and annual rankings in weekly news magazines. If you want an excellent education, go to Ivy University (if you can get in); steer clear of State College (even if it has the major you want at half the price). To appear excellent is to be excellent. This in turn means working to fashion conventional wisdom; aligning your school more closely in the popular press and on people's tongues with more prestigious institutions while distancing it from more mundane ones.

As Astin notes, unpacking these alternative models of excellence highlights some important issues. One is that the models tend to be interrelated in a self-perpetuating cycle. Undergraduate institutions with the most resources and most prestigious curricula typically are those that enjoy the best reputation and claim the most successful alumni, which in turn generates more resources, enables more curricular advancement, and attracts more highly skilled faculty and students. Institutions outside this cycle have a difficult time breaking in.

The other issue is more fundamental. None of the models, singularly or combined, convincingly captures the heart of educational excellence in terms of the actual learning of students. Each model is a partial representation, perhaps highlighting an aspect but failing to capture the essence. The resource-based model accounts for what an institution possesses, the content-based model documents curricular focus, the outcome-based model measures achievements of graduates, and the reputation-based model mirrors public perception. None of the models centers on the actual educational gains of students as a consequence of their undergraduate experience.

As Astin (1985) and Pascarella and Terenzini (1991) have emphasized, resources, curricula, and reputation do not inevitably translate into student learning, nor do student outcomes necessarily signify program effectiveness (high-scoring graduates might have scored just as high without ever having enrolled). Ultimately, how well an undergraduate program approximates educational excellence needs to be gauged in terms of the incremental difference in student learning in light of curricular goals and standards. Instructional quality, nature of interaction among teachers and students, intensity of academic experiences, and level of student engagement with learning experiences are much more important signifiers of educational excellence than institutional reputation, selectivity, or resources (Pascarella, 2001). From this perspective, the excellence of an undergraduate program depends less on which students are admitted and more on what is done in supporting student success once enrolled (Astin, 1990; Weingartner, 1994). The essential criterion for gauging educational excellence becomes: Given the competencies required for admission, how effectively does an undergraduate program support individual students in developing the competencies required for graduation?

Talent Development Model of Excellence

Astin (1985) calls this alternative view of educational excellence the talent development model. It is the model endorsed by this book. Applying it to undergraduate education, the measure of excellence becomes the extent to which each and every enrolled student successfully realizes the curricular competencies established for graduation. To the extent this "difference made" criterion is realized in practice, the undergraduate program approaches excellence. To the extent it is not, the program falls short of excellence, regardless of its relative status in resources, curriculum, alumni, or prestige. Approaching excellence according to this model, simply yet profoundly, translates into creating more instructional alternatives for supporting the academic success and eventual graduation of more enrolled students.

The talent development model of educational excellence is a guiding premise for this book, and so it is important to flesh out some of its implications. One is that an undergraduate program doubtlessly is better able to approach educational excellence when it has outstanding, rather than mediocre, resources and curricula (to choose key attributes from other models of excellence). The issue, however, is that these attributes by themselves do not signify educational excellence. Instead, an undergraduate program approaches excellence only when resources and curricula are effectively mobilized through actual teaching/learning interactions to support student accomplishment (Astin, 1987). The resources and curricula of an undergraduate program, and how it mobilizes them to support student success, are two different things. As we know too well in undergraduate education, the latter does not necessarily flow from the former.

Further, it is important to acknowledge that, from the talent development perspective, no undergraduate program ever fully realizes excellence. Educational excellence is an ideal, not an attainable reality. There are and always will be many individual students who, for whatever reasons, fail to achieve graduation competencies, no matter how skilled or motivated they be, or how collectively supportive and innovative their teachers and educational community. The issue is not the inherent impossibility of fully realizing excellence, but the criterion we choose to measure progress. The point echoes throughout this book. Using the talent development model, the essence of educational excellence is not ivy-covered walls, selective admissions, high tuition, famous alumni, or international scholars (Haworth & Conrad, 1997). Instead, simply and profoundly, it is the difference made in supporting individual students, wherever they begin upon admission, in achieving whatever competencies are established for graduation.

Finally, educational excellence in terms of talent development establishes some key premises about the meaning of learning and teaching:

- The sole reason for teaching is to promote student learning in light of established curricular goals and standards. Without this link to student learning, teaching is without meaning. No other rationale for it exists, not as a pulpit for personal views, a means of ego gratification, or a necessary filler activity balancing out the opportunity to pursue scholarly interests.

- Faculty expertise and program resources are allocated first and foremost to creating alternative ways for supporting individual students in realizing the target competencies established by the curriculum, not to enhancing institutional prestige, building scholarly reputation, or serving administrative convenience (Astin, 1985; Pascarella & Terenzini, 1991; Shuell, 1986).

- Assessing students primarily serves learning and teaching activities such as figuring out better instructional approaches for individual students and gauging attainment of target competencies, not bureaucratic tasks such as student sorting and labeling (Astin, 1990; Astin, 1999).

- The reasons for success and failure in achieving learning outcomes are framed in terms of the interaction between the student and the instructional setting (as created by the teacher), rather than strictly in terms of dynamics within the student (Coles, 1987; Porter, 1994).

- Educating students with histories of low or average achievement is of no less value than educating students with records of high achievement. What matters is supporting the academic success and graduation of all students able to benefit from an undergraduate education and doing so in ways that acknowledge and act on the reality that individual students benefit from alternative instructional approaches in accomplishing course and graduation requirements (Astin, 1985; Cross, 1987).

LEARNER DIVERSITY AND REFLECTIVE TEACHING

As earlier noted, colleges are places of increasing differences among students. More and more, students participating in undergraduate education represent those who are economically disadvantaged, academically underprepared, older, part-time, from other countries, of diverse ethnic or cultural backgrounds or are characterized as disabled (Hughes et al., 1991; Landscape, 1993; Magolda & Terenzini, n.d.; Wagener, 1989).

It is important to emphasize, however, that students differ as individuals, not as groups (Wang, 1991). Demographic categories only crudely capture diversity among undergraduate students as it affects actual teaching/learning dynamics and academic success. At a more refined level, Claxton and Murrel (1987) summarize theoretical models and empirical findings describing more than 15 learning styles characterizing college students. Claxton and Murrel define learning styles as ways of "perceiving, interacting with, and responding to the learning environment" (p. 71). They view learning styles as reflecting differences along a variety of dimensions (e.g., personality, information processing, organization and depth of existing knowledge, social interaction style, motivation).

The use of learning styles beyond demographic variables to characterize student diversity is significant in that it addresses, at least theoretically and in some cases empirically, the core issue of how individual students learn. This level of analysis in turn potentially provides guidance for teachers trying to decide which instructional approaches make sense for which students in supporting their achievement of the curricular goals under consideration.

Caution, even humility, is needed however in teasing out the implications of student differences for instructional decisions, even when differences are framed in terms of learning styles instead of demographic categories. Each student's way of learning represents a complex and unique mix of learning characteristics and strategies, shaped by that student's nervous system and personal history and interacting with the learning task and instructional approach of the moment. While we share a multitude of characteristics with our fellow humans, each of us (even identical twins) is interestingly unique from every other member of the human species (and from the way we were five years ago and five days hence!) (Gardner, 2001).

No two students are precisely alike in their learning characteristics and strategies, in how they receive, process, and make meaning of new information; in the organization and level of their current knowledge and competencies with respect to curriculum goals; in how they access their existing knowledge and competencies in integrating new content; in how they apply new learning to the task at hand and make refinements based on feedback from such application; in how they experience purpose in making the effort (or not) to learn; in how they monitor and revise their learning strategies during task engagement; and in how they evaluate the significance of the learning experience upon completion. To further complicate the picture, but also to make it more real, the specifics composing an individual's "constellation" of learning characteristics and strategies can change with the nature of the learning task and the demands and supports of the instructional context (Pintrich, 1988; Snow, 1978).

The learning characteristics and strategies of a particular student cannot be inferred from the demographic category applied to that student. There is not one homogeneous set of learning characteristics and strategies uniquely describing male students, a second characterizing Hispanic students, and a third applicable to students labeled as having a learning disability. Just as clearly, adequate representation of a particular student's engagement in a particular learning task cannot be captured by any one learning style model (Davis, 1993). The uniqueness and complexity of each and every learner, and the implications of this reality for instruction, defies meaningful taxonomic representation.

As Corno and Snow (1986) underscore, considerable overlap exists in practice among learning style models put forth as conceptually discrete. Further, the validity and reliability of many learner style assessment instruments are suspect (Fincher, 1985; Grasha, 1990; Wang, 1991). Their use too often results in viewing students as representing discrete categories within contrived frameworks without convincing connection between the assigned category and the "instructional approach of choice." Recognizing these problems, Grasha emphasizes the need for assessing learning differences among students and analyzing their instructional implications in ways grounded naturally in the daily experiences and interactions of learners and teachers. This "grounded approach" should at least complement the use of paper-and-pencil learning style measures, applied "out of context" from actual learning tasks and derived from preconceived theoretical frameworks.

Whether used singularly or in combination, current learning style constructs help illuminate, but do not do justice to, the daily complexities teachers face in pursuing common curricular goals and standards while accommodating the endless variety of learning differences among students. These constructs are useful in the conceptual realm of generalities about the various ways learning can happen and the various instructional approaches that might support such variety. They are less helpful, however, in informing the practical realm of teachers attempting to support this or that student trying to realize this or that learning outcome. For any given learning task within any particular instructional approach, students exhibit tremendous learning variation, variation only crudely and partially captured by demographic categories and learning style taxonomies. In the day-to-day practice of teaching and learning, theoretical frameworks establishing discrete categories of students or kinds of learning styles are swamped by actual variation among unique learners. The comforting fiction of the typical student fades quickly against the reality of the individual student. Undergraduate teachers cannot aim for the "middle" of the class when the "middle" doesn't exist (Clark, 1981).

The challenge for teachers in supporting the academic success of individual students is to consider, but see beyond, demographic indicators and learning style profiles. It is to come to know each student as a unique learner. It is divining, through artistry, plain old trial and error, ongoing partnerships and dialogue with students, insights passed along by colleagues, and the incorporation of pertinent research findings, those individual learning characteristics and strategies having the most significance for developing supportive instructional approaches (Amundsen, Gryspeerdt, & Moxness, 1993; Claxton & Murrel, 1987; Sherman, Armistead, Fowler, Barksdale & Reif, 1987; Shuell, 1986). It is becoming a "pedagogical researcher" (Plater, 1995), building on the outcomes and insights from past teaching/learning experiences in assessing and improving future instructional practice. It is viewing learner diversity in the context of common goals and standards not as a problem, but as a source of pedagogical innovation and educational enrichment (Smith, 1989). It is reflective teaching.

Supporting the academic success of individual students is a daunting challenge for teachers. It also is a generative one; particularly when approached from the perspective of "teacher as reflective practitioner" (Schon, 1983). It is generative in that what teachers come to know about supporting individual learners evolves from their own history of experimentation, reflection, and learning (Amundsen et al., 1993). As opposed to "teacher as technical production manager," seeking to maximize the average yield across large numbers of students, reflective teaching entails "teacher as problem solver," seeking to maximize the learning of each individual student (Lampert, 1985). Using Lampert's distinction, the reflective teacher works collaboratively with students as unique learners, creatively blending research findings, hunches, and personal experience in making instructional choices that help support successful learning. Reflective teachers gather feedback from the students they support, reflect on their expectations, beliefs, and values in setting goals and standards, and experiment with new ways of designing instructional approaches to support student success (Menges, 1991). All this within real-world settings where flawlessly (or even adequately) supporting the learning of each student every time is impossible, yet endures as the guiding criterion of educational excellence.

Research findings over the years consistently demonstrate that one best teaching or assessment technique for all students does not exist (Anderson, 2001; Davis, 1993; Dubin & Taveggia, 1968; Prégent, 1994; Siegel & Shaughnessy, 1994). Further, although findings from scientific research can greatly assist reflective instructional problem solving in figuring out better ways for supporting the learning of this or that student, such problem solving ultimately is beyond scientific prescription. Not only does science lose potency in explaining reality as it moves along the continuum of human experience from neurosensory processes to perceptual interpretations to guiding beliefs. It also loses potency when moving along the continuum of individuality, from group averages to unique personal experiences. When it comes to an individual student with a particular personal history living in a particular culture wrestling with a particular learning task, science's foreseeable future holds exciting promise for increasingly precise predictions about that student's neurosensory, perceptual, and memory processes. Most likely it will remain limited to informed speculation, however, about that same student's sophisticated cognitive and motivational processes and personal experience of learning and how best to support it (Gardner, 2001).

The effectiveness of any particular instructional approach chosen or developed by a teacher depends on a great many factors, chief among them the guiding curricular objectives, the content and design of the learning task, and the learning characteristics and strategies of the student. As portrayed by Shulman (1987a, 1987b), the teachers most skilled in their craft are those most reflective in monitoring and responding to both the difficulty and the nature of the learning task and the characteristics and strategies of the individual learner, all within the context of the guiding educational purpose. Including guiding purpose in this formulation is important, because reflective teaching means not only rethinking issues of "instructional means to ends," but the appropriateness of the "instructional ends," that is, what is worth learning in the first place (Paulsen & Feldman, 1995).

Reflective teaching also means assumption hunting (Brookfield, 1995), fleshing out and making explicit one's implicit theories and personal orientations about the meaning of learning and the related roles of student and teacher. Implicit assumptions made explicit become vehicles, in creative combination with pedagogical theory, research findings, past experience, intuitive hunches, collegial consultation, and student partnership, for supporting the educational progress of individual learners (McCombs & Whisler, 1997). Teaching that supports the learning of individual students ultimately depends on reflective practice exploring the hows and whys and what-ifs, rather than on prescribed practice determined by knowns, givens, and standard procedures.

The Importance of Individualizing Instruction

Students today, for all their diversity, expect the same life-changing benefit from higher education, given its pivotal role in socioeconomic advancement and personal fulfillment. In response, undergraduate education cannot be a "one size fits all" endeavor (Plater, 1995). Combining the talent development model of educational excellence with the reality of the individual learner underscores how important it is for undergraduate faculty to be skilled in individualizing their instructional approaches with students. If educational excellence is gauged by the extent to which every student develops the competencies established by the curriculum, and if each student ultimately is a unique learner, then faculty willingness and ability to respond instructionally to learning differences among individual students becomes a critical factor determining an undergraduate program's approximation of excellence. From this point of view, the traditional expectation that students adjust unilaterally to teachers' already established instructional approaches is not a viable path to program excellence. Rather, the reality of the individual learner within the talent development framework creates a very different expectation; that faculty and students work together to achieve academic success through creating alternative teaching and assessment strategies that support, but also expand over time, the learning characteristics and strategies of individual learners. This expectation represents a central challenge for undergraduate faculty as we begin the new millennium (Plater 1995).

Our ability to meet this central challenge is an open question. Our past track record is not encouraging. Traditions of graduate programs discourage prospective undergraduate faculty from worrying much about defining effective instruction in terms of effective learning (Cross, 1999). Traditions of undergraduate programs in turn discourage practicing faculty from valuing much the ongoing improvement of their teaching through purposeful attention to the success of individual students. (Eble, 1980). We remain obsessed with our students being smart rather than working with them to develop smartness (Astin, 1997).

Pascarella and Terenzini (1991), in their comprehensive research review of the impact of higher education, conclude that "greater content learning and cognitive development occur in classrooms where . . . systematic efforts [are made] to devise learning experiences that take into account the student's level of understanding, ways of structuring information, and learning style" (p. 651). They also emphasize that the notion of individualizing undergraduate instruction continues to be played out more in rhetoric than in practice, and that institutions of higher education remain better structured to process a large number of students than to maximize the development of individual students. There continues to be a lack of reflection by undergraduate programs in examining their own effectiveness, in figuring out what works and what does not for which students (Bok, 1992). Most undergraduate programs still try to achieve established curricular and program outcomes for students through selective admissions rather than through individualizing instruction (Astin, 1990, 1999).

The need for undergraduate faculty to become progressively skilled in individualizing their instruction with students is hard to argue against. Individualizing instruction represents a powerful means of accommodating the two realities of increasing student diversity and increasing levels of competencies required for functioning productively in today's society. It also represents a powerful means of furthering the transition of undergraduate education's function from filter to bridge.

Faculty efforts to become more adept in individualizing instruction clearly go against the grain of the prevalent culture throughout much of undergraduate education. Before highlighting the thoughts and actions of some skilled and dedicated faculty from various undergraduate disciplines who have done just that, a closer look at the notion of individualizing instruction is warranted. What does it mean to individualize instruction? What assumptions are entailed, and what are some general guidelines for its practice? What, in the first place, is going on when students learn, and what are ways that individualizing instruction can support such learning? These issues are taken up in the next three chapters.

REFERENCES

Amundsen, C., Gryspeerdt, D., & Moxness, K. (1993). Practice-centered inquiry: Developing more effective teaching. *Review of Higher Education, 16*(3), 329–353.

Anderson, J. (2001, March). Tailoring assessment to student learning styles. *AAHE Bulletin, 53*(7), 3–7.

Astin, A. W. (1985). *Achieving educational excellence*. San Francisco: Jossey-Bass.

Astin, A. W. (1987). Assessment, value-added, and educational excellence. In D.F. Halpern (Ed.), *Student outcome assessment: What institutions stand to gain* (pp. 89–107). New Directions for Higher Education, No. 59. San Francisco: Jossey-Bass.

Astin, A. W. (1990). Educational assessment and educational equity. *American Journal of Education, 98*(4), 458–478.

Astin, A. W. (1997). Our obsession with being "smart" is distorting intellectual life. *Chronicle of Higher Education, 44*(5), 60.

Astin, A. W. (1999). Assessment, student development, and public policy. In S. J. Messick (Ed.), *Assessment in higher education: Issues of access, quality, student development, and public policy* (pp. 157–175). Mahwah, NJ: Lawrence Erlbaum.

Blandin, D. M. (1994). Three realities: Minority life in the United States—the struggle for economic equity. In M. J. Justiz, R. Wilson, & L. G. Björk (Eds.), *Minorities in higher education* (pp. 22–43). Phoenix, AZ: Onyx Press.

Bok, D. (1992). Reclaiming the public trust. *Change, 24*(4), 12–19.

Bowen, H. R. (1977). *Investment in learning.* San Francisco: Jossey-Bass.

Boyer, E. L. (1987). *College: The undergraduate experience in America.* New York: Harper & Row.

Brookfield, S. D. (1995). *Becoming a critically reflective teacher.* San Francisco: Jossey-Bass.

Carnevale, A. P., & Desrochers, D. M. (2001). *Help wanted . . . credentials required: Community colleges in the knowledge economy.* Washington, DC: Community College Press.

Challenger, J. (2000, September/October). 24 trends reshaping the workplace. *Futurist, 34*(5), 35–41.

Chronicle of Higher Education. (2001, August 31). Almanac Issue 2001–2, *48*(1), 22.

Clark, T. F. (1981). Individualized education. In A. W. Chickering & Associates (Eds.), *The modern American college* (pp. 232–255). San Francisco: Jossey-Bass.

Claxton, C., & Murrel, P. (1987). *Learning styles: Implications for improving educational practices.* ASHE-ERIC Higher Education Report No. 4. Washington, DC: Association for the Study of Higher Education.

Coles, G. (1987). *The learning mystique.* New York: Pantheon Books.

Corno, L., & Snow, R. E. (1986). Adapting teaching to individual differences among learners. In M. C. Wittrock (Ed.), *Handbook of research on teaching* (3d ed., pp. 605–629). New York: Macmillan.

Cross, K. P. (1987, March 2). *Teaching for learning.* Paper presented at the annual meeting of the American Association of Higher Education, Chicago, IL.

Cross, K. P. (1999). Assessment to improve college instruction. In. S. J. Messick (Ed.), *Assessment in higher education: Issues of access, quality, student development, and public policy* (pp. 35–45). Mahwah, NJ: Lawrence Erlbaum.

Davis, B. G. (1993). *Tools for teaching.* San Francisco: Jossey-Bass.

Dubin, R., & Taveggia, T. C. (1968). *The teaching-learning paradox.* Eugene, OR: University of Oregon Press.

Eble, K. E. (1980). Future considerations and additional resources. In K. E. Eble (Ed.), *Improving teaching styles* (pp. 95–104). San Francisco: Jossey-Bass.

Edgerton, R. (1993a). The new public mood and what it means for higher education. *AAHE Bulletin, 45*(10), 3–7.

Edgerton, R. (1993b). The re-examination of faculty priorities. *Change, 25*(4), 10–25.

Edgerton, R. (1993c). The tasks faculty perform. *Change, 25*(4), 4–6.

Ewell, P. T. (1991, November/December). Assessment and public accountability. *Change, 23*(6), 12–17.

Fairweather, J. S. (1993). Faculty rewards reconsidered: The nature of tradeoffs. *Change, 25*(4), 44–47.

Fincher, C. (1985). Learning theory and research. In J. C. Smart (Ed.), *Higher education handbook of theory and research* (Vol. 1, pp. 63–96). New York: Agathon Press.

Fram, E. H., & Camp, R. C. (1995). Finding and implementing best practices in higher education. *Quality Progress, 28*(2), 69–73.

Gardner, D. (1999). Meeting the challenges of the new millennium: The university role. In W. Z. Hirsch & L. E. Weber (Eds.), *Challenges facing higher education at the millennium* (pp. 18–25). Phoenix, AZ: American Council on Education/Oryx Press.

Gardner, H. (2001, March 9). The philosophy-science continuum. *Chronicle of Higher Education, 47*(26), B7–B10.

Gordon, E. W. (1999). Human diversity and equitable assessment. In S. J. Messick (Ed.), *Assessment in higher education: Issues of access, quality, student development, and public policy* (pp. 203–211). Mahwah, NJ: Lawrence Erlbaum.

Grasha, T. (1990). The naturalistic approach to learning styles. *College Teaching, 38*(3), 106–113.

Gumport, P. J., Iannozzi, M., Sharman, S., & Zemsky, R. (1997). *Trends in United States higher education from massification to post massification.* Stanford, CA: National Center for Postsecondary Improvement.

Gumport, P. J., & Pusser, B. (1997). *Restructuring the academic environment.* Stanford, CA: National Center for Postsecondary Improvement.

Halpern, D. F., & Associates (1994). *Changing college classrooms.* San Francisco: Jossey-Bass.

Haworth, J. G., & Conrad, C. F. (1997). *Emblems of quality in higher education: Developing and sustaining high quality programs.* Needham Heights, MA: Allyn & Bacon.

Hughes, K. S., Frances, C., & Lombardo, B. J. (1991). *The impact of demographic and workforce trends on higher education in the 1990s.* Washington, DC: National Association of College and University Business Officers.

Justiz, M. (1994). Demographic trends and the challenge to American higher education. In M. J. Justiz, R. Wilson, & L. G. Björk (Eds.), *Minorities in higher education* (pp. 1–21). Phoenix, AZ: American Council on Education/Oryx Press.

Kerr, C. (1994). Expanding access and changing missions: The federal role in U.S. higher education. *Educational Record, 75*(4), 27–31.

Knox, W. E., Lindsay, P., & Kolb, M. N. (1993). *Does college make a difference?* Westport, CT: Greenwood Press.

Kuh, G. (2001, May/June). Assessing what really matters to student learning. *Change, 33*(3), 10–17, 66.

Kuh, G., Baird, L. L., & Leslie, D. W. (1992). A landmark in scholarly synthesis. *Review of Higher Education, 15*(3), 347–373.

Lampert, M. (1985). How do teachers manage to teach? Perspectives on problems in practice. *Harvard Educational Review, 55*(2), 178–194.

The Landscape (1993). The changing faces of the American college campus. *Change, 24*(4), 57–60.

The Landscape (2001, May/June). A report to stakeholders on the condition and effectiveness of postsecondary education: Part one. *Change, 33*(3), 27–42.

Lazerson, M., Wagener, U., & Shumanis, N. (1999). *What makes a revolution: Teaching and learning in higher education, 1980–2000.* Stanford, CA: National Center for Postsecondary Improvement.

McCombs, B., & Whisler, J. S. (1997). *The learner-centered classroom and school: Strategies for increasing student motivation and achievement.* San Francisco: Jossey-Bass.

McPherson, M. S., & Schapiro, M. O. (1995). Skills, innovations, values: Future needs for postsecondary education. *Change, 27*(4), 26–32.

McPherson, M. S., & Schapiro, M. O. (1999). *Reinforcing stratification in American higher education: Some disturbing trends.* Stanford, CA: National Center for Postsecondary Improvement.

Magolda, M. B., & Terenzini, P. T. (n.d.). Learning and teaching in the 21st century: Trends and implications for practice. In C. S. Johnson & H. E. Cheatham (Eds.), *Higher education trends for the next century: A research agenda for student success.* American College Personnel Association. Retrieved 2/8/02, http://www.acpa.nche.edu

Menges, R. J. (1991). The real world of teaching improvement: A faculty perspective. In M. Theall & J. Frankin (Eds.), *Effective practices for improving teaching* (pp. 21–37). New Directions for Teaching and Learning, No. 48. San Francisco: Jossey-Bass.

National Center for Education Statistics (2000a). *The condition of education 2000.* Retrieved 10/22/01, http://www.nces.ed.gov/pubs2000/coe2000.

National Center for Education Statistics (2000b). *Digest of Education Statistics, 1999.* Retrieved 10/22/01, http://www.nces.ed.gov/pubs2000/Digest99.

National Center for Education Statistics (2001). *Projections of education statistics to 2011.* Retrieved 10/22/01, http://www.nces.ed.gov/pubs2001/proj01/highlights.asp.

Noel, L. (1987). Increasing student retention: New challenges and potential. In L. Noel, R. Levitz, D. Saluri, & Associates (Eds.), *Increasing student retention* (pp. 1–27). San Francisco: Jossey-Bass.

Orfield, G. (1993). Federal policy and college opportunity. *Change, 25*(2), 10–15.

Pascarella, E. T. (2001, May/June). Identifying excellence in undergraduate education. *Change, 33*(3), 19–23.

Pascarella, E. T., & Terenzini, P. T. (1991). *How college affects students*. San Francisco: Jossey-Bass.

Paulsen, M. B., & Feldman, K. A. (1995). *Taking teaching seriously: Meeting the challenge of instructional improvement*. ASHE-ERIC Higher Education Report No. 2. Washington, DC: ERIC Clearinghouse on Higher Education, Graduate School of Education and Human Development, George Washington University.

Pintrich, P. R. (1988). Student learning and college teaching. In R. E. Young & K. E. Elde (Eds.), *College teaching and learning: Preparing for new commitments* (pp. 71–86). New Directions for Teaching and Learning, No. 33. San Francisco: Jossey-Bass.

Plater, W. M. (1995). Futurework: Faculty time in the 21st century. *Change, 27*(3), 22–23.

Porter, J. (1994). Disability in higher education: From person-based to interaction-based. *Journal on Excellence in College Teaching, 5*(1), 69–75.

Prégent, R. (1994). *Charting your course: How to prepare to teach more effectively*. Madison, WI: Magna.

Reich, R. B. (2000, September 15). How selective colleges heighten inequality. *Chronicle of Higher Education, 47*(3), B7–B10.

Reich, R. B. (2001, June 20). Standards for what? *Education Week, 20*(41), 64, 48.

Riesman, D., & Jencks, C. (1968). *The academic revolution*. Garden City, NY: Doubleday.

Schon, Donald A. (1983). *The reflective practitioner*. New York: Basic Books.

Sherman, T. M., Armistead, L. P., Fowler, F., Barksdale, M. A., & Reif, G. (1987). The quest for excellence in university teaching. *Journal of Higher Education, 58*(1), 66–84.

Shuell, T. J. (1986). Individual differences: Changing conceptions in research and practice. *American Journal of Education, 94*(3), 356–377.

Shulman, L. S. (1987a). Knowledge and teaching: Foundations of the new reform. *Harvard Educational Review, 57*(1), 1–22.

Shulman, L. S. (1987b). Learning to teach. *AAHE Bulletin, 40*(3), 5–9.

Siegel, J. S., & Shaughnessy, M. F. (1994). Educating for understanding: An interview with Howard Gardner. *Phi Delta Kappan, 75*(7), 563–566.

Smith, D. G. (1989). *The challenge of diversity: Involvement or alienation in the academy?* ASHE-ERIC Higher Education Report, No.5. Washington, DC: ERIC Clearinghouse on Higher Education, Graduate School of Education and Human Development, George Washington University.

Snow, R. E. (1978). Theory and method for research on aptitude processes. *Intelligence, 2*(3), 225–278.

Tinto, V. (1987). Dropping out and other forms of withdrawal from college. In L. Noel, R. Levitz, D. Saluri, & Associates (Eds.), *Increasing student retention* (pp. 28–43). San Francisco: Jossey-Bass.

Trow, M. (1989). American higher education—Past, present, and future. *Studies in Higher Education, 14*(1), 5–22.

Wadsworth, D. (1995). The new public landscape: Where higher education stands. *AAHE Bulletin, 47*(10), 14–17.

Wagener, U. E. (1989). Quality and equity: The necessity for imagination. *Harvard Educational Review, 59*(2), 240–250.

Wang, M. C. (1991). Adaptive instruction: An alternative approach to providing for student diversity. In M. Ainscow (Ed.), *Effective schools for all* (pp. 134–160). London: David Fulton.

Weingartner, R. H. (1994). Between cup and lip: Reconceptualizing education as student learning. *Educational Record, 75*(1), 13–19.

Chapter 2

Learning and Individualizing Instruction

Jeffrey E. Porter

Through the talent development lens, supporting student learning is the focal mission of undergraduate education. To be sure, we learn prolifically on our own, beyond formal courses and without assistance from an institutional infrastructure of approved curricula, credentialed teachers, or academic policies (Fincher, 1985; Pascarella & Terenzini, 1991). The sole justification for creating and maintaining this infrastructure, from the talent development perspective, is to support student learning in light of the specific curricular goals required for a particular course and the overall competencies established for graduation. Given the centrality of student learning, it is important to consider it more closely.

THE NATURE AND DYNAMICS OF STUDENT LEARNING

Learning can be defined as progressive, relatively enduring change in a student's capabilities, based on experience and practice (Shuell, 1986a). It represents advancement from ignorance to knowledge, ineptness to competence, misunderstanding to insight, and unawareness to appreciation (Fincher, 1985).

As with most things fundamental, student learning is more speculated about in discourse than attended to in practice. For being such a central topic of undergraduate education's ongoing discourse, the nature and dynamics of actual student learning in classroom settings remain impressively unanalyzed and unaccounted for in day-to-day practice. When we do focus on learning and how best to support it, we gloss too easily over what is essential and dwell too readily on the peripheral; the number of credits for this course or which department should offer that course, the desirability of requiring that all courses be posted on the Web, or the advantages and disadvantages of a semester versus a quarter calendar.

Student learning is complex. It resists single-factor explanations and encourages multiple theoretical orientations (Eble, 1980; Fincher, 1985; Stage, Muller, Kinzie, & Simmons, 1998). Specifically related to college students, more than twenty theoretical models of learning and development have been enumerated (Pascarella & Terenzini, 1991).

Complex, however, does not mean mysterious (Fincher, 1985). Most contemporary views of learning, one way or another, incorporate the key processes of acquisition, integration, application and refinement. Students acquire and integrate new content in light of their existing knowledge, skills, and conceptual understandings. The acquisition and integration of the new with the existing generates emergent learning, which the student then applies to related problems and situations. The student's application of learning in turn leads to ongoing refinements of emergent learning based on generated feedback and the acquisition and integration of these refinements along with subsequent new content (Fincher, 1985; Shuell, 1986a).

The related processes of acquisition, integration, application, and refinement represent a common thread through most models of learning, although the particular mechanisms hypothesized as explaining these processes vary with the theoretical orientation (Stage et al., 1998). It is critical to note that almost all views of learning (save perhaps Freudian or radical behaviorism schools of thought) hold these key processes as controlled directly by the learner. Environmental factors (such as the expertise of a teacher's instructional approach or the adequacy of surrounding educational facilities and resources) clearly can enhance or undermine these processes so essential to learning, but they are under the voluntary control of no one but the student.

The French or biology I am learning now, I am integrating with what I remember and bring forward from yesterday's or last year's learning. The emergent learning I construct as a result of this integration I apply to the next practice problem or pertinent real-life situation. On the basis of the results of such application (i.e., the feedback I receive and interpret), I refine my emergent learning and carry it forward to future encounters with new content. This set of voluntary learning processes accounts for how students realize (or do not) curricular goals defining the first introductory course required of all new majors. It accounts as well for how students ultimately realize (or do not) graduation outcomes constituting their entire undergraduate degree.

The key processes of acquisition, integration, application, and refinement are noticeably cognitive in nature, reflecting what Gardner (1985) has termed the cognitive revolution in psychology, and in learning theory specifically. It would be a distortion, however, to portray learning as strictly cognitive. As I elaborate shortly, learning centrally involves motivational, affective, and behavioral dimensions as well. Learning constitutes holistically what a person does and feels, not just thinks. It constitutes as well the why, or motivation, for such doing, feeling, and thinking. Social scientists and educators too easily accept as real the discrete, artificial realms of functioning we create (like "cognitive," "affective," "behavioral") in attempting to describe and explain human action. Human action such as learning clearly is complex, but it is unitary and indivisible.

One of the ways to look at learning is types of learning outcome. Guskin (1994) describes three types of learning outcomes: accumulation of facts, development of procedural skills, and creation of conceptual perspectives or ways of analyzing and understanding the world. Memorizing the names and characteristics of reactions in organic chemistry, refining dissection skills in the laboratory, and applying alternative psychological frames of reference in interpreting human behavior illustrate respectively these three types of outcomes. Most theorists and educators agree that the first type of learning outcome, accumulation of facts, is relatively rudimentary, and most meaningful when serving the latter two "higher" types of learning outcomes, developing skill and creating conceptual understanding. Further, all three types of learning outcomes can be viewed as enabling yet a fourth type, learning how to learn. This last type of learning perhaps is highest of all in significance for negotiating our daily worlds, where learned facts, skills, and frameworks frequently are overturned by new ones. "Learning how to learn" refers to the ability to oversee and guide the success of one's own learning efforts in mastering new content and adapting to new situations. It includes being able to divine the goals of a learning event, planning and organizing available resources in accomplishing those goals, choosing a learning strategy to accommodate the demands of the learning event, monitoring the effectiveness of the chosen strategy, and modifying the strategy as needed to realize eventual success (Shuell, 1986a).

Another way to look at learning is in terms of its dynamics. From this perspective, Kolb (1981) provides a helpful model, termed experiential learning theory. According to this model, learning involves movement along and between two basic dimensions of experience. One dimension represents the experiencing of concrete events at one pole and the abstract interpretation of those experiences at the other pole. The second dimension is framed by active experimentation with concrete events and reflective observation on the outcomes of such experimentation. In this model, then, a student generates learning through active experimentation with concrete experience, with this activity fueling reflective observation and abstract interpretation. Such observation and interpretation generates hypotheses about the meaning and implications of what has been experienced. These hypotheses in turn lead to more experimentation with concrete experience, yielding yet further observation, interpretation, and hypothesis generation.

Whether I am learning calculus, counseling skills, or karate, my experience in doing so entails, more or less, interacting with concrete facts or givens and interpreting these interactions in light of not only the established wisdom of the particular discipline or tradition, but also in light of my personal background and set of developed understandings. It also entails testing the correctness of my interpretations through generating what-if hypotheses; applying these in experimenting with additional facts and givens, observing the consequences, and revising my interpretations as necessary.

These learning dynamics require the student to shift roles continuously: from actor to observer, from conceptualizer to experimenter. Remembering that complexity (if not mystery) is the name of the game here, it is important to recognize that different learning events by their nature call upon these different roles to different degrees. Learning calculus may emphasize disproportionately the role of conceptualizer, counseling the role of observer, and karate the role of actor. As well, each role entails different learning capabilities and strategies, with individual students varying in their strengths, weaknesses, and preferences regarding such qualities. Kolb's model ultimately relies on the individual student as responsible, in a "learning how to learn" way, for figuring out which roles and respective sets of capabilities and strategies best support which learning events. In doing so, the model captures both the diversity of capabilities and strategies involved in the act of learning and the central responsibility of individuals for controlling and overseeing their own learning.

FUNDAMENTAL FEATURES OF LEARNING

As noted earlier, learning incorporates the full range of human capabilities: cognitive, behavioral, affective, and motivational (Fincher, 1985). The variables influencing these capabilities are rich and diverse. Reflecting this, research on student learning in college classrooms has evolved over the past decades from simple snapshots of what has been learned to more complex analyses of ongoing learning processes and from studies of outcomes to studies of students' thoughts, feelings, and actions during learning experiences (McKeachie, 1990). The results of this research have culminated in consensus about some fundamental features of learning.

One such fundamental feature is that learning is *student-centered*. In accounting for learning, the student, not the teacher, curriculum, or well-equipped laboratory, is at center stage. On this stage the student purposefully interacts with learning tasks to construct learning outcomes, outcomes that are self-created rather than transplanted from elsewhere (see Angelo, 1993; Chickering & Gamson, 1987; Cross, 1987; Graman, 1988; Jones, Palinscar, Ogle, & Carr, 1987; Shuell, 1986a; Wagener, 1989). Learning does not happen to the student, it is brought about by the student. In the "physics of learning," people cannot move one another; only individuals can move themselves (Vella, 2000). The student is the subject, not the object, of learning.

Even as students are the central players in learning, they are not the only players. Learning outcomes also reflect factors and dynamics that are not solely internal to the student. Environmental factors, such as teacher expertise in setting and communicating curricular goals and designing the learning tasks that lead toward them, opportunities for collaborating with fellow learners, and the richness of available educational resources all interact strongly with the efforts and activities of students to influence learning outcomes—for better or worse (Fincher, 1985; Shuell, 1986a). It is important however to appreciate the nature of this interaction. Environmental factors, when supportive, can facilitate significantly student learning. When inadequate, they can hinder student learning. In neither case do they cause (or prevent) learning. Students are the causal agents for their own learning. In terms of learning outcomes, what students do during learning is determinative, and is fundamentally more pivotal than what teachers do (Shuell, 1986a).

It follows as a second fundamental feature that student learning is *constructive*. Learning is not a passive process, with students simply receiving transmitted content from others (Brown, 1994; Fincher, 1985; Jones et al., 1987). Through interactions with learning tasks, students construct knowledge, skills, and conceptual frameworks through acquiring, integrating, applying, and refining new content in relation to existing learning. The more students work with new content to understand it meaningfully in relation to what they already know and can do, the more likely they are to learn it. Students derive, not duplicate, the meaning of new content. What they derive depends specifically on the learning characteristics they bring to the learning task and the learning strategies they are motivated to use and revise throughout the learning task, all as influenced by the teacher's instructional approach and the task's expected outcomes (Vella, 2000). In the interface between existing and emergent learning, the student transforms the old by constructing the new (Brown & Ellison, 1995; Jones et al., 1987; Spence, 2001; Wagener, 1989).

Finally, as implied from the above discussion, a third fundamental feature of learning is that it is *personal* in nature. New learning has meaning for a student only in terms of learning already possessed. Nothing is learned in isolation from the student's existing archive of skills, knowledge, and conceptual perspectives (Davis, 1993; Gagne, 1985; McKeachie, Pintrich, Lin, Smith, & Sharma, 1990; Shuell, 1986a). What students already know, can do, and understand, and the extent to which they bring all of this into play during new learning, defines the nature and meaning of any resultant learning. Individual students are unique in the precise characteristics of their existing knowledge, skills, conceptual perspectives and motivational orientations and in the strategies they use to organize, integrate, and construct new learning (Angelo, 1993). They actively explore the meaning of new learning in terms of their own histories and experiences (Silberman, 1996; Vella, 2000). Learning, then, at heart is an extremely personal and idiosyncratic process (Vella, 2000). Only at the level of formal curricular goals and program competencies can we think of common learning outcomes for all students undertaking the same learning events. At the experiential level of individual students, given the personalized dynamics noted above, learning outcomes constructed by individual students are most uncommon. The learning I construct and take with me from my freshman geology course is unique to me. It is unlike what any of my classmates take with them. It is influenced (in part) by my prior knowledge and understanding of geology, how I learn, what I consider to be important (in my life and in this course), my respect for the teacher, how well the teacher's instructional approach supports my preferred learning strategies and stretches me to practice less familiar ones, whether the course was required or elective, and the vocation I envision for myself along with the avocations I enjoy. Similarly, what I take with me from my undergraduate degree in literature reflects the same sort of variables, only writ large and cumulatively.

LEARNING AND MOTIVATED ENGAGEMENT

If learning is *student-centered, constructive*, and *personal*, it follows that a student must engage new content to make learning happen (Bloom, 1976; Brophy & Alleman, 1991; Haertel, Walberg, & Weinstein, 1983; Shuell, 1986a; Vella, 2000). Students engage new content when they incorporate the goals of the learning task as their own, work to integrate and interpret the new content in light of their existing learning, strive to apply emergent learning to related problems and situations and make refinement along the way on the basis of generated feedback, and take responsibility for monitoring and revising their learning strategies to better achieve successful learning. Learning does not result when teachers teach; it results when students engage. Pascarella and Terenzini (1991), in their comprehensive research review on the impact of higher education, conclude that the greater a student's engagement in academic work, the greater the resulting level of knowledge acquisition and overall cognitive development. Their conclusion echoes the assertions of others (Astin, 1985; Gamson, 1991; Sherman, Armistad, Fowler, Barksdale, & Reif, 1987). The amount of student learning in college is proportional to the quality and quantity of student engagement. Likewise, the effectiveness of any educational practice is related to its ability to foster student engagement. A recent initiative at the national level, the National Survey of Student Engagement, provides data to colleges and universities on the extent to which their campuses provide experiences fostering student engagement, measured in terms of level of academic challenge, active and collaborative learning, student interactions with faculty members, enriching educational experiences, and supportive campus environment (Cambridge, 2001). Learning depends on student engagement with the learning task, with students ultimately in control of the extent and nature of such engagement.

In this regard, the role of student motivation becomes pivotal. If learning depends on student engagement, such engagement in turn is fueled by student motivation. As research amply demonstrates, and as teachers and students know in their bones, the nature of learning processes and outcomes is strongly related to the degree and quality of student motivation (Fincher, 1985). As noted earlier, learning is not only a function of students' cognitive capabilities: their accumulated knowledge, conceptual perspectives, and learning strategies. Learning also depends on whether and how students choose to activate such capabilities in the first place and sustain their activation throughout the learning experience (Pintrich, 1989).

By motivation, I refer to a related set of phenomena: the goals and purposes explaining a person's action; why that person selects and initiates this activity rather than that one; why the person persists (or doesn't) in the selected activity; why the person sooner or later brings the activity to conclusion; and how he or she ultimately interprets the personal significance of the activity (Ames & Ames, 1984; deCharms, 1984). A great many theoretical constructs attempt to account for motivational dynamics; attributional theory, sense of self-efficacy, and ownership of goals are a few examples.

Like learning theory, the last thirty years of research and theoretical speculation about motivation has a decidedly cognitive slant. More and more, motivation is explained in terms of the information a person takes in, how the person transforms information into beliefs or interpretations of one kind or another, and how these interpretations then explain the person's action (whether it be aversion, activation, persistence, or cessation). As applied to student learning, contemporary research generally holds that students will be more motivated to engage new learning to the extent that motivational beliefs and interpretations emphasize (1) a positive value for the student of the goals characterizing the learning task; (2) the experiencing of these goals as more mastery-oriented ("what I can learn") rather than performance-oriented ("how others will evaluate me"); (3) experience of "personal ownership" for these goals; (4) perceived expectancy that one can perform effectively the actions leading to accomplishment of these valued and personally owned goals; (5) student attribution of setbacks in reaching those goals to factors that are under one's control to change (e.g., effort, strategy, skill level); (6) correspondingly, student attribution of successes in realizing learning goals to personal characteristics (e.g., ability, effort) rather than external factors (luck, task demands); and (7) a sense of challenge in mastering new skills and knowledge coupled with a sense of being supported in doing so (deCharms, 1984; Dweck, 1999; McKeachie et al., 1990; McCombs & Whisler, 1997; Stage et al., 1998).

LEARNING AND INDIVIDUAL DIFFERENCES

Individual differences among students are a fact of life; no two people experience, organize, interpret, and act on the world in precisely the same ways (Clark, 1981; Cross, 1987; McCombs & Whisler, 1997; Ramsden, 1988). This reality precludes generalities about fixed relationships among instructional approaches, learning processes, and learning outcomes (Fincher, 1985).

Individual students uniquely transform learning content into learning outcomes. This transformation depends partly on what students bring to the learning event: their unique personal histories and existing sets of knowledge, skills, conceptual perspectives and motivational orientations. Different students bring different learning characteristics of these kinds to the same learning task. The transformation also depends on the learning strategies applied by students in acquiring, integrating, applying, and refining new learning. Different students engage the same learning task with different learning strategies (Shuell, 1986b).

Learning strategies are conceptualized in many ways. One way is to view them as differing among individual students along an affective dimension (e.g., motivational dynamics influencing self-confidence, perceived probability of success, task focus, and task persistence), an organizing dimension (e.g., how new content is taken in, represented, and integrated with existing content), and a monitoring dimension (e.g., self-questioning, error detection, and corrective strategies) (Weinstein & Mayer, 1986). Even people's particular epistemological beliefs, not necessarily explicitly formulated, about what knowledge is and how it is acquired can influence how they approach and monitor learning, and how they persist in the face of difficulty (Schommer, 1994). Our individual life experiences (in the family, at home, school, and work), and our particular cognitive and behavioral capabilities and affective dispositions in experiencing our interactions with the world, dispose each of us over time to develop unique learning strategies, with concomitant strengths, weaknesses and preferences (Anderson, 2001; Kolb, 1981). If it is true that learning requires student engagement with content, it also is true that students use individual learning strategies in doing so, resulting in individual learning outcomes.

Because it is student engagement with a learning task that generates learning, the effectiveness of any instructional approach depends on its capacity to foster and support such engagement. Further, since each student ultimately represents a unique configuration of learning characteristics and learning strategies in engaging a particular learning task, an instructional practice effectively fostering engagement for one student will not do so for another (Lidman, Smith, & Purce, 1995; Shuell, 1986b; Silverman & Casazza, 2000). To improve success in the classroom, undergraduate students need to learn in ways that work for them (Chickering & Gamson, 1987) as well as practice new learning strategies that will enable them to become more versatile learners (Shuell, 1986a). Undergraduate teachers, as a consequence, need as much skill as possible in developing diverse instructional approaches that support and extend the learning of diverse individual students (Vella, 2000).

REFERENCES

Ames, R., & Ames, C. (1984). Introduction. In R. Ames & C. Ames (Eds.), *Research on motivation in education* (Vol. 1, pp. 1–11). Orlando, FL: Academic Press.

Anderson, J. (2001, March). Tailoring assessment to student learning styles. *AAHE Bulletin, 53*(7), 3–7.

Angelo, T. A. (1993). "A teacher's dozen": Fourteen general research-based principles for improving higher learning in our classrooms. *AAHE Bulletin, 45*(8), 3–7, 13.

Astin, A. W. (1985). *Achieving educational excellence.* San Francisco: Jossey-Bass.

Bloom, B. S. (1976). *Human characteristics and school learning.* New York: McGraw-Hill.

Brophy, J., & Alleman, J. (1991). Activities as instructional tools: A framework for analysis and evaluation. *Educational Researcher, 20*(4), 9–23.

Brown, A. L. (1994). The advancement of learning. *Educational Researcher, 23*(8), 4–12.

Brown, D. G., & Ellison, C. W. (1995). What is active learning? In S. R. Hatfield (Ed.), *The seven principles in action: Improving undergraduate education* (pp. 39–53). Boston: Anker.

Cambridge, B. (2001, January). Assessing the real college experience. *AAHE Bulletin, 53*(5), 7–11.

Chickering, A. W., & Gamson, Z. F. (1987). Seven principles for good practice in undergraduate practice. *AHHE Bulletin, 39*(7), 3–7.

Clark, T. F. (1981). Individualized education. In A. W. Chickering & Associates (Eds.), *The modern American college* (pp. 232–255). San Francisco: Jossey-Bass.

Cross, K. P. (1987, March 2). *Teaching for learning.* Paper presented at the annual meeting of the American Association of Higher Education, Chicago, IL.

Davis, B. G. (1993). *Tools for teaching.* San Francisco: Jossey-Bass.

deCharms, R. (1984). Motivation enhancement in educational settings. In R. Ames & C. Ames (Eds.), *Research on motivation in education* (Vol. 1, pp. 275–310). Orlando, FL: Academic Press.

Dweck, L. S. (1999). *Self-theories: Their role in motivation, personality, and development.* Philadelphia: Psychology Press.

Eble, K. E. (1980). Future considerations and additional resources. In K. E. Eble (Ed.), *Improving teaching styles* (pp. 95–104). San Francisco: Jossey-Bass.

Fincher, C. (1985). Learning theory and research. In J. C. Smart (Ed.), *Higher education handbook of theory and research* (Vol. 1, pp. 63–96). New York: Agathon Press.

Gagne, R. M. (1985). *The conditions of learning* (4th ed.). New York: Holt, Rinehart & Winston.

Gamson, Z. F. (1991). Why is college so influential? *Change, 23*(6), 50–53.

Gardner, H. (1985). *The mind's new science.* New York: Basic Books.

Graman, T. (1988). Education for humanization: Applying Paulo Freire's pedagogy to learning a second language. *Harvard Educational Review, 58*(4), 433–448.

Guskin, A. E. (1994, September/October). Restructuring the role of the faculty. *Change, 26*(5), 16–25.

Haertel, G. D., Walberg, H. J., & Weinstein, T. (1983). Psychological models of educational performance: A theoretical synthesis of constructs. *Review of Educational Research, 53*(1), 75–91.

Jones, B. F., Palinscar, A. S., Ogle, D. S., & Carr, E. G. (Eds.). (1987). *Strategic teaching and learning: Cognitive instruction in the content areas.* Alexandria, VA: Association for Supervision and Curriculum Development.

Kolb, D. A. (1981). Learning styles and disciplinary differences. In A. W. Chickering & Associates (Eds.), *The modern American college* (pp. 232–255). San Francisco: Jossey-Bass.

Lidman, R. M., Smith, B. L., & Purce, T. L. (1995). Good practice respects diverse talents and ways of learning. In S. R. Hatfield (Ed.), *The seven principles in action: Improving undergraduate education* (pp. 95–106). Boston: Anker.

Magolda, M.B.B. (1992). Students' epistemologies and academic experiences: Implications for pedagogy. *Review of Higher Education, 15*(3), 265–287.

McCombs, B., & Whisler, J. S. (1997). *The learner-centered classroom and school: Strategies for increasing student motivation and achievement.* San Francisco: Jossey-Bass.

McKeachie, W. J. (1990). Research on college teaching: The historical background. *Journal of Educational Psychology, 82*(2), 189–200.

McKeachie, W. J., Pintrich, P. R., Lin, Y., Smith, D.A.F., & Sharma, R. S. (1990). *Teaching and learning in the college classroom: A review of the research literature* (2d ed.). Ann Arbor, MI: National Center for Research to Improve Postsecondary Teaching and Leaning, University of Michigan.

Pascarella, E. T., & Terenzini, P. T. (1991). *How college affects students.* San Francisco: Jossey-Bass.

Pintrich, P. R. (1989). The dynamic interplay of student motivation and cognition in the college classroom. In M. Maehr & C. Ames (Eds.), *Advances in motivation and achievement*: Vol. 6. *Motivation enhancing environments* (pp. 117–160). Greenwich, CT: JAI Press.

Ramsden, P. (1988). Context and strategy: Situational influences on learning. In R. R. Schmeck (Ed.), *Learning strategies and learning styles* (pp. 159–184). New York: Plenum Press.

Schommer (1994). An emerging conceptualization of epistemological beliefs and their role in learning. In R. Garner & P. A. Alexander (Eds.), *Beliefs about text and instruction with text* (pp. 25–40). Hillsdale, NJ: Lawrence Erlbaum.

Sherman, T. M., Armistead, L. P., Fowler, F., Barksdale, M. A., & Reif, G. (1987). The quest for excellence in university teaching. *Journal of Higher Education, 58*(1), 66–84.

Shuell, T. J. (1986a). Cognitive conceptions of learning. *Review of Educational Research, 56*(4), 411–436.

Shuell, T. J. (1986b). Individual differences: Changing conceptions in research and practice. *American Journal of Education, 94*(3), 356–377.

Silberman, M. (1996). *101 strategies to teach any subject.* Needham Heights, MA: Allyn & Beacon.

Silverman, S. L., & Casazza, M. E. (2000). *Learning and development: Making connections to enhance teaching.* San Francisco: Jossey-Bass.

Spence, L. D. (2001, November/December). The case against teaching. *Change, 33*(6), 10–19.

Stage, F. K., Muller, P. A., Kinzie, J., & Simmons, A. (1998). *Creating learning centered classrooms: What does learning theory have to say?* ASHE-ERIC Higher Education Report (Vol. 26, No. 4). Washington, DC: George Washington University, Graduate School of Education and Human Development.

Vella, J. (2000). *Taking learning to task: Creative strategies for teaching adults.* San Francisco: Jossey-Bass.

Wagener, U. E. (1989). Quality and equity: The necessity for imagination. *Harvard Educational Review, 59*(2), 240–250.

Weinstein, C. E., & Mayer, R. F. (1986). The teaching of learning strategies. In M. C. Wittrock (Ed.), *Handbook of Research on Teaching* (pp. 315–327). New York: Macmillan.

Chapter 3

Individualizing Instruction: A Framework

Jeffrey E. Porter

Teaching is not telling. Although probably not obvious from visiting the many classes throughout undergraduate education that rely primarily, if not exclusively, on the lecture format, instruction encompasses more than disseminating information. For classroom instruction to realize its purpose, the teacher must center on student learning, not telling or information dissemination. What is the purpose of classroom instruction? To support each student in acquiring new and refining existing knowledge, skills, and conceptual understanding represented by curricular goals (Fincher, 1985; McCombs & Whisler, 1997). Using this end of the telescope, classroom instruction includes (1) establishing the set of learning outcomes that constitute a course's overall curricular goals; (2) organizing the overall course format and general classroom structure to be compatible with student achievement of learning outcomes and curricular goals; (3) designing and sequencing learning tasks that incorporate the target knowledge, skills, and conceptual understanding represented by the expected learning outcomes and provide opportunities for applying and revising emergent learning on the basis of corrective feedback; (4) implementing learning tasks through teaching strategies that include mixtures of demands and supports to foster student engagement; (5) creating strategies for ongoing assessment of student learning; and (6) revising expected learning outcomes, learning tasks, and teaching strategies to better support student learning in the light of assessment results. These six elements constitute instruction anchored in student learning. The cyclical nature of the way that these elements interact and inform one another is represented in Figure 1.

Different from the logic of commercial transaction, where the act of selling necessarily results in, and cannot happen without, the act of buying, the logic of educational transaction is only loosely coupled. Acts of instruction often do not result in acts of learning, and acts of learning often happen unrelated to acts of instruction. When student learning is held up as the endpoint of instruction (Lisska, 1997), instruction is effective only when it actually supports student learning. If a student is not realizing intended learning outcomes and

Figure 1
Components of Classroom Instruction

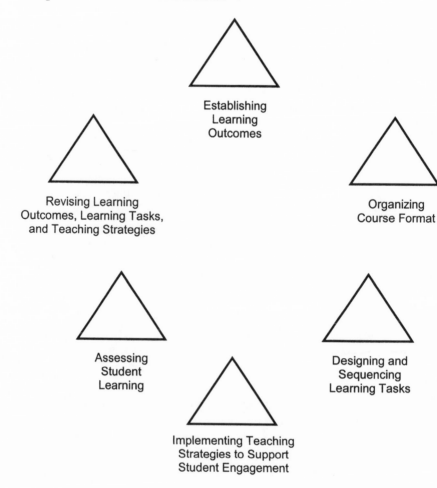

Establishing
Learning
Outcomes

Revising Learning
Outcomes, Learning Tasks,
and Teaching Strategies

Organizing
Course Format

Assessing
Student
Learning

Designing and
Sequencing
Learning Tasks

Implementing Teaching
Strategies to Support
Student Engagement

curricular goals as supported by a teacher's instructional approach, then that teacher is not practicing effective instruction for that student. Perhaps the teacher is engaged in telling or disseminating information, but not effective instruction. Students can learn without effective instruction, or even in the face of poor instruction, but teachers are not practicing effective instruction if students are not learning.

In meeting the challenge of effective instruction, teachers must consider and support the learning characteristics and strategies unique to each student, qualities such as current level of knowledge and competency, motivational orientation, preferred ways of processing and applying new information, etc. (Shuell, 1986). The reality of individual differences translates into the reality of there being no one best instructional approach for all students. Effective instruction comes down to what works in supporting the learning of individual students (Davis, 1993). A teacher's instructional challenge for a given course is as varied as the number of enrolled students.

INDIVIDUALIZING INSTRUCTION

"Individualizing instruction" captures the notion we are developing of a teacher "radiating," to use Joyce and Weil's (1972) term, an array of alternative instructional approaches to support individual learners. The goal of individualizing instruction is to support academic success for each individual learner. Individualizing instruction acts on the insight that a student's academic progress is neither an exclusive function of learner factors (e.g., existing competencies, motivation, or preferred learning strategies) nor one of instructional factors (e.g., teacher's content mastery, expertise in designing learning tasks, or assessment skills) (Tobias, 1994; Whitener, 1989). Academic progress reflects instead adaptive interaction between students (with their individual mix of learning characteristics and strategies) and teachers (with their array of alternative instructional approaches), in light of the immediate learning task outcomes and the long-term curricular goals.

Individualizing instruction has been a theme in education generally, and undergraduate education in particular, for a long time. Variations of this theme go back at least to the beginnings of audio tutorials, programmed instruction, and Keller's personalized system of instruction (Keller & Sherman, 1974), if not to Socrates and Plato! Common threads throughout these variations, and consistent with the idea of individualizing instruction presented here, include (1) acknowledging individual differences among students and adapting instruction according to these differences, (2) making the goals of the learning experience explicit and providing continuous feedback to students on progress toward these goals through ongoing assessment, and (3) emphasizing the active engagement of students in fueling and constructing their own learning (Fincher, 1985; Pascarella & Terenzini, 1991). The additional meaning this book brings to the notion of individualizing instruction is this: Individualizing instruction is not simply an instructional technique, one option among many for teachers to consider and perhaps choose in working with students. Individualizing instruction instead represents the essential approach for any form of effective instruction, given the nature of student learning and the reality of individual differences.

Individualizing instruction requires focusing on students' learning characteristics and strategies, rather than pedagogical preferences, in figuring out how to best support students in their accomplishment of curricular goals and standards. This focus represents a growing trend within undergraduate education (Plater, 1995; Rouche & Rouche, 1987). Plater sees it as a trend destined to change dramatically how undergraduate teachers define their role and invest their time. With individualizing instruction, student learning, rather than teaching habits or the dissemination of academic disciplines, is at the hub of the enterprise. From the perspective of individualizing instruction, the primary role of the undergraduate biology professor is supporting students, each and every one, in realizing the learning outcomes represented by the biology curriculum. It is not disseminating the discipline of biology to generically defined students.

IMPLICATIONS OF INDIVIDUALIZING INSTRUCTION

Individualizing instruction obligates teachers to design learning tasks and create teaching and assessment strategies that foster the engagement and success of individual students. It requires holding constant expected standards of student performance while varying instructional approaches from student to student. Individualizing instruction runs counter, then, to traditional undergraduate instructional practices of holding constant learning activities and teaching strategies while accepting variable performance levels among students (Astin, 1990; Cross, 1976).

Teachers who commit to individualizing instruction commit to creating alternative instructional approaches for individual students. Such commitment requires a reflective, experimental attitude in divining which approach best supports which students. It also requires revising existing approaches and developing new ones, based on assessment feedback, when instruction proves ineffective for a particular student (Eble & McKeachie, 1985; Sherman, Armistead, Fowler, Barksdale, & Reif, 1987; Wang, 1991). Individualizing instruction means therefore practicing the assessment of student learning as an embedded aspect of the learning/teaching transaction, not as separate, disconnected activity (Huba & Freed, 2000). This critical element of individualizing instruction is taken up further in Chapter 4.

It is important to clarify what individualizing instruction as discussed in this book does not mean. It does not imply teachers are bound to support unquestioningly the preferred learning strategies of individual students, never requiring students to expand existing ways of learning in making sense of new content. Indeed, if a valued goal of undergraduate education is to help students become more versatile and adept lifelong learners (along with mastering discipline-based content), then it is a serious obligation of teachers to do just that. Individualizing instruction holds simply that when the development of new learning strategies is a curricular goal, teachers consider the existing learning characteristics and strategies of individual students in tailoring instructional approaches to help students practice and realize these new ways of learning.

Further, individualizing instruction is not synonymous with students undertaking independent learning tasks in isolation. Teaching and assessment strategies reflecting the learning characteristics and strategies of individual students clearly can include independent learning activities and one-on-one tutorials. At the same time, they also can happen in the communal context of classrooms. Multimedia presentations and simulations (encompassing numerous sensory and expressive modalities and various ways of processing and structuring information), menus of alternative culminating projects to demonstrate learning outcomes (including collaborative small-group options), learning contracts reflecting individual choices, group work that brings to the surface learning differences among individual students and incorporates them into an enriched exploration both of the topic at hand and of the tremendous variation in how people learn, student choice regarding assessment methods and multiple opportunities for reassessment, and different levels of classroom content (from introductory to advanced) simultaneously available for learners with different levels of experience and expertise are just a few examples of ways teachers can individualize instruction within the group setting of the classroom.

Finally, individualizing instruction does not mean watering down curricular goals or academic standards (Chism, 1994). In individualizing instruction, teachers strictly maintain established course goals and standards of academic performance and they actively vary how students reach those goals and satisfy those standards in ways reflecting individual differences. To treat students differently based on learning differences is preferential treatment only if course goals and standards are changed for this or that student. Indeed, it is in treating all students the same in the face of individual differences that inequity is introduced. If equity means providing students sufficient opportunity to realize their own optimal level of learning, then inequity means precluding such opportunity by applying the same instructional approach to all learners (Gordon, 1999).

LEVELS OF INDIVIDUALIZING INSTRUCTION

Strategies for individualizing instruction happen at the level of overall course design, as well as at the level of minute-to-minute learning/teaching interactions during and outside of class. Individualizing instruction at this first level, the "macro level" (Corno & Snow, 1986), means organizing course structure and classroom design (syllabus, teacher expectations, classroom procedures, the use of space within the classroom, for a few examples) in ways that set the stage for differences among students to reveal themselves, be recognized as legitimate, and incorporated within the classroom experience. In supporting the success of individual students at this level, alternative learning outcomes, learning tasks, and teaching and assessment options leading to the same curricular goals and standards can be designed into the course syllabus. Classroom tone and operating procedures can be established that encourage students to become more aware, with reference to themselves and others, of the endless diversity of learning characteristics and strategies, more open to experimenting with new ways of learning, and more appreciative of the responsibility they have for their own learning.

We know well that teachers too often design undergraduate courses in ways that assume all students learn in the same way. The syllabus establishes and maintains one and only one mode of learning/teaching interaction and applies that mode to all students. Students are required to complete the same learning tasks and demonstrate in the same ways what they have learned. The teacher's instructional approach provides for no variation in how new content is presented to students or in how students are encouraged to engage, practice, and apply this content. Courses are designed and managed in such ways that the reality of individual learning differences is ignored or stifled, rather than recognized, valued, and seized upon.

The macro level of individualizing instruction is complemented by the micro level, the realm of teachers' moment-to-moment instructional decisions and ongoing adaptations among students and teachers. It is at the micro level that teachers and students can collaborate on which combinations of instructional and learning approaches best foster academic engagement and success. Individualizing instruction at the micro level is the ongoing learning/teaching transaction of how teachers choose, structure, and present a learning task to foster student realization of short-term learning outcomes and long-term curricular goals, how the individual student performs in engaging the task so structured, how the teacher responds, and what the student does next. Issues abound. What learning outcome and task was decided upon, perhaps by both the teacher and student, to support eventual achievement of a long-term curricular goal? What kind of strategy is the student using to acquire and organize the new information or skill represented by the learning task? How is the student relating the new content to information already stored, skills already mastered, and habitual ways of thinking? How skillfully is the student going beyond the current learning activity to make new applications? What creative links to other information and skills is the student forming? Does the student possess the prerequisite skills, the required prior knowledge? Is the student practicing enough with the new content in applying it to new situations? Do these applications generate feedback sufficient to enable the student to revise and improve upon learning? How is the teacher assessing the status of these and other such issues? How are the teacher and student interpreting the assessment results, and how do their interpretations influence them in maintaining or modifying the instructional and learning approaches under way?

This is the ceaseless dance of learning and teaching at the micro level of individualizing instruction, given the uniqueness of students, the reflective practice of teachers, and the constancies of curricular goals and standards. It is a dance blending the roles of teacher and student; teachers doing their best to learn new ways for making content as meaningful and accessible as possible in light of the learning characteristics of their individual students, and students instructing their teachers and themselves on the endless variety of ways to approach and construct new learning.

INDIVIDUALIZING INSTRUCTION: A FRAMEWORK

Individualizing instruction responds to one of undergraduate education's central challenges: how to provide effective instruction for diverse learners (Wagener, 1989). This challenge confronts an academic culture traditionally devoting considerably more time and discourse to the curricular issue of what rather than the pedagogical issue of how in considering the education of students (Bok, 1992).

Most undergraduate instruction continues to be delivered through the deeply ingrained practice of lecturing, an approach that assumes learning is primarily an act of passively taking in information (Guskin, 1994; Nemko, 1995; Pascarella & Terenzini, 1991, 1994; Weingartner, 1994). Following Guskin's (1994) call, and consistent with the aim of individualizing instruction, undergraduate teachers need to invest more collective time and energy focusing on how individual students go about constructing their own learning beyond taking in information. Within such a focus, they need to invest in more reflective and creative experimentation in what it takes to support successful learning by individual students. The sincere intentions of undergraduate teachers to provide effective instruction are not at issue. Realizing these intentions more effectively nevertheless requires a fundamental shift in focus and more open, adaptive, and learning-centered instructional approaches.

Figure 2 presents a framework for understanding the variables and processes in individualizing instruction. It represents a problem-solving tool for teachers to use in individualizing their efforts to support student learning.

A learning event encompasses a student's engagement with a specific learning task as supported by a teacher's instructional approach. Student performance in any learning event is influenced by a common set of interrelated factors: the expected outcomes and requirements of the learning task, student factors, and teacher factors (Fincher, 1985; Salvia & Ysseldyke, 1998). These variables are represented in Figure 2 as the givens.

Figure 2
A Framework for Individualizing Instruction

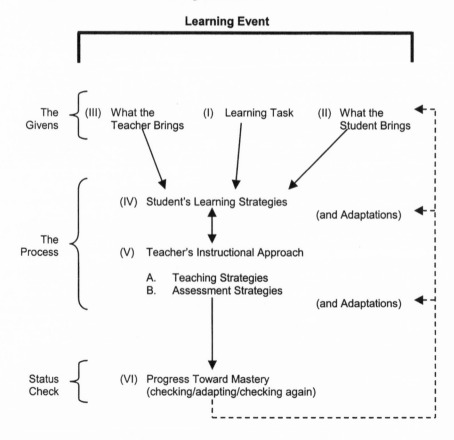

Given I is the learning task. Learning tasks are activities, either teacher-designed or codesigned with students, intended to help students acquire, integrate, and construct the target knowledge, skills, and conceptual understandings specified by the task's learning outcomes. Well-designed learning tasks provide opportunities for applying and revising emergent learning. Learning tasks are educational steppingstones, intended to foster the achievement of learning outcomes incrementally leading to overall curricular goals. Examples of learning tasks include such knowledge, skills, and conceptual understandings as distinguishing between the concepts of validity and reliability, mastering a sequence of turns in a dance performance, and analyzing differences among various rhetorical voices. Learning tasks can be the focus of a single class session, or several. They often are reintroduced and elaborated in subsequent sessions.

As noted, learning tasks are designed to help students realize expected learning outcomes, as framed by overall curricular goals. Productive learning requires that expected learning outcomes be explicit and clearly understood by both students and teachers (Angelo, 1993; Cross, 1987; Ewell, 1991). Without this, teachers and students are hard pressed to assess progress toward realizing expected outcomes, identify obstacles to more productive learning, and evaluate whether efforts to resolve obstacles have been effective.

Given II is what the student brings. This given refers to a student's existing learning characteristics as the learning event begins. Such characteristics include already acquired knowledge, skills and conceptual abilities, habitual learning strategies for processing and relating emergent with acquired learning, and typical motivational orientations. These entering learning characteristics play a profound role in learning. Since learning outcomes are brought about by acts of construction, the foundation for this constructive process is represented by what the student brings to the learning event. The foundation fundamentally shapes resultant learning outcomes. The more solid and differentiated the foundation, the more solid and differentiated the outcome (Gagne, 1985).

Given III is what the teacher brings. This given refers to the set of guiding assumptions, based on past experience, a teacher brings to the learning event. Such assumptions relate to the nature of learning and the corresponding roles of teacher and student. They include as well assumptions about the structure, content, and modes of inquiry characterizing the teacher's discipline. Finally, they define the educational goals the teacher finds worthy in the first place and the academic standards applied to student work. These guiding assumptions frame the teacher's personal orientation in approaching the learning event.

Student's learning strategies and adaptations (IV) and teacher's instructional approach and adaptations (V) are the process variables within the learning event. These variables interact with each other to generate what happens throughout the educational transaction. Within the context established by the givens, the nature of learning at any given moment reflects the ongoing reciprocal influence of how the teacher structures and presents the learning task, how the student engages with the learning task, how the teacher assesses this engagement and responds, and what the student does next (note the bidirectional arrows between IV and V).

Student's learning strategies and adaptations (IV) involve a great many important issues. How is the student acquiring and organizing new learning? How is the student relating to existing learning? Does the student demonstrate a variety of learning strategies complementing the variety of learning task requirements, or does the student rely on one way of learning regardless of the nature of the learning task and the demands and supports of the teaching strategy? What is the student's motivational orientation? Does the student exhibit ownership of the expected learning outcomes? How is learning success and failure being interpreted by the student? What is the significance of the new learning for the student? How skilled is the student in stepping back during the learning process to observe and evaluate how well or poorly the operative learning strategy is bringing about desired results? How adaptive is the student in generating more productive learning strategies or in trying out new learning strategies that others suggest?

The second process variable, teacher's instructional approach and adaptations (V), comprises both (A) teaching strategies and (B) assessment strategies. Teaching strategies aim to foster student engagement, persistence, and success. They do so through a mix of demands, supports, and incentives in presenting the learning task to students. They also do so through revising the learning task to accommodate and expand student learning characteristics and strategies. Assessment strategies serve to illuminate such student learning qualities in terms of overall learning progress. They provide information to the student and teacher that guides the revision of learning and teaching strategies to promote more effective student learning.

The issues that teachers wrestle with in process variable V mirror those that students wrestle with in process variable IV (not surprising if indeed effective instruction and student learning represent two sides of a common transaction). What additional structure, incentive, or demand should the teacher provide to help encourage and support a student's engagement with the learning task? What is the teacher's rhythm in phasing out added structure within the learning task and requiring the student more and more to provide his or her own structure? What is the teacher's pace in introducing greater challenge throughout the sequence of learning tasks in helping the student move toward the level of sophistication represented by the long-term curricular goals? What approaches can the teacher experiment with to marshal student motivation (from involving students in defining the expected learning outcomes to incorporating their interests in the learning tasks in the first place to tweaking the point system for arriving at final course grades)? What strategies does the teacher use to assess a student's learning characteristics, strategies, and progress? How is the assessment information used to revise the learning task in ways that better support student achievement of expected outcomes?

Revising learning tasks and teaching and assessment strategies to support more effectively the success of individual students is an act of reflective instructional problem solving. It is guided by assessing the learning characteristics, strategies, and actual performance of the individual student in light of expected learning outcomes and long-term curricular goals. It is fueled by findings from pedagogical research, past instructional experiences, ongoing trial and error, re-evaluation of pedagogical assumptions, and creative intuition (Lacey, 1980; Wang, 1991).

Assessment strategies (VB) underlie the remaining variable in Figure 2 under status check, progress toward mastery (VI). This variable refers to the monitoring of student learning in light of expected learning outcomes, revised learning strategies, and modified instructional approaches. The checking/adapting/checking again process optimally occurs early and often throughout the learning event (Angelo, 1993; Chickering & Gamson, 1987; Norman, 1993). Restricting such monitoring to the end of a learning event precludes opportunities for enhancing learning productivity along the way.

The assessment activities chosen for status checks need to generate feedback about student learning that aligns accurately with the nature of expected learning outcomes and long-term curricular goals. It is alarmingly easy to check on student progress using assessment activities that are familiar and easy to use but provide feedback about student learning that only partially reflects expected outcomes and goals. (See Angelo & Cross, 1993, for a valuable resource of diverse assessment strategies fitting a variety of learning outcomes.)

The effectiveness of efforts to enhance learning is made known to teachers and students through ongoing status checks. This process of checking/adapting/checking again is at the heart of tailoring instruction to support every student's successful learning. As should be clear by now, effective instruction in the context of Figure 2 is not one-way, from teacher to student. It consists instead of mutual accommodation and extension between the student's evolving repertoire of learning characteristics and strategies and the teacher's evolving repertoire of guiding assumptions and instructional approaches—all with the aim of supporting student mastery of curricular goals. The ideal outcome of a learning event transacted through individualizing instruction is one in which both students and teachers leave with more than they entered.

Finally, the recursive path in Figure 2, circling back from progress toward mastery (VI) to the other learning event variables illustrates a critical dynamic of the learning/teaching dance characterizing individualizing instruction. If a periodic status check shows either no student progress or noticeably inefficient progress toward learning outcomes, what adaptations in the learning event variables might be needed? Following a line of analysis traced by Salvia and Hughes (1990), is the learning task and associated outcomes appropriate, given the learning characteristics of the student? Does the student possess prerequisite skills? Does the learning task provide enough opportunities for applying and practicing new learning in different contexts? Is the student getting meaningful feedback on that application and practice? Does the teaching strategy sufficiently foster and support student engagement? Is the teacher's assumption about what learning entails and personal orientation about the roles of teacher and student consistent with the learning task's expected outcome? The posing of such questions as hypotheses, and then collecting assessment information in response, captures the notion of teacher as pedagogical researcher/instructional problem solver. It is a process central for informing a teacher's efforts to individualize instruction.

A quick point is worth emphasizing. In preceding comments, it is the teacher who conducts periodic status checks. It is desirable of course (in terms of helping to develop skills of learning how to learn) for students to share in this responsibility, and to follow through in figuring out what learning strategy adaptations might make sense for improving learning effectiveness. This kind of student involvement, as fostered by the teaching strategy crafted by the teacher, is a powerful means of furthering students' metacognitive skills of self-assessment and self-adjustment (Angelo & Cross, 1993; Wiggins, 1997).

In putting forth this framework for individualizing instruction, it is important to remind ourselves of the essential elusiveness, uncertainty, and reflectiveness of instructional problem solving (Lampert, 1985; Plater, 1995; Salvia & Ysseldyke, 1998; Shulman, 1999). Frameworks often wrongly imply fixed systems, definitive variables and processes, cut-and-dried decision making. These implications poorly match the realities of wrestling with how best to support productive student learning. In contrast, the orientation best fitting this framework's application is a pragmatic one, recognizing the undeniable need for teachers and students to work together in combining experience, insight, research, and trial-and-error experimentation (all as informed by ongoing assessment) in coming up with instructional and learning approaches that support student success (Angelo & Cross, 1993). Less fertile orientations would be those tied to preconceived theoretical stances that limit ways of thinking about learning and teaching and reject potentially effective approaches out of hand.

REFERENCES

Angelo, T. A. (1993). "A teacher's dozen": Fourteen general research-based principles for improving higher learning in our classrooms. *AAHE Bulletin,* *45*(8), 3–7, 13.

Angelo, T. A., & Cross, K. P. (1993). *Classroom assessment techniques: A handbook for college teachers* (2d ed.). San Francisco: Jossey-Bass.

Astin, A. W. (1990). Educational assessment and educational equity. *American Journal of Education, 98*(4), 458–478.

Bok, D. (1992 July/August). Reclaiming the public trust. *Change, 24*(4), 12–19.

Chickering, A. W., & Gamson, Z. F. (1987). Seven principles for good practice in undergraduate practice. *AHHE Bulletin, 39*(7), 3–7.

Chism, N. (1994). Taking student diversity into account. In W. J. McKeachie, N. Chism, R. Menges, M. Svinicki, & C. Weinstein (Eds.), *Teaching tips: Strategies, research, and theory for college and university teachers* (pp. 223–237). Washington, DC: D.C. Heath.

Corno, L., & Snow, R. E. (1986). Adapting teaching to individual differences among learners. In M. C. Wittrock (Ed.), *Handbook of research on teaching* (3d ed., pp. 605–629). New York: Macmillan.

Cross, K. P. (1976). *Accent on learning.* San Francisco: Jossey-Bass.

Cross, K. P. (1987, March). *Teaching for learning.* Paper presented at the annual meeting of the American Association of Higher Education, Chicago, IL.

Davis, B. G. (1993). *Tools for teaching.* San Francisco: Jossey-Bass.

Eble, K. E., & McKeachie, W. J. (1985). *Improving undergraduate education through faculty development.* San Francisco: Jossey-Bass.

Ewell, P. T. (1991). To capture the ineffable: Newer forms of assessment in higher education. In G. Grant (Ed.), *Review of Research in Education* (pp. 75–125). Washington, DC: American Educational Research Association.

Fincher, C. (1985). Learning theory and research. In J. C. Smart (Ed.), *Higher Education Handbook of Theory and Research* (Vol. 1, pp. 63–96). New York: Agathon Press.

Gagne, R. M. (1985). *The conditions of learning* (4th ed.). New York: Holt, Rinehart, & Winston.

Gordon, E. W. (1999). Human diversity and equitable assessment. In S. J. Messick (Ed.), *Assessment in higher education: Issues of access, quality, student development, and public policy* (pp. 203–211). Mahwah, N.J.: Lawrence Erlbaum.

Guskin, A. E. (1994, September/October). Restructuring the role of the faculty. *Change, 26*(5), 16–25.

Huba, M. E., & Freed, J. E. (2000). *Learner-centered assessment on college campuses.* Needham Heights, MA: Allyn & Bacon.

Joyce, B., & Weil, M. (1972). *Models of teaching.* Englewood Cliffs, NJ: Prentice-Hall.

Keller, F. S., & Sherman, J. G. (1974). *The Keller Plan handbook.* Menlo Park, CA: W. A. Benjamin.

Lacey, P. A. (1980). *Teaching as a double dialogue*. New Directions for Teaching and Learning, 4, 71–80.

Lampert, M. (1985). How do teachers manage to teach?: Perspectives on problems in practice. *Harvard Educational Review, 55*(2), 178–194.

Lisska, A. J. (1997). Teaching through the curriculum: The development of a comprehensive honors program. In J. K. Roth (Ed.), *Inspiring teaching: Carnegie professors of the year speak* (pp. 90–99). Bolton, MA: Anker.

McCombs, B., & Whisler, J. S. (1997). *The learner-centered classroom and school: Strategies for increasing student motivation and achievement*. San Francisco: Jossey-Bass.

Nemko, M. (1995). Preface. In S. R. Hatfield (Ed.), *The seven principles in action: Improving undergraduate education* (pp. ix–x). Bolton, MA: Anker.

Norman, D. (1993). *Things that make us smart: Defending human attributes in the age of the machine*. Reading, MA: Addison-Wesley.

Pascarella, E. T., & Terenzini, P. T. (1991). *How college affects students*. San Francisco: Jossey-Bass.

Pascarella, E. T., & Terenzini, P. T. (1994). Living with myths: Undergraduate education in America. *Change, 26*(1), 28–32.

Plater, W. M. (1995). Future work: Faculty time in the 21st century. *Change, 27*(3), 22–33.

Rouche, J. E., & Rouche, S. D. (1987). Teaching and learning. In L. Noel, R. Levitz, D. Saluri, & Associates (Eds.), *Increasing student retention* (pp. 283–330). San Francisco: Jossey-Bass.

Salvia, J., & Hughes, C. (1990). *Curriculum based assessment: Testing what is taught*. New York: Macmillan.

Salvia, J., & Ysseldyke, J. E. (1998). *Assessment* (7th edition). Boston: Houghton Mifflin.

Sherman, T. M., Armistead, L. P., Fowler, F., Barksdale, M. A., & Reif, G. (1987). The quest for excellence in university teaching. *Journal of Higher Education, 58*(1), 66–64.

Shuell, T. J. (1986). Individual differences: Changing conceptions in research and practice. *American Journal of Education, 94*(3), 356–377.

Shulman, L. S. (1999, July/August). Taking learning seriously. *Change, 31*(4), 11–17.

Tobias, S. (1994). The contract alternative. *AAHE Bulletin, 46*(6), 3–6.

Wagener, U. E. (1989). Quality and equity: The necessity for imagination. *Harvard Educational Review, 59*(2), 240–250.

Wang, M. C. (1991). Adaptive instruction: An alternative approach to providing for student diversity. In M. Ainscow (Ed.), *Effective schools for all* (pp. 134–160). London: David Fulton.

Weingartner, R. H. (1994). Between cup and lip: Reconceptualizing education as student learning. *Educational Record, 75*(1), 13–19.

Whitener, E. M. (1989). A meta-analytic review of the effect on learning of the inter-
    action between prior achievement and instructional support. *Review of Edu-
    cational Research, 59*(1), 65–86.
Wiggins, G. (1997, November). Feedback: How learning occurs. *AAHE Bulletin,
    50*(30), 7–8.

Chapter 4

Individualizing Instruction: Guidelines

Jeffrey E. Porter

Teachers face substantial challenge in tailoring existing instructional approaches or generating new ones to enhance learning by individual students. Meeting this challenge, however, can have an impressive payoff. Considerable research in undergraduate education shows that students learn more when teachers individualize their instruction in ways responsive to such differences among learners as level of preparation, learning rate, and learning strategy (Pascarella & Terenzini, 1994).

The guidelines below focus selectively on the learning task, what the teacher brings, teacher's instructional approach (including both teaching and assessment strategies), and progress toward mastery as presented in Figure 2 of Chapter 3. These guidelines are culled both from research findings and practitioner insights. They represent cross-disciplinary instructional heuristics for fueling the reflections and shaping the efforts of teachers attempting to support the success of individual learners.

In setting forth these guidelines, it is important to clarify their heuristic nature. As grounded as they are in solid research and skilled practice, they serve as reference points only. They do not rise to the level of prescriptive truths, ensuring certain success in supporting productive learning by individual students. Assuming such status would be not only presumptuous but antithetical to the notion of teacher as reflective practitioner; each interaction between student and learning task should be approached as a unique episode of instructional problem solving. These guidelines are offered touchstones to help to anchor the process of instructional problem solving. They require deft translation because of the complex nuances constituting actual learning/teaching events with individual students.

Individualizing instruction relies on creative problem solving in collaboration with individual students, not application of prescribed guidelines. Teaching and learning are social activities comprising the idiosyncratic qualities of unique participants (Roth, 1997). No blueprints, no formulae exist for determining which instructional approach will support which learner in mastering which learning outcome in which discipline area. As Brookfield (1995) notes, the answers to such queries are not "out there somewhere." They are embedded in the improvisations of teachers and students as committed partners in a common enterprise. Ultimately, teachers attempting to support the learning of individual students represents interpretive, not ballroom, dancing!

GUIDELINES

- As part of their personal orientation towards learning and instruction, effective teachers care passionately about the success of individual students (Granrose, 1980). They demonstrate this care through personal interactions with students, developing relationships of respect and empathy (McCombs & Whisler, 1997; Pascarella & Terenzini, 1991; Reynolds, 1992; Rouche & Rouche, 1987). Effective teachers know that interacting with students in ways that demonstrate care and support can powerfully promote student engagement with learning (Angelo, 1993; Chickering & Gamson, 1987; Norman, 1993; Sherman, Armistead, Fowler, Barksdale, & Reif, 1987). Such interactions enable teachers to learn about their students as individuals, their backgrounds, their ways of looking at the world, their preferred learning strategies, and their motivational orientations. This kind of knowledge is critical for informing efforts to individualize instruction (Roth, 1997).

- As another aspect of their personal orientation, effective teachers strive for the sake of each student's intellectual development as much as for the sake of their own (Woditsch, Schlesinger, & Giardina, 1987). They adopt a role of working with students as partners. "Teacher as unassailable expert," possessing all answers and defining the correct way of learning, represents the traditional role of the undergraduate teacher. Such a role is less effective in supporting engaged learning by students than that of "teacher as senior partner," with students viewed not as intellectual pawns but as learning companions (Kuh, Baird, & Leslie, 1992; Welker, 1991). Taking on this latter role within teaching/learning relationships provides teachers numerous natural opportunities to validate the strivings of students, assure students that with effort and adaptability they can be successful learners, and recognize students as valued partners with legitimate experiences and insights to bring to the learning experience (Terenzini et al., 1994).

- Effective teachers demonstrate such thorough command of their disciplines that they are able to make them accessible, meaningful, and coherently organized for students representing great varieties of learning characteristics and strategies. Such expertise enables a teacher to generate alternative and personalized metaphors, analogies, models, reinforcing examples, linkages, and learning tasks—all with the aim of helping individual students relate to new learning (Baiocco & DeWaters, 1998; Jones, Palinscar, Ogle, & Carr, 1987; Lacey, 1980; McKeachie, Pintrich, Lin, Smith, & Sharma, 1990; Sherman et al., 1987; Woditsch et al., 1987).

- Effective teachers are "bridge builders" between the knowledge and skills individual students bring to the learning task and the knowledge and skills constituting expected learning outcomes (Eble & McKeachie, 1985; Jones et al., 1987). Such bridge building entails stimulating students' pertinent knowledge and skills in introducing new learning activities (Gagne, 1985); fostering meaningful connections between new content and existing knowledge and skills (Angelo, 1993; Pascarella & Terenzini, 1991); and providing opportunities for applying emergent knowledge and skills to new problem situations (Angelo, 1993; Gagne, 1985). As noted above, discipline expertise (in content mastery, theoretical lay of the land, and associated modes of inquiry) is essential for effective instruction, but it is not enough (National Research Council, 1999). Effective teachers also demonstrate expertise both in assessing the current learning characteristics and strategies of individual students relative to the expected learning outcomes and in working with individual learners to craft alternative paths for bridging current with expected competencies (Davis, 1993). They are skilled in designing learning activities that connect what students need to know and how they need to learn with what they currently know and how they currently learn (Vella, 2000). Research shows that expert teachers take into account students' existing profiles of knowledge and skill as starting places more often than novice teachers (Reynolds, 1992). Further, effective teachers analyze how the learning task is being processed and understood by individual students throughout the learning experience (Ramsden, 1988). Without a dual focus both on expected learning outcomes and the student's current functioning, and without responsive adaptations along the way, a teacher's bridge building won't meet in the middle!

- To support learning more likely to be retained and used, effective teachers encourage students to generate as much personal meaning as possible from their engagement with learning tasks (Angelo, 1993; Loeffelbein, 1963; Wagener, 1989). Instructional strategies serving this purpose include establishing personally meaningful contexts through structuring learning tasks not only to be internally coherent, but externally linked to the backgrounds and interests of individual learners (Gagne, 1985; Ramsden, 1988); providing opportunities for students to reflect on related learning experiences in other settings, anticipate what is to come, generate questions, summarize information, and clarify unclear concepts and vocabulary (Jones et al., 1987); and structuring the learning task to provide opportunities for processing and interacting with the content from a variety of conceptual perspectives (Brophy & Alleman, 1991).

- Effective teachers engage in ongoing assessment and reflective instructional problem solving. They assess those learning characteristics (e.g., structures and extent of existing knowledge and skills, nature of motivational orientation) and learning strategies (e.g., ways of processing and organizing information, ways of solving problems) of individual students crucial for success with the learning task at hand. This kind of assessment depends on being able to see through the eyes of the student (Brookfield, 1995). Effective teachers fold the results of such assessment into reflective instructional problem solving, incorporating as well findings from pedagogical research, past instructional experiences, assumptions about the nature of learning and teaching, personal orientations about the roles of student and teacher, and hunches. Ongoing assessment and instructional problem solving inform the progress toward mastery variable in Figure 2 of Chapter 3: the selecting, creating, trying out, evaluating, reflecting upon, and revising of instructional and learning approaches aimed at supporting an individual student's academic success (Davis, 1993; Lacey, 1980; Pascarella & Terenzini, 1991; Wang, 1991). Such activity is critical in attempting to bridge the idiosyncrasies of individual learners with the constants of curricular objectives and performance standards (Bennet & Dyer, 1994).

- Effective teachers assume responsibility for supporting successful student learning (Chickering & Gamson, 1987; Ericson & Ellett, 1990). It is a responsibility shared between teachers and students, but not in the sense of something split down the middle. Clearly, learning is what teachers and students work at together. As emphasized in Chapter 3, learning and effective instruction are not discrete processes; they are reciprocal aspects of a common transaction. Just as clearly, the contributions of teachers in supporting successful student learning are important. Learning ultimately is nevertheless the direct result of effort and processes initiated and controlled by the student; therefore it ultimately is the responsibility of the learner (McKeachie, Pintrich, & Lin, 1985). This reality implies that effective teachers view themselves as responsible agents within the learning/teaching transaction—not for learning itself, but for effectively supporting learning through the effective design, implementation, and refinement of their instructional approaches (Vella, 2000). A coresponsibility for learning exists between students and teachers, even if it applies to different aspects of the learning/teaching transaction. This coresponsibility is most fully realized between teachers and students within educational settings of mutual cooperation, respect, and investment (Smith, 1989).

- Coresponsibility for learning between teachers and students has clear implications for the issue of power sharing. Undergraduate teachers typically exercise control in staking out curricula, the what of teaching. Whether at course, program, or collegewide levels, faculty today (certainly compared to the 1960s!) more often than not assume final authority for discriminating between what is worth learning and what is not. However, in figuring out the successful how of learning and teaching, effective teachers have learned to give up exclusive decision-making power and to share control with learners (Clark, 1981; Graman, 1988; Welker, 1991). They work collaboratively, rather than hierarchically, with individual students to create instructional and learning approaches that lead to academic success (Plater, 1995). If students and teachers truly are cocreators in the learning/teaching transaction, then students need to be viewed as partners by teachers in the decision making underlying that transaction (McCombs and Whisler (1997). The teacher-centered notion that curricular goals are realizable only through learning tasks unilaterally designed and imposed by the teacher is counterproductive to student academic success. It needs to yield to a student-focused instructional approach, one that allows some degree of student control and choice over the selection and design of learning tasks, assessment strategies, and even expected short-term learning outcomes (within parameters set by long-term curricular goals). The responsibility shared by all members of an educational community for maintaining standards for the quality of learning outcomes need not translate into a fixed standardization of how those outcomes are achieved. In fact the opposite is true. Highest-quality learning happens when individual students engage in learning tasks within instructional approaches designed to support and expand their unique learning qualities. Creating alternative learning/teaching paths to support the success of individual students cannot be undertaken by teachers alone; it requires the shared efforts and decision making of students and teachers working together.

- Teacher and student coresponsibility for learning also means that both success and failure in realizing expected learning outcomes is accounted for by interactions between students and teachers, not exclusively by dynamics within students (Porter, 1994). Assuming genuine effort by both, the accomplishment of learning outcomes in light of established standards is attributable to both student and teacher—likewise when outcomes are not accomplished.

- Effective teachers understand and act on the simple, profound reality that learning results from the actions of learners (Angelo, 1993; Cross, 1987; Norman, 1993). They encourage students to apply themselves in figuring out the meaning, implications, and applications of new content, instead of just reproducing or recalling it as given (McCombs & Whisler, 1997). They do this through creating instructional strategies and learning tasks that constitute open, rather than closed questions and that require students to use available educational resources in constructing their own best answers (Vella, 2000). As Vella emphasizes, a teacher's lecture might very well be an important component of an overall instructional strategy, but only as a means for efficiently disseminating a large amount of new information to students in a short time. Active learning involves what students directly do with new content beyond receiving it, through analysis, critique, integration, reconstruction, and application. When students challenge assumptions or conclusions, find flaws, explore implications through discussion with others, write about new content from a variety of perspectives, relate emergent learning to past experiences through comparison and contrast, create real-life applications and refine emergent learning based on the results of such application, they actively learn (Chickering & Gamson, 1987;

McCombs & Whisler, 1997; Norman, 1993; Pascarella & Terenzini, 1991; Vorkink, 1995).

- Effective teachers help students motivate themselves to initiate and sustain engagement in learning tasks (Angelo, 1993; Brophy & Alleman, 1991; Gagne, 1985; Norman, 1993). They do so through their overall instructional approach with students and in their specific design of the learning tasks. First, regarding overall instructional approach, students experience greater motivation to engage in learning when teachers establish with them a collaborative, senior/junior partner relationship. Such a partnership is demonstrated through activities that include deciding upon expected learning outcomes open to the interests of students (and compatible with long-term curricular goals); codesigning learning tasks that are instrumental to those learning outcomes and that also support and expand preferred learning strategies; figuring out and assembling the needed educational resources responding to a particular learning task; and developing alternative strategies for assessing whether, and how, students are progressing (Chickering & Reiser, 1993). Instructional approaches foster student engagement with learning when they communicate and affirm, from the first through the last day of class in a variety of ways, that students are in control of and primarily responsible for the outcomes of their learning and that they are able to navigate learning tasks successfully with effort, persistence, and a willingness to experiment with and develop new learning strategies (McCombs & Whisler, 1997). Instructional approaches also foster student engagement when they help students frame the meaning of learning failure as temporary rather than terminal and as reflecting a lack of effort or an ineffective learning approach (perhaps in combination with an ineffective instructional approach) rather than a lack of ability (Jones et al., 1987). When teachers work with students in ways that portray ability as an acquirable skill and that help students view progress and accomplishment in terms of self-growth rather than comparison with others, students experience greater motivation for learning engagement (Stage, Muller, Kinzie, & Simmons, 1998).

- Effective teachers also are aware that student motivation for learning engagement can be fostered by the way specific learning tasks are designed. One such design feature is fashioning learning task content to spark curiosity and creative association for students while also forging links to their personal experiences, to the broader community, and to events and issues on the world stage (McCombs & Whisler, 1997). As well, the more a teacher designs learning tasks that challenge the existing capabilities of students, the more students will be motivated to engage it. By "challenge," I mean that elusive balance between boredom and panic. It is a balance realized and maintained through refining the nature of the learning task and the demands and supports constituting the teaching strategy, with a view to advancing the student's progress toward expected learning outcomes (Angelo, 1993; Bruner, 1966; Cross, 1987; Norman, 1993). Learning engagement is enhanced by this sense of disequilibrium between what a student does not know or cannot do and what that student needs or wants to know and be able to do. When the condition of "challenge" is achieved, the student is motivated to engage the learning task; learning is charged

(Graman, 1988; Pascarella & Terenzini, 1991). Other learning task design features available to teachers for fostering student motivation include stipulating clearly and explicitly the expected learning outcomes defining the learning task and ensuring they are understood by students (Angelo, 1993; Bruner, 1966; Cross, 1987); and establishing and communicating high standards for student performance (Angelo, 1993; Chickering & Gamson, 1987; Kuh et al., 1992; Reynolds, 1992). For better or worse, teacher expectations expressed both verbally and nonverbally exert considerable influence on student performance (Rouche & Rouche, 1987).

- Effective teachers translate long-term curricular goals into a sequence of expected learning outcomes that define individual learning tasks, tasks that are manageable and that with effort and adaptiveness students can engage and master (whenever possible, at their own pace) (Cross, 1976; Pascarella & Terenzini, 1991). In this way, effective teachers build in ongoing student success as a basic dynamic of their daily interactions with students (Rouche & Rouche, 1987).

- Effective teachers act on the well-supported research finding that student learning is significantly enhanced by performance feedback (Brophy & Alleman,1991; Ewell, 1991; Fincher, 1985; Pascarella & Terenzini, 1991). For optimal enhancement, such feedback needs to specifically address where individual students stand now, in light of where they started and the expected learning outcome (Guskin, 1994). Performance feedback can be formal or informal but it needs to be of high intensity (Norman, 1993) and useful to students in their self-adjustments toward realizing the learning outcome (Wiggens, 1997). Performance feedback should occurr early, often, and promptly (Angelo, 1993; Chickering & Gamson, 1987). Effective teachers capitalize on the power of performance feedback not only in enhancing student learning but also in shaping it. How students are assessed, what they are assessed on, and the kind of feedback provided influence powerfully how students interpret the meaning of the learning experience and the kind of learning they generate and take with them (Angelo, 1993).

- Effective teachers hold as their ultimate goal supporting students to become progressively skilled and self-sufficient learners, beyond accomplishing this or that discipline-based set of learning outcomes and curricular goals. In this way, effective teachers view transactions with students and among students themselves as fertile opportunities for modeling the generative power and importance of learning itself, and for considering, acquiring, and practicing new learning strategies, perspectives, and attitudes that will enable them to become more expert learners.

A FINAL WORD ABOUT INDIVIDUALIZING INSTRUCTION AND ASSESSMENT

Figure 2 (Chapter 3) emphasizes the relationship between assessment and instruction in efforts to support effectively the learning of individual students. What is the nature of this relationship that a static, two-dimensional diagram attempts to capture? Three key qualities define the relationship. First, assessment is an inherent aspect of effective instruction; the act of effective instruction necessarily embodies the act of assessment. Second, assessment is critical to effective instruction, in that it is impossible to conceive of effective instruction that does not stem from effective assessment. Finally, assessment is pervasive throughout effective instruction, in that it illuminates variables and informs teaching/learning decisions in all phases of a learning event.

Assessment in undergraduate education has taken on assorted meanings for teachers and students beyond those captured by Figure 2. Unfortunately, many of them are negative. For teachers, examples are figuring out what questions to include on the mid-term exam with that uneasy feeling that the expected learning outcomes thus far have been as ambiguous for the students as they have been for you; slogging through students' final projects to meet the registrar's deadline for course grades, knowing that an occasion such as this for providing students with feedback about the effectiveness of their learning efforts (so they can self-adjust in better approximating expected learning outcomes) has occurred too rarely throughout the course; and regretting the assessment strategies you have chosen to use throughout the course because they provide, in the end, too superficial a glimpse of the kind of learning you feel is most important. For students, examples include: showing up for the final exam representing 50% of the final grade, and hoping that what you think is important jives with your teacher's judgment; getting back your mid-term, figuring out what the score means, and hurriedly tucking it away in your notebook as the teacher begins to cover the material assigned for the rest of the week; and realizing that, although there are several ways to demonstrate a correct answer to the teacher's test question, if you want to do well in the course you need to state your answer in the one way sanctioned by this particular teacher.

Assessment in undergraduate education frequently is externally imposed, bureaucratically fashioned, and competitively driven. It centers too often on evaluating and fixing accountability for end products and too rarely on the heart of the enterprise: understanding the dynamics of student learning and informing teachers and students how to better support it. In today's culture of undergraduate education, assessment is associated more with forming comparative judgment of final products than with enhancing individual learning toward curricular goals (Ewell, 1999).

In the context of individualizing instruction, assessment has a clear if uncustomary role. It is linked directly to student learning and the instructional challenge of how best to support it. It is a core dimension of student-focused instruction. The countless questions fueling reflective instructional problem solving, the moment-to-moment ones guiding interactions with students within the context of discrete learning events and more sweeping ones such as monitoring student progress throughout the overall course curriculum require the ongoing assessment of student learning. Figure 2 in Chapter 3 brings such questions to the surface. What are this student's learning characteristics in terms of educational background, motivational orientation, and current structure of knowledge and skills that bear on the expected learning outcomes? Are learning outcomes explicit and clear, and understood by the student? Will mastery of such outcomes indeed lead to achieving long-term curricular goals? What seems to be the student's learning strategy in engaging the learning task? Is the student monitoring the relative effectiveness of this chosen strategy and making appropriate refinements along the way? Is the instructional approach providing sufficiently clear corrective feedback for the student? What progress is the student making toward realizing the expected learning outcomes? What is the final extent to which the student has realized the established learning outcome? The results of these kinds of ongoing queries inform the continuous problem solving between teacher and student in individualizing instruction to support productive learning.

Figure 2 (Chapter 3) makes explicit the important variables of any learning event and the relationship among them. Assessing these variables and their influence on one another, and incorporating the results of such assessment in ongoing instructional problem solving, is critical in supporting the productive learning of individual students. Without assessment, teacher and students lack the navigational tools and reciprocal feedback necessary for achieving learning task outcomes and curricular goals.

In crafting assessment strategies to support the learning of individual students (see Figure 2 VB, Chapter 3), there are some helpful rules of thumb:

- The most effective assessment strategies for figuring out how best to support productive student learning are those developed and implemented by teachers and students themselves in answering their own learning/teaching questions, not those prescribed by someone's packaged wisdom about types of learners and teacher-proof instructional strategies (Angelo & Cross, 1993).

- The most useful assessment techniques are context-specific and formative. They focus on specific learning characteristics and strategies of individual students in relation to the established outcomes and requirements of the specific learning task, rather than on general learning characteristics and strategies independent of the actual learning event. They monitor a student's ongoing progress in light of the established learning outcomes, in addition to that student's final level of learning once instruction is concluded.

- Of all the learning characteristics and strategies that could be assessed, effective teachers focus on those that are (1) functionally related to alternative instructional approaches that could be applied differentially in enhancing a student's learning productivity and (2) alterable by the student within existing time and energy constraints (regarding both the learning event at hand and the overall curriculum) (Angelo & Cross, 1993).

When assessment is keyed to student learning, it is not externally imposed. It arises from dynamics inherent in the learning/teaching transaction. It is shaped by the knowledge, personal orientation, pedagogical assumptions, insights and hunches, and trial-and-error experimentation of teachers committed not merely to transmitting their disciplines but helping individual students realize productive discipline-based learning. It is not undertaken for the purpose of comparatively ranking final student products at the conclusion of learning. It aims instead to illuminate the process of learning and enhance the effectiveness of instruction in supporting student success (Angelo, 1995).

REFERENCES

Angelo, T. A. (1993). "A teacher's dozen": Fourteen general research-based principles for improving higher learning in our classrooms. *AAHE Bulletin, 45*(8), 3–7, 13.

Angelo, T. A. (1995, February). Classroom assessment for critical thinking. *Teaching of Psychology, 22*(1), 6–7.

Angelo, T. A., & Cross (1993). *Classroom assessment techniques: A handbook for college teachers* (2d ed.). San Francisco: Jossey-Bass.

Astin, A. W. (1985). *Achieving educational excellence.* San Francisco: Jossey-Bass.

Baiocco, S. A., & DeWaters, J. (1998). *Successful college teaching: Problem-solving strategies of distinguished professors.* Needham Heights, MA: Allyn & Bacon.

Bennet, J. B., & Dyer, E. A. (1994). On complaining about students. *AAHE Bulletin, 46*(8), 7–8.

Brookfield, S. (1995). *Becoming a critically reflective teacher.* San Francisco: Jossey-Bass.

Brophy, J., & Alleman, J. (1991). Activities as instructional tools: A framework for analysis and evaluation. *Educational Researcher, 20*(4), 9–23.

Brown, A. L. (1994). The advancement of learning. *Educational Researcher, 23*(8), 4–12.

Bruner, J. S. (1966). *Toward a theory of instruction.* Cambridge, MA: Harvard University Press.

Chickering, A. W., & Gamson, Z. F. (1987). Seven principles for good practice in undergraduate practice. *AHHE Bulletin, 39*(7), 3–7.

Chickering, A. W., & Reiser, L. (1993). *Educational and identity* (2nd ed.). The Jossey-Bass higher and adult education series. San Francisco: Jossey-Bass.

Clark, T. F. (1981). Individualized education. In A. W. Chickering & Associates (Eds.), *The modern American college* (pp. 252–255). San Francisco: Jossey-Bass.

Cross, K. P. (1976). *Accent on learning.* San Francisco: Jossey-Bass.

Cross, K. P. (1987, March 2). *Teaching for learning*. Paper presented at the annual meeting of the American Association of Higher Education, Chicago, IL.

Davis, B. G. (1993). *Tools for teaching*. San Francisco: Jossey-Bass.

Eble, K. E. (1980). Future considerations and additional resources. In K. E. Eble (Ed.), *Improving teaching styles* (pp. 95–104). San Francisco: Jossey-Bass.

Eble, K. E., & McKeachie, W. J. (1985). *Improving undergraduate education through faculty development*. San Francisco: Jossey-Bass.

Ericson, D. P., & Ellett, F. S. (1990). Taking student responsibility seriously. *Educational Researcher, 19*(9), 3–10.

Ewell, P. T. (1991). To capture the ineffable: Newer forms of assessment in higher education. In G. Grant (Ed.), *Review of Research in Education* (pp. 75–125). Washington, DC: American Educational Research Association.

Ewell, P. T. (1999). Assessment of higher education quality: Promise and politics. In S. J. Messick (Ed.), *Assessment in higher education: Issues of access, quality, student development, and public policy* (pp. 147–156). Mahwah, NJ: Lawrence Erlbaum.

Fincher, C. (1985). Learning theory and research. In J. C. Smart (Ed.), *Higher education: Handbook of theory and research* (Vol. 1, pp. 68–96). New York: Agathon Press.

Gagne, R. M. (1985). *The conditions of learning* (4th ed.). New York: Holt, Rinehart & Winston.

Graman, T. (1988). Education for humanization: Applying Paulo Freire's pedagogy to learning a second language. *Harvard Educational Review, 58*(4), 433–448.

Granrose, J. T. (1980). Conscious teaching: Helping graduate assistants develop teaching styles. In K. E. Eble (Ed.), *Improving teaching styles* (pp. 21–30). San Francisco: Jossey-Bass.

Guskin, A. E. (1994, September/October). Restructuring the role of the faculty. *Change, 26*(5), 16–25.

Haertel, G. D., Walberg, H. J., & Weinstein, T. (1983). Psychological models of educational performance: A theoretical synthesis of constructs. *Review of Educational Research, 53*(1), 75–91.

Jones, B. F., Palinscar, A. S., Ogle, D. S., & Carr, E. G. (1987). *Strategic teaching and learning: Cognitive instruction in the content areas*. Alexandria, VA: Association for Supervision and Curriculum Development.

Kuh, G., Baird, L. L., & Leslie, D. W. (1992). A landmark in scholarly synthesis. *Review of Higher Education, 15*(3), 347–373.

Lacey, P. A. (1980). Teaching as a double dialogue. *New Directions for Teaching and Learning, 4*, 71–80.

Loeffelbein, R. L. (1963). My best teachers. *Improving College and University Teaching, 11*, 25–26.

McCombs, B., & Whisler, J. S. (1997). *The learning centered classroom and school: Strategies for increasing student motivation and achievement*. The Jossey-Bass education series. San Francisco: Jossey-Bass.

McKeachie, W. J., Pintrich, P. R., & Lin, Y.-G. (1985). Teaching learning strategies. *Educational Psychologist, 20*(3), 153–160.

McKeachie, W. J., Pintrich, P. R., Lin, Y.-G., Smith, D.A.F., & Sharma, R. S. (1990). *Teaching and learning in the college classroom: A review of the research literature* (2d ed.). Ann Arbor, MI: National Center for Research to Improve Postsecondary Teaching and Learning, University of Michigan.

National Research Council, Committee on Learning Research and Educational Practice. (1999). *How people learn: Bridging research and practice.* Washington, DC: National Academy Press.

Norman, D. (1993). *Things that make us smart: Defending human attributes in the age of the machine.* Reading, MA: Addison-Wesley.

Pascarella, E. T., & Terenzini, P. T. (1991). *How college affects students.* San Francisco: Jossey-Bass.

Pascarella, E. T., & Terenzini, P. T. (1994). Living with myths: Undergraduate education in America. *Change, 26*(1), 28–32.

Plater, W. M. (1995). Future work: Faculty time in the 21st century. *Change. 27*(3), 22–33.

Porter, J. (1994). Disability in higher education: From person-based to interaction-based. *Journal on Excellence in College Teaching, 5*(1), 69–75.

Ramsden, P. (1988). Context and strategy: Situational influences on learning. In R. R. Schmeck (Ed.), *Learning strategies and learning styles* (pp. 159–188). New York: Plenum Press.

Reynolds, A. (1992). What is competent beginning teaching? A review of the literature. *Review of Educational Research, 62*(1), 1–35.

Roth, J. K. (1997). What this book teaches me. In J. K. Roth (Ed.), *Inspiring teaching: Carnegie Professors of the Year Speak* (pp. 226–232). Bolton, MA: Anker.

Rouche, J. E., & Rouche, S. D. (1987). Teaching and learning. In L. Noel, R. Levitz, D. Saluri, & Associates (Eds.), *Increasing student retention* (pp. 283–330). San Francisco: Jossey-Bass.

Sherman, T. M., Armistead, L. P., Fowler, F., Barksdale, M. A., & Reif, G. (1987). The quest for excellence in university teaching. *Journal of Higher Education, 58*(1), 66–84.

Smith, D. G. (1989). *The challenge of diversity: Involvement or alienation in the academy?* ASHE-ERIC Higher Education Report, No. 5. Washington, DC: ERIC Clearinghouse on Higher Education, Graduate School of Education and Human Development, George Washington University.

Stage, F. K., Muller, P. A., Kinzie, J., & Simmons, A. (1998). *Creating learning-centered classrooms: What does learning theory have to say?* ASHE-ERIC Higher Education Report, No. 4. Washington, DC: ERIC Clearinghouse on Higher Education, Graduate School of Education and Human Development, George Washington University.

Terenzini, P. T., Rendon, L. I., Upcraft, M. L., Allison, K. W., Gregg, P. L., & Jalomo, R. (1994). The transition to college: Diverse students, diverse stories. *Research in Higher Education, 35*(1), 57–73.

Tobias, S. (1994). The contract alternative. *AAHE Bulletin, 46*(6), 3–6.

Vella, J. (2000). *Taking learning to task: Creative strategies for teaching adults.* San Francisco: Jossey-Bass.

Vorkink, S. (1995). Time on task. In S. R. Hatfield (Ed.), *The seven principles in action* (pp. 67–78). Bolton, MA: Anker.

Wagener, U. E. (1989). Quality and equity: The necessity for imagination. *Harvard Educational Review, 59*(2), 240–250.

Wang, M. C. (1991). Adaptive instruction: An alternative approach to providing for student diversity. In M. Ainscow (Ed.), *Effective schools for all* (pp. 134–160). London: David Fulton.

Welker, R. (1991). Expertise and the teacher as expert: Rethinking a questionable metaphor. *American Educational Research Journal, 28*(1), 19–35.

Wiggins, G. (1997). Feedback: How learning occurs. *AAHE Bulletin, 50*(3), 7–8.

Woditsch, G. A., Schlesinger, M. A., & Giardina, R. C. (1987). The skillful baccalaureate. *Change, 19*(6), 48–57.

PART II

ENGLISH CURRICULA

Chapter 5

Whitman Among the Engineers: Teaching Poetry at a Technological Institution

Anne C. Coon

SETTING AND PERSONAL BACKGROUND

Although the term "technological institution" accurately describes Rochester Institute of Technology (RIT), it is much more difficult to find a single term to characterize the multitude of individuals who constitute the institute's student body. Not only are there students from every state and more than eighty foreign countries, those students are enrolled in over 200 different programs, ranging from engineering and computer science to business and photography. RIT has about 12,000 undergraduates, more than one-third of whom are women, and 1,100 of the 9,500 full-time undergraduates are deaf. As a university, RIT comprises eight separate colleges offering certificates, diplomas, and associate degrees; undergraduate BS and BFA degrees; and graduate MS, MBA, and Ph.D. degrees.

Despite the emphasis on technological studies, almost all undergraduate students at RIT are required to take fifty-four credit hours in the general education curriculum of the College of Liberal Arts. In addition to offering the introductory core courses and advanced coursework of the general education curriculum, the College of Liberal Arts offers undergraduate degrees in criminal justice, economics, professional and technical communication, psychology, public policy, and social work. There is, however, no English major.

Nonetheless, there are many options for students interested in studying literature beyond the introductory level. These students may take several advanced or upper-division courses grouped together to fulfill either a concentration (three courses) or a minor (five courses) in literature, or they may take individual elective courses in literature. As a faculty member in the Department of Language and Literature, I teach the required two-quarter Writing and Literature I and II sequence, as well as several upper-division courses, including courses in poetry and mythology. In these advanced literature courses, where the typical enrollment is thirty-two, there are great differences among the students: differences in demographics, academic majors, critical reading and writing skills, knowledge of literature, and learning styles. In this chapter I will focus primarily on my approach to teaching the course Modern Poetry, with occasional references to a second course, Myth, Legend, and Folklore.

GUIDING ASSUMPTIONS ABOUT LEARNING AND TEACHING

In the poem "Eating Poetry," Mark Strand uses a clever analogy to describe the enthusiasm of one who reads poetry.

> Ink runs from the corners of my mouth.
> There is no happiness like mine.
> I have been eating poetry.
> (Strand, 1968, pp. 1436–1437)

Since RIT students will not be "majoring" in literature, their decision to take a course such as Modern Poetry is most often motivated by a love of poetry, a curiosity about the particular period, or simply the desire to "try something different." Regardless of their background or major, I invite students to enter into a common inquiry to which we all bring our individual experiences, perspectives, and questions, along with a healthy appetite for reading poetry.

One of my objectives as a teacher is to help students develop an intellectual curiosity and informed understanding of literature that will enable them to read with insight and pleasure long after they have completed a particular course. I also hope to make them aware of the expressive and transformative power of literature. As Strand's poem continues,

> The librarian does not believe what she sees.
> Her eyes are sad
> and she walks with her hands in her dress.

The poems are gone.
The light is dim.
The dogs are on the basement stairs and coming up.

Their eyeballs roll,
their blond legs burn like brush.
The poor librarian begins to stamp her feet and weep.
She does not understand.
When I get on my knees and lick her hand,
she screams.

I am a new man.
I snarl at her and bark.
I romp with joy in the bookish dark.
(Strand, 1968, pp. 1436–1437)

If the enthusiasm of individual students is encouraged, if they can feel "new," or "snarl," or "bark," or even "romp with joy" at their own discoveries, they may be well on their way to developing an appreciation of literature that will continue long after the class is completed. Such an appreciation is built on the students' understanding of the many elements, aesthetic to historical, that make up a literary work. Arising in a particular time and place, drawing upon a particular impulse, a work of literature may celebrate, reject, or transcend those particulars. And just as students are moved by the pleasures and complexities of literature, especially poetry, they are also eager to know more about the particulars: the lives and circumstances of writers, the influences on their craft. Who, for instance, is the woman who was moved to write these lines?

This is my letter to the World
That never wrote to Me—
(Dickinson, 1890, p. 49)

What can we learn about her life? How will that help us understand her art?

In all my courses, I present literature as a body of written, spoken, and performed creative work; a reflection of human experience and emotion. The familiar mode of inquiry in a literature course is careful, reflective reading, followed by response, analysis, and expression of ideas. When approaching new material, teachers often encourage students to make connections between the literature and their own experience; to place themselves imaginatively in the position of the author, the original audience, or the subject of a work. As part of the process of inquiry, I also try to challenge students' initial or unexamined responses to literature by exposing them to writers whose opinions, culture, and view of the world may be quite different from their own. At the same time, I believe it is important to add breadth to the students' experience of literature by bringing in as many outside sources as possible (literary, visual, aural) beyond the required "texts."

Learning begins to take place when students appreciate literature as more than words on a page; when they begin to see connections between themselves and the material they are reading, among different texts, and among the subjects they are studying. Then students go on to make critical observations, ask questions, challenge assumptions, and formulate new understanding on their own. The process by which each student formulates his or her understanding of the material is complicated. It may occur during class or out of class when the student later reflects on a reading assignment or a class discussion. Likewise, the manifestation of the student's new understanding of the material may appear in several ways, through a comment made in class, an essay written on an exam, or perhaps, in the way the student selects, organizes, or presents material for a research presentation.

Sometimes, working individually with a student will serve as a catalyst, sparking the student's interest in learning. In meetings with students I provide what may sometimes sound like little more than a personalized version of things I have already said in class, as I clarify an assignment, help with course material, or provide guidance in identifying an appropriate research topic. And yet, these individual meetings provide more than the one-on-one delivery of information. For example, helping students select a poet for their research projects poses some logistical difficulties, since the students select their topics and begin working on the projects fairly early in the term, while much of the course material is still unfamiliar. When meeting with a student who is having difficulty choosing a poet for the research project, I will spend time talking with the student about his or her own background and interests before talking about the course. Whether a student is fascinated by science, writes lyrics for a local band, or owns every book by Maya Angelou, I try to build on those interests and commitments as I offer suggestions.

Individual meetings also provide an opportunity to extend the teaching and learning of the classroom in a more general way. For example, as I skim a student's draft to see whether the paper makes sense, I will provide tips for future proofreading. Likewise, if a student says there's nothing in our library on the topic in which he or she is interested, I will log onto the library's electronic databases through my office computer and—working through each step aloud with the student—casually try out several on-line search strategies. In both these instances, my teaching is informal, almost indirect. My goal is to make the student more independent, more confident about his or her skills and, perhaps, more curious. Indeed, encouraging this triad of student characteristics—independence, confidence, and curiosity—is critical to how I perceive my role as a teacher, whether I am working individually with a single student in my office or meeting with a class of thirty-two people.

Measuring the effectiveness of encouraging and supporting student learning is not easy. Certain changes can be observed. Improved writing skills, increased classroom participation, greater facility with the material, and more willingness to ask questions are all indicators that the student is engaged in the course and understands the instructor's expectations. There are often unexpected surprises, however, more dramatic indicators that the student is actively involved in learning the material and is engaging personally with that material. For example, I recall a student who went home for the weekend and returned with an audiotape of Robert Frost, specifically wanting to play it for the class in order to compare that tape to the Robert Frost recording I had played earlier. Another student brought in all the equipment needed to set up his laptop computer and show the class a poetry Web site he had found. When this serendipitous teaching and learning takes place, it is clear to me that the students are thinking about the course material in a new way and are also eager to add to the experience of others in the class. Likewise, when a student began her research presentation by giving a dramatic performance in the character of her chosen poet or when another student created a beautifully illustrated book of a poet's work, they were both demonstrating in a powerful way the personal and aesthetic connections they had made with the subjects of their research. A professor cannot design a course in order to ensure that such learning will happen. Indeed, only the student can make the leap from merely completing assigned tasks to the active engagement required for comparing, demonstrating, performing, or illustrating what he or she has learned. As a teacher, my goal is to create an environment in which the power of individual learning is both valued and visible. By treating the students and the material with respect and enthusiasm, by conveying an active interest in the subject—and its complexities—I try to create an environment where engineers, business majors, graphic designers and social workers want to learn about poetry and want to share what they have learned with others.

APPROACHES AND TECHNIQUES FOR INDIVIDUALIZING INSTRUCTION

Students at RIT are, in general, serious and career-oriented. They put a great deal of effort into their studies, and their priority, not surprisingly, is the work demanded by their majors. Thus even those with a strong interest in poetry or mythology may struggle to find the time and attention needed for an upper-division literature course. There are some advantages to this environment: first, I try to plan the work for the ten-week quarter as carefully as possible, making it clear from the beginning what is expected and that I see the course syllabus as a contract between us. If I make revisions to the syllabus, I distribute them in writing. I try to pace the workload evenly throughout the quarter and give ample time for assignments, especially research projects. Next, I emphasize that I have high expectations for the students: I consider attendance mandatory, I do not accept late work, and I grade written assignments for the quality of writing as well as the originality and clarity of thought. Having established these expectations, I stress throughout the quarter that the policies I set, as well as decisions (and any exceptions) I make, are guided by my desire to be fair. I will not, for example, offer one student an extra credit assignment unless I am willing to make that option available to the entire class. My experience has been that students respond well to an environment in which there are consistent and fair expectations.

From Walt Whitman and Emily Dickinson through the Harlem Renaissance to the Beat Poets and contemporary Hip-Hop, I arrange the course syllabus for Modern Poetry chronologically, framing individual poets and poetic movements within a social and historical context. I use the 110–minute class period in many ways, usually dividing the time into two 50–minute segments with a brief break at the midpoint. Class sessions include lectures on specific poets, poetic movements, and theories of poetics, discussion, group activities, watching/listening to and discussing recordings and films of individual poets, in-class writing, and student presentations. By varying how the class period is used and the ways in which material is presented, I try to engage the interest of each student in the class, while also being responsive to the differences in student learning styles.

I know that some students will do well if given a fairly traditional literary analysis assignment, but others will respond with more enthusiasm and do much better work if given the opportunity to choose from a variety of topics and types of assignments. Whether it is a brief in-class piece of writing or a research project and class presentation, I try to design assignments that are themselves creative and that allow students choices in the topic and often in the mode of presentation.

Within the classroom, I make an effort to learn students' names as soon as possible. On the first day of class, I ask my students to write a brief introduction of themselves, describing what brings them to the course. This helps me in learning their names, but it also serves to provide an initial impression of the students' writing skills, as well as some indication of their experience with literary materials and their level of interest and expectations for the course.

After introducing the course, the requirements, and myself and asking students to write their own introductions, I distribute and read one or two poems chosen to engage the students' interest and to provide examples of the readings they will encounter during the quarter. Two of my favorite poems to use here are "Piano" by D. H. Lawrence and "The Boy Died in My Alley" by Gwendolyn Brooks. Reading the first stanza of each poem reveals some of their differences:

> Softly, in the dusk, a woman is singing to me;
> Taking me back down the vista of years, till I see
> A child sitting under the piano, in the boom of the tingling strings
> And pressing the small, poised feet of a mother who smiles as she sings.
> (Lawrence, 1988, p. 358)

> Without my having known.
> Policeman said, next morning,
> "Apparently died Alone."
> "You heard a shot?" Policeman said.
> Shots I hear and Shots I hear.
> I never see the dead.
> (Brooks, 1988, pp. 985–986)

The differences in form, voice, and subject matter are obvious, yet the poems are similar in that each invites an immediate response. Right from the beginning, I jump in, asking students what they believe Lawrence and Brooks want us to think about as we read the poems. This relatively simple question invites a range of informal responses on which I build, drawing in the students and allowing them to reveal that they already have knowledge and insights that will serve them well in the class. Whether it is volunteering the definition of a perhaps-unfamiliar word such as "vista" or describing the physical sensations of sitting beneath a piano or offering a response to Brooks's line "I never see the dead," students will begin to make comments based on their individual experiences and on the knowledge they bring to the class. The poems are also emotionally powerful. The students leave with something to think about and, I hope, an interest and heightened readiness for what the course will offer.

The reading assignments for Modern Poetry begin with the work of Walt Whitman. One of the first things I do after students have read selections from Whitman's "Song of Myself" on their own is to ask the entire class to take turns reading those selections aloud, beginning with the words,

> I celebrate myself, and sing myself,
> And what I assume you shall assume,
> For every atom belonging to me as good belongs to you.
> (Whitman, 1988, p. 22)

We go around the room, reading in turn, with each person having the option to pass at his or her turn. My goal here is to emphasize the fact that most poetry is written to be read aloud and that it is often easier to understand poetry when it can be heard. In addition, I don't want the class to expect to listen to my voice only throughout the term, and I emphasize the value in hearing poetry read in different ways, by voices of varying timbre and pitch. I believe it is important that students understand from the beginning that there is not a single, "correct" way to read a poem, and that each one of them should be confident about reading and experimenting with oral interpretation of a poem. To illustrate this point, I will sometimes ask several individuals to read the same passage during the course of a discussion, in order for us to hear and reflect on the different impressions created by the various readers. Once they can set aside any initial self-consciousness, I usually find that students do not mind—and often enjoy—being asked to read or reread a poem aloud. Since there are often deaf students in the class, reading a poem may involve having the student sign the poem while the interpreter voices or, as is often the case, the deaf student may choose to read in his or her own voice. For this activity, as in many other instances, I ask the students to arrange themselves so they can see one another. The ability for students to make eye contact and to see one another's responses to questions and comments is critically important. The physical arrangement of the room, where each person can see and be seen by others, also enforces the point that each student's voice and opinions are valuable. However, arranging a class to ensure such visibility is not always easy. In some classrooms, it involves moving desks to form a large circle; in classrooms with long tables, I ask all the students to turn their seats to face an imaginary center point in the room.

In part because of the richness it adds to the classroom, and in recognition of the fact that many students will learn best from the visual or oral presentation of information, I build a variety of materials and media into each course. I complement the required readings with visual materials, including videos, photographs, works of art, and maps. In Modern Poetry, driven by the belief that it is especially important that students hear a poet's own voice reading his or her work, I often play audiotapes as well, beginning with an early sound recording of Walt Whitman. To further emphasize the power and pleasure of experiencing poetry live, I invite area poets to visit and read their work in the poetry class and encourage the students to attend and write about poetry readings in the community or on campus. The class visits by poets are especially effective in drawing out individual students. On several occasions, students have shared their own writing, exchanged e-mail addresses with the visiting writers, and gone on to attend readings in the community after meeting a local poet in class. This kind of contact allows the individual student to experience modern poetry in a very personal way and to recognize that his or her voice and ideas may resonate far beyond the classroom.

In addition to making the course design clear, presenting information through different media, and including a variety of in- and out-of-class experiences, I use several strategies to try to help each student master the course material. For example, when we discuss poetic form, I give students an optional assignment of memorizing a poem. Then, either in class or as a short writing assignment, the students describe how they memorized the piece. This assignment not only gives the students the opportunity to get inside the language and structure of a poem, it always generates interesting classroom discussion as the students describe what works for them when memorizing. Students enjoy explaining how they learned a poem, and the strategies they use illustrate well the differences in learning styles: some describe visualizing the poem, others imagine hearing it set to music, and still others learn by simply repeating the poem over and over, line by line.

In Myth, Legend, and Folklore, where the reading assignments in classical mythology are lengthy and the material is complex, I use several techniques to help students learn. Beyond lecture and classroom discussion, I give weekly ten-point reading quizzes on key terms, names, and concepts in order to provide each student with constant feedback on his or her mastery of the information. In this way, both the student and I can quickly discover whether he or she is having difficulty, and before we get too far into the quarter I can meet with the student to discuss reading or study strategies. Students frequently comment on the helpfulness of having this weekly check on their understanding.

Another more lively approach to helping students master the material is to have them work in small groups and develop mnemonic strategies for learning new material. This works very well in the myth class when each group is asked to develop a mnemonic device or trick for remembering the physical traits, powers, epithets, and realm of influence associated with a specific god or goddess in the Greek pantheon. Each group then instructs the rest of the class in the use of their mnemonic and poses "Jeopardy" questions to the class to enforce the material. Working together in an informal setting, students have a great deal of fun with the material; at the same time the challenge and usefulness of creating mnemonic devices encourage each student to get involved in sharing memorization strategies. Here, too, the range of student learning styles becomes obvious, as some groups design acrostics, some create rhymed jingles, and others create visual aids.

A more general strategy I have found useful for reaching students individually, regardless of the course, is to invite them to bring in and talk about material that complements the class readings and discussion. Over the years, students have brought an array of books, videos and tapes, and clippings to class. In Modern Poetry particularly, I also encourage students to make links between the material presented in the class and that covered elsewhere, not only in liberal arts courses such as history, political science, and music, but especially in courses in the students' respective majors. "What does 'modern' mean to an engineer? Or to a photographer?" "What changes in technology were occurring at the beginning of the twentieth century? Or in the fifties?" or, more specifically, "What principles of cubism can a design major observe in Gertrude Stein's writing?" These questions serve to open a broad, cross-disciplinary discussion of modern poetry to which individual students contribute their own, often highly specialized, expertise and knowledge. At the same time, the learning process is extended as each student constructs for himself or herself a cognitive and intellectual bridge linking material learned across the disciplines.

SELECTED ASSIGNMENTS AND FINAL EXAMS

In structuring writing assignments for Modern Poetry, I build in increasing complexity, links to classroom discussion and group work, and opportunities for individual approaches and creativity. The following pair of assignments illustrates this progression.

Given early in the quarter, the Emily Dickinson assignment allows the student to benefit from an in-class group discussion and presentation before writing a more individualized response—and ideally, a more reflective one—on elements of the poem he or she finds compelling.

Assignment 1–Emily Dickinson

Part One: In-class group work

Within your group, read, reread, and discuss your assigned poem. Be prepared to read and present the poem to the class. Consider the question of theme, or the main idea of the poem and then look specifically at how the particular features of the poem (for example, rhyme, figurative language, word choice, rhythm, etc.) help develop that theme.

Part Two: Response Paper

After discussing your assigned poem with your group, write a brief (1–page) response in which you carefully analyze one aspect of the poem. This should not be the same material you cover in your presentation to the class. Instead, it should be your individual response to some aspect of the poem that interests you.

In the following assignment on Robert Frost, given later in the quarter, the group seminar activity is not announced in advance but takes place in class on the day the students hand in a two- to three-page analytical essay. Students are assigned to a group according to which poem they selected for the essay. Each group is given an overhead transparency of their poem to use in the class presentation. In this assignment, each student is prepared by having already written his or her own paper, and the seminar setting allows for a dynamic, informed conversation on each poem.

Assignment 2–Robert Frost

Part One: Analytical Paper

In his 1994 New Yorker essay "On Grief and Reason" [attached to the assignment], the poet Joseph Brodsky provides a close reading of two of Robert Frost's poems and argues that many of the usual assumptions about Frost ("a folksy, crusty, wisecracking old gentleman farmer, generally of positive disposition") may be incorrect. Brodsky goes on to say "Nature for this poet is neither friend nor foe, nor is it the backdrop for human drama; it is this poet's terrifying self-portrait." After you have read closely one of the poems listed below, write a careful, line-by-line explication in which you explain what you think the poem means. Then respond to Brodsky's thesis, showing how the poem you have chosen does or does not support Brodsky's opinion of Frost as a dark, "terrifying" poet.

Part Two: In-class Seminar

As a group, discuss carefully the poem on which you wrote your papers. In your presentation to the class, explain what the group members believe the poem means and present your response(s) to Brodsky's thesis.

Another assignment allows students to demonstrate their understanding of a particular poet while also engaging in creative writing. I have titled this assignment "In the Manner of . . . ." Students are asked to write a poem in which they attempt to replicate the style and subject matter associated with a poet whose work they have studied. After creating the new poem, the students then analyze the piece they have written as an "example" of the poet's work. I also encourage them to describe some of the challenges they encounter in writing the poem. The results of this assignment can be quite extraordinary, as the students have the opportunity to experiment creatively while making critical connections between the poems they write and the course material. Just as each student's response to a poet will be nuanced in many ways, so too will the new poem reflect the student's own personality and understanding. This is another assignment that serves as an excellent starting point for class discussion. Students are often quite articulate about the challenges they face when writing "in the manner of" a famous poet, and they very much enjoy hearing, reading, and discussing the poems produced by the class.

For the major final assignment, students in Modern Poetry complete a research project and oral presentation on the work of a single poet. I make it clear from the beginning that I regard the information students present to the class as supplementary course material. In addition to asking each student to become the authority and teach a poem written by his or her chosen poet, I also encourage each student to find a unique way to present the class with a "snapshot" of the poet. Some students prepare one-page mini-posters featuring the poet, samples of his or her work, and biographical or historical information. These sheets may be distributed to each member of the class or displayed on the wall. In other instances, students produce a photo montage or a small book describing the poet's life and work. Still other students "bring the poet into" the classroom by logging onto a Web site or showing part of a video or interview featuring the poet. In any case, the process of locating and selecting different media and visual images helps each student gain a better understanding of the writer, while enjoying the freedom to present the material according to the student's own sense of aesthetics and design.

In the final exam for Modern Poetry, I bring together several means of evaluating students' understanding of the material. The first part of the exam is a short-answer section of factual information on individual poets, poetic movements, and literary terms, including questions based on the student presentations. The second part of the exam is an analytical essay that requires students to make broad connections among poems they have read but have not discussed in class. Here is a recent example:

In general, modern poets probably choose nature as the subject of a poem less often than many earlier writers. Using the poems in the packet [selections from Walt Whitman, Emily Dickinson, William Carlos Williams, Langston Hughes, Dudley Randall, and H.D.], develop a thesis about modern poets and their relationship to or attitude toward nature, as demonstrated in their work. You may wish to compare and contrast the works of two or more of the writers. Write a well-developed essay of at least four pages in which you support your thesis using specific references to at least two of the poems.

The third section of the exam is designed to allow students to use alternative means of demonstrating what they have learned. The format and topics are quite varied: Students are asked to choose among topics such as the following.

- Write an interview in which Allen Ginsberg interviews the character J. Alfred Prufrock. Use the questions and answers to reveal and explore important elements of (and differences between) each person's character, beliefs, and personality.

- Write an interview in which Sylvia Plath interviews Emily Dickinson. Use the questions and answers to reveal and explore important elements of (and differences between) each person's character and feelings about her poetry.

- You have been asked to chair the search committee to select the next United States poet laureate. Write a detailed job description and statement of goals for this position, including qualifications, necessary prior experience, and the kinds of activities the person would be expected to take on. Remember this is a two-year public appointment; you want to clearly define what should be expected of someone in this position and why.

- The poetry read in this class has spanned more than 130 years of history. During the same period, many scientific discoveries and inventions have taken place. Select one discovery or invention that you believe has had an influence on modern poetry. Write an essay in which you discuss how you think this influence was important and refer to a poet (or poets) who you think illustrates your point.

Taken together, the three sections of the final exam make it possible to evaluate several increasingly sophisticated types of learning, as outlined in Chapter 2. Students first demonstrate their mastery of factual material; second, they engage in a critical analysis of literary texts; and third, they go beyond the course material itself and create new ways of organizing and interpreting what they have learned.

Throughout the term, I make it very clear to students that I enjoy experimenting in class, and I may say "Let's try this . . ." or "This is the first time I've used this poem . . ." as a way of inviting them to join me in exploring something new. Despite the possible risks, presenting new material in new ways when I am not sure of the outcome is always exhilarating. I continually try to incorporate innovative approaches, sometimes inspired by ideas from colleagues and sometimes simply on the basis of an intriguing problem, question, or juxtaposition I want to bring to the class. Often I will return to an unresolved question raised in an earlier class, acknowledging the student who first brought it up. "Sharon raised an interesting question the other day and we didn't really have a chance to think about it carefully. Let's go back to that same question and apply it to the following poem." This strategy not only creates continuity between class sessions, it also demonstrates that questions can be left open-ended, to be returned to later, and most important, that the student's inquiry merits extended reflection and deserves to be taken up as the focus of class discussion.

In trying new things and consciously experimenting in class, I am careful not to abandon things that do work, whether it is a tried and true assignment or the use of lecture to present background information or critical material. Indeed, taking notes in a lecture setting is very familiar to RIT students, and for many of them it is the most effective way to process new material. As much as I enjoy trying new approaches to the classroom, I have learned to test and carefully refine new ideas, especially the use of group assignments. In a university where teamwork is a familiar buzzword, group assignments must have a clearly defined outcome and not appear to be busywork. Each student must be expected to participate in the process and presentation of the group. Assigning specific questions or problems to groups and linking group work to individual assignments are two strategies that enforce the learning that takes place in a group setting. In order to emphasize the value of each student's viewpoint and contribution and to make the point that the goal in assigning a problem to a group of individuals is not to arrive at a single, simple answer, I encourage students to articulate the points on which group members disagree and to outline those differences for the rest of the class as part of the group's presentation. Agreeing that there may be different and conflicting ways to respond to a writer or interpret a poem opens the way for greater and more vocal involvement by individual students who at first may be reluctant to offer differing views or views that others may consider wrong.

IDENTIFYING LEARNING DIFFERENCES AMONG STUDENTS

I rely upon multiple cues—some informal, others formal; some obvious, others less obvious—in order to identify and assess learning differences among students. The written introductions I request from students on the first day of class (discussed earlier) provide me with some information on each student's background and skills. Subsequent assignments, of course, provide much more information. In response to a student's poor performance on an assignment, I may ask the student to meet with me. In that meeting, I will spend some time trying to find out what may be causing the problem. I ask about the student's past performance in other English classes and whether this class seems different and why. I will also ask the student what he or she thinks is the problem. In the case of a student who seems to need additional assistance with reading strategies or writing skills, I will often make a referral to the Learning Development Center. For some students, the difficulties may be not weak skills but a learning disability. Students receiving institutional support services for learning disabilities are required to present their instructors with a letter outlining their needs for accommodation early in the academic term. The accommodations may include having a note taker and/or scribe, being provided with recorded books on tape, or being allowed extra time for exams. Occasionally, it is necessary to arrange for an alternative means of completing an assignment, and in such circumstances, I work out specific arrangements that will accommodate the student's needs while meeting the objectives for the course. Although infrequent, these arrangements usually involve finding evaluation alternatives for students unable to be evaluated by conventional testing or oral presentation methods.

In addition to the information provided by students, my class list will indicate which students, if any, are cross-registered in the National Technical Institute for the Deaf, and the presence of sign language interpreters will confirm that there are deaf or hard-of-hearing students in the class. Speaking slowly, remembering not to "talk to the blackboard," and reminding students to speak one at a time are strategies that help ensure that all students—not only the deaf and hard of hearing—will be able to learn and participate in the class. I also pay close attention to the interactions among students and the dynamics within small groups to see who may be having difficulty. I make a concerted effort to call on students and to draw even the reluctant ones into class discussions. I try—with encouragement and humor—to make sure all students are included, even asking myself aloud, "who hasn't had a chance to speak yet today?"

USING TECHNOLOGICAL TOOLS IN AND BEYOND THE CLASSROOM

Because of the nature of the materials covered in Modern Poetry, there are many traditional technological resources available to the instructor. As mentioned earlier, I include several videotape productions and sound recordings as important supplements to the course reading. Turning to newer technologies, I also introduce the students to appropriate Web sources, especially materials that may be useful in their research. Of course, at a technological institution, the students themselves are an excellent source of information on the newest electronic tools. Students are very aware of the ways in which such tools can assist them in learning new material and presenting their ideas. Although the technology changes so fast that any example may soon appear outdated, student use of certain technological resources has become routine in my classroom, especially the use of laptop computers to log on to an existing Web site or to demonstrate a Web site the student has created for the course. Students will also adapt tools used in other courses to the classroom environment of Modern Poetry. This is especially true of PowerPoint technology, widely used on campus to organize and illustrate oral presentations. Going beyond the tools used within the classroom, the technological resource that has most altered my out-of-class contact with individual students is e-mail. In general, students are very much at ease with this electronic medium and use it frequently to make appointments, check on assignments, pose questions, or make comments related to the class. I, too, will use e-mail to initiate contact with a student if I have a question or concern or if I want to follow up on a point raised in class. For me and for my students, the ease of e-mail communication extends learning beyond the classroom in a forum that is personal, immediate, and by now very familiar to all of us.

ENGAGING STUDENTS IN THEIR OWN LEARNING

The creativity and variety that I build into assignments pose significant challenges for some students. Those who are accustomed to a certain kind of writing assignment or classroom experience in an English course sometimes just want me to tell them what topic to choose or what poet to select for a research project. In those cases, as described earlier, I work with the student to guide him or her in the research before the research. My goal is to help the student make a decision or selection that is not entirely arbitrary but is informed by his or her own interests, experiences, or questions about the subject.

Another strategy for helping students become responsible for their own learning is to shuffle the groups in the class. Although group work is by no means a daily activity, it does not take long to observe whether one or two students dominate the conversation when students group themselves or when they work in assigned groups. When this happens, I deliberately reassign the groups for the next assignment, composing groups of students who don't know one another, separating those who like to talk to one another, putting a reticent student with someone who seems to be a good listener. My objective here is to maximize the opportunity for each student to feel as though his or her contribution is important by creating a group setting where the conversation stays on task and is not monopolized by one or two students.

My primary strategy for engaging students in their own learning is to encourage them to ask questions, of me and of each other. As Roger Schank (1988) has written, "teaching people to think means teaching people to ask questions" (35). In a first-year writing and literature class, I ask students to hand in anonymous questions, large or small. This works especially well for breaking the ice before the class discusses a novel the students have read on their own. They may have genuine confusion about the book but be reluctant to ask a question in front of the class. In Modern Poetry, I ask the students to generate their own lists of questions, the answers to which they believe would improve their understanding of the material. Finding the answers to these questions may then be woven into the work of the class. Some questions, such as those dealing with a poet's biography, may be relatively easy to answer. Others may introduce larger thematic issues that will continue to be addressed throughout the quarter. Formulating questions, at the introductory or advanced level, allows each student the opportunity to make an important cognitive leap: to articulate what he or she needs to know in order to better understand the material and to frame the unknown in relation to what is already known.

CONCLUSION

Teaching literature at a technological institution such as RIT provides exciting opportunities for a faculty member. RIT students bring to the classroom a variety of backgrounds, demographics, learning characteristics, and career interests that creates endless possibilities for teaching and learning. By consciously examining the intersections among the arts, science, and technology that abide implicitly within our institution, my students and I can extend our exploration of literature beyond the boundaries of a single academic discipline. As I reflect on the ways in which I try to reach and draw in each student, I am continually reminded that my efforts are rewarded many times over by the contributions the students themselves make to the dynamics and learning in the literature classroom.

REFERENCES

Brodsky, J. (1994, September 26). On grief and reason. *New Yorker*, pp. 70–85.

Brooks, G. (1988). The boy died in my alley. In R. Ellmann and R. O'Clair (Eds.), *The Norton Anthology of Modern Poetry* (2d ed., pp. 985–986). New York: W.W. Norton. [Original work published 1981.]

Dickinson, E. (1988). This is my letter to the world. In R. Ellmann and R. O'Clair (Eds.), *The Norton Anthology of Modern Poetry* (2d ed., pp. 49–50). New York: W.W. Norton. [Original work published 1890.]

Lawrence, D. H. (1988). Piano. In R. Ellmann and R. O'Clair (Eds.), *The Norton Anthology of Modern Poetry* (2d ed., p. 358). New York: W.W. Norton. [Original work published 1918.]

Schank, R. (with P. Childers). *The creative attitude: Learning to ask and answer the right questions.* New York: Macmillan, 1988.

Strand, M. (1988). Eating poetry. In R. Ellmann and R. O'Clair (Eds.), *The Norton Anthology of Modern Poetry* (2d ed., pp. 1437–1438). New York: W.W. Norton. [Original work published 1968.]

Whitman, W. (1988). From song of myself. In R. Ellmann and R. O'Clair (Eds.), *The Norton Anthology of Modern Poetry* (2d ed., pp. 22–35). New York: W.W. Norton. [Original work published 1855.]

Chapter 6

The Vocation of a Writing Coach: Teaching Composition and Creative Writing to Individual Learners

Bunny Paine-Clemes

SETTING AND PERSONAL BACKGROUND

Since 1993 I have been teaching at the California Maritime Academy, a residential campus of approximately six hundred students in the town of Vallejo, nestled in a bend of Morrow Cove between San Francisco and the Napa Valley.

The college became an institution of higher education in 1940 and the twenty-third campus of the California State University System in 1995. Students earn degrees in business administration, marine transportation, mechanical engineering, facilities engineering, and marine engineering technology. Most receive Coast Guard licenses, and some receive certification as plant engineers or commissions as naval officers. The centerpiece of education is the training ship Golden Bear, completed for the U.S. Navy in 1989 and on loan to Cal Maritime for cruises as far away as China or Australia.

As the first maritime academy to admit women, Cal Maritime continues to become more diverse in ethnic composition and gender, though the majority of students are white males who have recently graduated from high school. In the fall of 2000 the student body was 20% female, with 24% of all students identifying themselves as non-Caucasian (American Indian or Alaskan native, Asian, Hispanic, African American, or other). The SAT scores are among the

highest in the CSU system, and students enjoy 100% employment at graduation, with starting salaries in the mid-$40Ks.

At Cal Maritime I have a half-time assignment as campus assessment coordinator and regularly teach Psychology of Success (an entry-level social science
elective) and literature (the course required after freshman composition). I
have also taught other electives: Introduction to Psychology (advanced), Psychology and Literature (advanced), and Creative Writing (advanced). Class
sizes range from 15 to 25 students.

However, my experience is eclectic. I have taught at two high schools, five
two-year colleges, and three universities. At times I have focused on composition and creative writing as well as literature. I have taught developmental
writing and freshman composition (entry-level), beginning and advanced creative writing (advanced), business and technical writing (advanced), and semi-
nars in the novel (advanced). I have taught minority students taking labs and
freshman English at California two-year colleges and thirtysomething and
fortysomething professional women learning to perfect their romance novels
at Houston Community College. I have taught numerous workshops and am
founder and leader of the Vallejo Writers' Group. Whether in California or
Texas, whether in a remedial lab with reluctant scribblers or a critiquing session
with published authors, the problems remain the same.

GUIDING ASSUMPTIONS ABOUT LEARNING AND TEACHING

In a lecture delivered at the annual convention of ECCTYC (community
college English teachers in California), Silver (1993) announced a remarkable
fact: a century of composition research indicates that comments on student
papers create no measurable improvement in writing. Silver cited the research
of Stiff (1967), who found "no significant improvement" whether the comments were in the margin, at the end, or a combination of both. Then Silver
cited Bata (1972), who not only drew the same conclusion but discovered that
reading an essay without making the comments takes half as long. Finally, Silver cited King (1979), who found that neither marking grammar, nor describing rules, nor doing exercises has any relationship to student success.

King was also interested in how students get derailed in following teachers'
suggestions and found the following, according to Silver: they "don't read the
comment, may not understand the terminology, may not be able to identify the
place in the text, and may make corrections without knowing what they are doing." Silver handed out his summary of the research, which indicated that none
of the following made any difference: "locations of written comments, length of
written comments, explicitness of written comments, frequency of written com-

ments, intensity of written comments, comments asking for clarification or directing revision, tape-recording of teachers' comments, peers' written evaluation of writing, 'unimproved' student self-evaluation and revision." He found that, in fact, "Teachers' written comments can contribute to fragmented or superficial revision by students." More recent assessment studies at the University of Hawaii, Manoa, yield the same data ("Writing Matters #2").

What does improve student writing? According to Silver's research, two factors make a difference: prewriting exercises and revision after an individual conference with the instructor. In the application of these strategies, five other useful practices emerge: "teacher evaluation between drafts and revision; improving students' revision practices; better student–teacher communication; focus on students' writing intentions, their realization, and responsibilities; a recursive writing process offering opportunity for multiple drafts and appropriate teacher response along the way."

These findings correlate with what I have learned in thirty-four years of teaching, practice, and research. Writing is communication from one mind to another. Unfortunately, we cannot transfer the picture of our idea from the right brain, where it occurs: we have to use the medium of language, a left-brain symbol system. As communicators we think our messages are clear because we know what we mean, but often what we mean is more in our minds than on the page. We use what Flower (1985) calls "code words" that convey associations to us because of past experience but mean something different to the audience.

There is no way to check this miscommunication except by getting feedback, and doing so in person is much more effective than on paper: We can check the body language of the audience and engage in a mutual question-and-answer session and then determine precisely what is needed to clarify the confusion. Deciphering a teacher's cryptic scribbles often entails playing a guessing game and guessing wrong. This problem is as germane to experts or professionals as it is to beginners. Most articles or reports that I have written have entailed conferences with an editor who wanted revisions, and usually I have had to quiz the editor to determine what he or she meant. (For instance, the first submitted draft of this chapter involved a forty-five minute phone conference with the editor!) As if this miscommunication problem were not enough, according to the research of Mary Dosin (*WAC Faculty Handbook 2000–2001*), "indecipherable handwriting and obscure jargon or abbreviations" are major student irritants (p. 10). Hence marginal scribbles are annoying as well as confusing.

A major reason for this annoyance is that writing expresses the self in a way that quadratic equations do not. Our egos get identified with the work. For those who have done their best and are proud of the results, it is discouraging to receive feedback in the form of scribbles picking at trivia. Hence students confronted with a marked-up paper tend to toss it in the trash and tell themselves that the teacher was being irrational and subjective. However, if they are required to take a few days to cool off and then read the comments again and then make a plan of how to respond to them in a conference, sometimes the criticisms begin to make sense.

In addition, meeting face to face enables both instructor and student to see one another as human beings (see "Responding to Student Text"), not as scribbles on a page. The instructor may realize that this paper was treated too harshly during the exhaustion of a marathon grading session. The student may realize that the feedback does, indeed, have justification, now that there is less emotional upheaval from the impact of receiving a low grade. In the light of day and intimacy of a conference, the two communicators can meet more easily on a common ground.

Finally, prewriting furnishes the detail that can prevent confusion in the first place. More of the idea is on the paper, and less has to be teased out of the brain of the student. Writing itself generates ideas. It is a truism in the field that we can't know what we say until we see what we write.

It is also a truism that writing is a process, both unconscious creation and conscious control (Elbow, 1973, 1981). To create, one enters the flow state so well defined by Csikszentmihalyi (1990); then one steps back and analyzes the results. Prewriting promotes flow; conscious revision refines the creative product for the audience. Writing is both art and skill, a process that draws on both intuition and conscious control (Elbow, 1981).

In fact, the concept of writing as process has supplanted an earlier emphasis on writing as product. Now instructors help students through all stages: prewriting, drafting, revising, and editing. Conferences may be held on the idea, the thesis, the outline, the creativity exercises, and one or more rough drafts. At each stage the instructor has a chance to assess progress and suggest directions. When the final version is submitted, along with the prewriting exercises, notes, and revisions, the evolution of ideas and the development of style are clear. Throughout this process the teacher has served as a counselor or coach, encouraging individual learners to hone their skills, guiding them from one level of expertise to the next as a master stonecutter guides an apprentice.

The following section explains how creativity exercises and one-on-one conferences contribute to this individualized learning experience.

APPROACHES AND TECHNIQUES FOR INDIVIDUALIZING INSTRUCTION

The Macro Level and the Micro Level

Chapter 3 divides instructional activities into the macro level of course design and the micro level of moment-to-moment teaching/learning adaptations. Silver's two recommendations, prewriting exercises and individual conferences, exemplify both levels. They can be built into the design of a process-oriented writing course as stages in the creation of each essay. In addition, they can furnish the teaching/learning adaptations suggested in Chapters 3 and 4. The creativity exercises furnish active engagement, which is "the goal of individualized instruction . . . and thus academic success for each individual learner" (Chapter 3, p. 41). The conference can help determine to what extent the student is learning, where unique problems or blockages exist, and whether adjustments should be made to modify the needs of that particular student.

Let us see how applying Silver's recommendations can work to improve student writing, reach students as unique learners, and support the instructional problem-solving process explained in Chapters 3 and 4 of this anthology. The methods are largely the same, whether the class is beginning (developmental writing), intermediate (freshman composition), or advanced (creative writing). What is different is their specific application to the individual student, with his or her level of skill and special needs or goals.

Instructional Method One: Prewriting Exercises

All writing texts now specify prewriting or invention exercises, which can be done as homework or in class. Such exercises usually include listing ideas; brainstorming in small groups; free writing (usually credited to Elbow, 1973, and adapted by authors such as Goldberg, 1986); and idea trees or designs, called clustering by Rico (1983) and mind mapping by Buzan (1983). Cowan and Cowan (1980) suggest focused free writing in a three-stage process, as well as classical invention questions based on Aristotle's topoi and "cubing," or viewing a subject from six perspectives (also summarized, along with exercises adapted from Jacqueline Burke, in "Planning" at the Owl Online Writing Lab, Purdue University). Murray (1989) brainstorms the questions he thinks a reader would ask and then answers them. Avery, Cole, Ford, and Lindemann (1988) recommend stating audience, purpose, thesis, tone, and strategy as their prewriting exercise. Paull and Kligerman (1972) recommend in-class observations during which writers study ordinary objects and then note and reflect on their details in journal entries. Ford and Ford (1992) have constructed a composition text around journal exercises that apply to both reading and writing assignments. In fact, many experienced teachers stress the benefits of keeping a journal. An excellent resource is The Journal Book (Fulwiler, 1987), which discusses the use of journaling in courses across the curriculum.

These prewriting strategies, which are commonly mentioned in academic texts, provide the active engagement whereby students' vague inspirations are converted into coherently expressed ideas. By jotting down impressions and ideas without editing or censoring, learners practice more than one of Kolb's (1981) modalities. By answering questions or free writing, they engage in active experimentation that leads to concrete experiencing and abstract interpretation of an idea; they may even use reflective observation if they scrutinize an object in the way recommended by Paull and Kligerman (1972). In this way a classroom of thirty students becomes a communal laboratory in which each learner is grappling with material in a unique and creative way. In accordance with the talent development model, each writer draws on his or her own private store of experiences and ideas. Each, according to his or her ability, recalls incidents or facts, experiences insights, makes connections, and constructs meaning. Without these active learning techniques, students often complain that they can't choose a topic or find supporting details. (See Elbow & Belanoff, n.d.)

In my thirty-four years as a teacher, I have found all these strategies useful in helping writers to discover and structure their unique ideas. One of the most useful, though, is a prewriting exercise that I have never seen mentioned in any academic text. It is actually an idea derived from my research in creativity and right-brain functioning.

Visualization

Ask the students to sit up straight, close their eyes, and visualize something imagery connected with the writing task at hand. Turn off the lights, put on a tape of classical or New Age music, and ask the students to lean back, close their eyes, and begin relaxing, from the tips of their toes to the tops of their heads. Then direct an inner imagery experience like one of those described below. Finally, bring the students back and ask them to free-write quickly about the experience.

If you use this method in conjunction with the narrative essay, you can direct students to return to a past experience and then ask what they are hearing, seeing, and touching; probe for emotions and physical sensations; and, finally, the meaning of the incident. Then suggest that they bring themselves back and free-write quickly about what they have relived. If they lose the flow of words, they can close their eyes and reenter the experience briefly. After this exercise the details in the students' themes are precise and concrete. Gone are the vague statements that convey nothing ("The weather was bad"). In their place are sensory images ("The rain pelted like needles against my face").

With this technique, individual learners can draw on their own store of experiences and ideas and construct meanings unique to themselves, as mentioned during the discussion of active learning in Chapter 2. One student may compose an entire rough draft. Another may experience, for the first time, the specific sensations that will make a narrative come alive. Yet another may, in this intuitive right-brain state, experience the connections that give meaning to the incident. As Chapter 2 discussed, the meanings of our experiences are unique to each of us. The active learning strategy of visualization has drawn them out as a lecture on visualization could never have done. In addition, a combination of inner imagery and writing helps learners who process information visually or kinesthetically.

When introducing this exercise, you might want to consider adjusting your explanation to student demographics. In the Bay Area, where I began teaching in 1991, students are familiar with visualization and ready to get on with it. When I taught in Texas during the 1970s and 1980s, though, I found that preliminary instruction was needed to help students understand what we were doing and why. I had to give examples from sports: football players who visualized kicking a goal beforehand, golf stars who visualized a swing. I had to assure them that there was nothing religious about the exercise but that if it made them uncomfortable, they need not participate.

At Cal Maritime, the business and engineering students are pragmatists. What I tell them is that we are about to do an exercise that may seem weird but that it works for many writers—including Stephen King! In fact, he says it is the only way to create imagery. He leans back, closes his eyes, and for several minutes visualizes a scene until he "really" sees it (King 1980).

There are usually a few students for whom this method works imperfectly or not at all. They will need to use some other strategy, such as clustering, free writing, or question answering. Still, in every class or workshop, somewhere between 75% and 95% of students are writing away busily, and many do not want to stop when I call time. During the question-and-answer period many discuss breakthroughs, and it is not uncommon to have students express gratitude after class and say they were worried about this paper but now have a whole draft. Visualization has helped them harness the image-making function of the subconscious mind and enter the flow state necessary for creation: to enlist the intuition that Elbow (1981) stresses as essential to writing.

This exercise can be adapted to various writing tasks. In creative writing or freshman composition, I lead students through an exercise in which they experience themselves writing easily and fluently and correctly. Many report later that they go home and immediately write, without stopping, a fluent draft that needs little revision. Gawain (1978), who pioneered creative visualization, provides a text that can be adapted for various imagery exercises. Clearly, such a technique empowers individual learners. Through it they can access their inspiration as well as drawing upon their unique experiences to provide the details essential for effective writing.

Instructional Method Two: The Individual Conference

Harris (1986, 1995) and Carnicelli (1980) stress the importance of the writing conference in helping students apply classroom theories to their individual circumstances. Much advice has been provided on how to plan, structure, and conduct such conferences so that the teacher and student work as partners, discussing not only drafts but prewriting exercises and discovering strategies to implement student intentions (see, for instance, Arbur, 1977; Carnicelli, 1980; Harris, 1986; Murray, 1989). In a common scenario, for instance, an essay may seem to be going in two or three directions. A teacher who jumps in to suggest a thesis will usually find that the student becomes irritated and says, as in T. S. Eliot's poem about the hapless Prufrock, "That is not what I meant at all." It is important to draw out what the student intends to say and help that idea find expression instead of imposing an intention that is not the writer's. Carnicelli and Harris establish that when a teacher becomes a collaborator instead of an error detector, students take more initiative in their own process and make substantial changes in drafts. Harris finds that other students often cannot provide this sort of direction in peer evaluation sessions but fall back on generalized compliments meant to be pleasant and supportive.

So crucial has Murray (1979) found the conference to be that, after years of teaching composition, he decided to structure his writing courses around this method alone. If you want to maintain a traditional class structure but have too many students to accommodate extra one-on-one sessions, you can convert the class to a writing workshop: consult with individuals in a corner of the room while you have the other students work on assignments (Carnicelli, 1980). Some suggestions for alternative class activities include the following: Have students review and critique one another's papers, either in small groups or in pairs; divide students into groups to study grammar or diction problems in their writing or discuss published models; have students work individually or in groups to generate questions about their writing ("FAQs about a Teacher/Student Writing Conference," n.d.). Conferences need be only three or four minutes long, especially if you conduct four or five conferences per essay, each one solving a specific writing problem for a unique learner.

Another alternative is to build into the course (at the macro level) one unit during which intensive problem solving in an individual conference occurs. For instance, a unit on the persuasive essay can begin with class sessions that establish the theory and practice of argumentation and then proceed to listing, questioning, and free writing to get ideas. Then the students can sign up for fifteen-minute conferences to which they must bring these invention exercises and a legible rough draft, as well as the answers to these process questions: (1) What am I trying to do in this paper? How do I want the audience to think, act, or believe? (2) Who is that audience, specifically? (3) What help do I need? Where is the paper not working for me? (4) What is working well in the paper, or what strengths do I see? Murray asks students, "What surprised you in writing the draft? What did you do differently in this draft than you've done before? What did you learn from writing the draft? What would you do differently if you had another chance at it?" (1989, p. 130). Such questions furnish a springboard for discussion so that the student's reaction and intent guide the conference. (More of them, by Murray and others, are summarized in "FAQs about a Teacher/Student Writing Conference," n.d., and *Traci's Fourth List of Ten*, n.d.).

Carnicelli (1980), after analyzing 1,800 student evaluations, found that conferences have the greatest value when the teacher resists the temptation to pontificate on his or her own reactions and suggestions but instead draws out the student's purpose, focus, and ideas. As nationally known educational critic Alfie Kohn once put it, "'Talk less, ask more'" (*Traci's Fourth List of Ten*). Resist the temptation to offer judgments and quick fixes; students like to generate their own answers (Harris 1995). An idea must be self-generated in order to be owned and experienced. A good therapist asks questions that lead the client to the insight; a good writing coach does the same.

During the conference, you can skim the draft and then focus Socratic questioning on problem areas defined by the student's responses to the process questions. The longer the paper, the more difficult it is to concentrate on the draft and formulate ideas while under the pressure of time and the anxious gaze of the student. An alternate idea is to collect drafts and read them in advance. This option, of course, increases the paper load. In addition, Carnicelli (1980) warns that it may focus the teacher too much on his or her judgment so that the conference becomes prescriptive and teacher-directed rather than collaborative. He finds that as teachers gain experience in conducting conferences, more of them prefer to scan drafts on the spot.

The creativity exercises, drafting, and questioning engage the student in ongoing self-assessment and problem solving of the sort mentioned in Chapters 3 and 4 of this anthology. Each student begins with a unique set of competencies, skills, and problems; each identifies how, with the instructor's help, there can be an incremental difference made in accordance with the talent development model outlined in Chapter 1. Even in a fifteen-minute session, a surprising amount of intensive problem solving can be done together if the student is prepared.

The less cooperative the student, of course, the more specific and innovative the follow-up questions must be. Harris (1986) details ways in which hostile or insecure writers can be resistant to the process. They may be passive, resistant, defensive, or argumentative. They may avert their eyes in silence and shrug. They may proudly hand over a paper that attacks the reader's religion or sexual orientation (*Tutor Stories*, n.d.; "When Tutoring Becomes Counseling," 1997). They may feel blocked, either by the demands of the task or their past negative experiences with English. They may need to consult more sources, create a timeline, outline their main points, or try more free writing. Perhaps they may even need to be given Elbow's (1973) suggestion for an early draft: give yourself permission to write badly. Sometimes as they explain why a part is unclear, it suddenly clarifies. Sometimes they have been editing the words (micro level) when they should consider reorganizing the ideas (macro level).

During this process the student and writing coach grapple with the issues mentioned in Chapter 1 of this anthology: the unique mix of learning characteristics, shaped by the student's personal history and the instructional context of the moment. The best metaphor for what transpires during such sessions is probably therapeutic. Like a good therapist, the teacher has to be an intent and careful listener, scanning body language, listening to emotional undercurrents. Often the crucial communication is not verbal. The message is in the defensive tone or slumped shoulders, in the intuitive sense that the student is troubled or confused or resentful. The writing coach must use what Goleman (1995) calls emotional intelligence and what Gardner (1983) names as one of his seven key intelligences: the ability to understand the emotions of others. Like any talent, this is a natural gift in some people but can be learned at least to some extent by all. The key is in trying to put aside one's own ideas and empathize with someone else's point of view. It is useful to relax, take a deep breath, and imagine opening up to the student, surrounding this special person with acceptance, trying to understand his or her unique ideas. At the same time one must make eye contact, nod, offer supportive remarks, and speak in a warm voice, with statements that feed back the student's words and empathize with his or her reactions. Eventually the student's language will become less stilted or defensive, the body language, more open and relaxed. For e-mail tutoring, where the process is different, see Coogan (1995).

Carnicelli (1980) offers some practical suggestions for methods to use in a conference setting: Offer encouragement and praise first, don't address too many problems in a session, and focus initially on matters of content, audience, and purpose. Elbow suggests how to phrase suggestions specifically rather than globally ("Feeling Good," 1994). Grammar can be addressed on later drafts, especially if a problem is chronic. Harris (1986) suggests several tactics for doing so, including one of my favorites, getting the student to read his or her prose aloud. I have found that such a conference, using the student's own writing, will clear up mechanical errors far better than class drill.

In fact, by working in a writing lab at a two-year college, I discovered that five or ten minutes of individual instruction can go far toward eradicating a persistent mechanical/grammatical error. I developed a methodology: Define the error; point out some examples in the draft; analyze one; lead the student through a step-by-step analysis of others; write three new examples on the spot; ask the student to correct and analyze them; and then find and analyze two other examples in the draft. Some students needed more time, more examples, or more intensive Socratic questioning, but all seemed able to solve the problem. At the very least, even if writing teachers are too beleaguered to offer this sort of one-on-one instruction, they ought to be supported by a college lab with trained instructors who can do it.

Grammatical instruction must be individualized in order to work. The contention of Carnicelli (1980), Harris (1986), King (1979), Silver (1993), and so many others is correct: General class attention to a grammatical problem does not transfer to the individual writing task. Perhaps the comma splices in a drill are easy to find because one is scanning for them alone; in one's own prose there may be too many other distractions of style and content. Perhaps getting the teacher's individual attention causes the student to focus his or her mind more fully. In developmental English classes, I can give a set of instructions to the class, and only five out of fifteen will understand; I go to the desks of the ten other students, say the same words, point to them on the written assignment sheet, and the students understand what to do.

With advanced students, of course, the individual conference can be a mentoring process, like Guy de Maupassant's as he studied fiction writing under Gustave Flaubert. One semester I taught an independent study course in creative writing with a senior engineering student at Cal Maritime. We discussed his goals: to become more creative and fluent and to use metaphors and imagery. We then devised and signed a contract. He wrote every day in a journal; we met once a week for an hour to discuss his entries and plan how to shape them into longer pieces; I assigned additional creativity exercises as needed and requested; we discussed which journal entries and exercises to develop into articles or op-ed pieces; he wrote the resultant drafts; I edited and commented on these revisions, which we discussed and then revised a few more times. At midterm and at the end of the semester, he turned in a portfolio of all his journal entries and drafts, as well as answers to these questions: (1) What strengths do you see in your writing? What do you like about it? What progress do you see? (2) On what problems are you still working? (3) What help do you need? (4) Do you want to change your contract? Together we undertook an intellectual voyage in which we were able to watch his writing achieve new dimensions. One argumentative essay had so much value for the college that the student photocopied and distributed it on campus and submitted a copy to the president, who changed school policy as a result.

Such mentoring creates the ongoing partnerships and dialogue mentioned in Chapter 1 of this anthology. It exemplifies the micro level of instructional strategies mentioned in Chapter 3, as well as the method of checking/adapting/checking again exemplified by Figure 2 of that chapter. Finally, such an independent study format also enables students and instructor to design the course on the macro level to fit each student's needs. An individual contract can be hammered out: the student contributing his or her goals, the teacher suggesting strategies and standards. An extra benefit is the increase in faculty–student contact that Chickering and Gamson (1987) have identified as one of the seven principles for good practice in higher education.

A private conference motivates those involved to take responsibility for their own learning. One of my independent-study students confided, "I have to prepare more carefully when I know I'm meeting you one on one. I can't just sleep in the back of the room." Besides, answering the process questions gives the student ownership of his or her writing. It is not some whimsical authority who has decided what the strengths and weaknesses of the portfolio are, what the intents and goals of the essay are; the problem areas and goals have been identified by the writer, who then takes ownership of the creative process.

This point is crucial in getting students to buy into their own learning and improve their own writing. The alternative is the often-heard complaint, "I don't know what you want." The veiled suggestion is that the student is subject to the tyrannical whims of a despotic god, whose irrational edicts must be satisfied. No doubt students have felt that way in the past. They have been given micro direction by past teachers who tell them to write five paragraphs, with a formula for what must go in each. They have been told to keep it simple in one class, use dependent clauses in another. Many are passive, waiting to be told what to do. Taking charge of their own creative process may seem intimidating but, for most, is ultimately liberating.

The Problem of Standards

A major problem of such joint collaboration between student and teacher is the necessity of assigning a grade to the results. A colleague once admitted with chagrin that he had copy-edited a barely passing paper, line by line; the student had dutifully plugged the corrections into the word-processed text and received an A! This faculty member highlighted a major problem: rewarding improvement while maintaining standards. Solutions include the following:

- Average the grades of the rough and the final draft.
- Mark errors on only a few pages.
- Mark one or two kinds of errors.
- Take off points if no revisions are done.
- Add points if revisions are done well.
- Allow revisions on some but not all papers.

For more about this problem, see "What Is 'Help' with Writing?" (1995) and the bibliography "Articles on Evaluating Student Writing" (n.d.). The key is finding some incentive for the student to collaborate with the process and feel rewarded for so doing while still awarding a grade that reflects the relative quality of the student's writing, not the quality of the teacher's revisions.

CONCLUSION: THE VOCATION OF WRITING COACH

Being a writing coach is like being a therapist; one can lead, question, and direct, but the illumination must come from within. And just as good therapists heed research in their field, we can benefit from the research that so many experts have conducted and that Silver has summarized. As Stewart (1988) says, "How can historical knowledge liberate composition teachers from theory and practice which are dated and ineffective? The obvious answer is that the teacher who has it is flexible. She knows what has been tried, what has worked, and what has not" (p. 22).

Theory and practice, research and intuition, trial and error: They all work together if we are to be the best mentors that we can be. How we assess our effectiveness is an ongoing part of the dialogue between teacher and student. When we confer with students on their creativity exercises, thesis statements, and rough drafts, we engage in periodic status checks (see Chapters 3 and 4) that keep the project on track and help the writer to move to the next level of proficiency. As Angelo and Cross (1993) show, this continual feedback can be much more significant in evaluating the learning process than the end-of-the-term formalities of a grade for the student and course evaluation for the teacher.

REFERENCES

Angelo, T. A., & Cross, K. P. (1993). *Classroom assessment techniques* (2d ed.). San Francisco: Jossey-Bass.

Arbur, R. (1979). The student-teacher conference. In R. C. Gebhardt (Ed.), *Composition and its teaching: Articles from college composition and communication during the editorship of Edward P.J. Corbett*. Findlay, OH: Ohio Council of Teachers of English Language Arts.

Articles on evaluating student writing.(n.d.). Available: www.indiana. edu/~wts/cwp/lib/evalbib.html [Retrieved May 8, 2001.]

Avery, L., Cole, S., Ford, M., & Lindemann, J. (1988). *Write on: An English resource*. Parts I & II (2d ed.). Dubuque, IA: Kendall Hunt.

Bata, E. J. (1972). *A study of the relative effectiveness of marking techniques on junior college freshman English composition*. Unpublished doctoral dissertation, University of Maryland.

Beach, R. (1979). The effects of between-draft teacher evaluation versus student self-evaluation on high school students' revising of rough drafts. *Research in the teaching of English, 13* (May), 111–119.

Buzan, T. (1983). *Use both sides of your brain* (2d ed.). New York: E. P. Dutton.

Carnicelli, T. A. (1980). The writing conference: A one-to-one conversation. In T. Donovan and B. McClellan (Eds.), *Eight approaches to teaching composition* (pp. 101–131). Urbana, IL: National Council of Teachers of English.

Chickering, A. W., and Z. F. Gamson (1987). Seven principles for good practice in undergraduate education. *AAHE Bulletin, 39*(7), 5–10.

Coogan, D. (1995). E-mail tutoring, a new way to do new work. *Computers and Composition 12*(2). [Online.] Available: www.cwrl.utexas.edu/~ccjrnl/Archives/v12_2_html/feature.html [Retrieved May 2, 2001.]

Cowan, E., & Cowan, G. (1980). *Writing*. New York: John Wiley.

Csikszentmihalyi, M. (1990). *Flow: The psychology of optimum experience*. New York: Harper and Row.

Elbow, P. (1973). *Writing without teachers*. New York: Oxford University Press.

Elbow, P. (1981). *Writing with power*. New York: Oxford University Press.

Elbow, P., & Belanoff, P. (n.d.). *Why freewriting is important from a community of writers*. [Online.] Available: www.people.virginia.edu/~kac3g/freewhy. html [Retrieved May 2, 2001.]

FAQs about a teacher/student writing conference. (n.d.). PSSA Classroom Connections. [Online.] Available: www.pasd.com/PSSA/WRITING/wri4345. htm [Retrieved May 2, 2001.]

Feeling good. (1994). Word works, learn through writing at Boise State University 16 [Online.] Available: www.boisestate.edu/wcenter/ww69flow.htm

Flower, L. (1985). *Problem-solving strategies for writing* (2d ed.). San Diego: Harcourt Brace Jovanovich.

Ford, M., and Ford, J. (1992). *Writing as revelation*. New York: HarperCollins.

Fulwiler, T. (Ed.). (1987). *The journal book*. Portsmouth, NH: Boynton-Cook/Heinemann.

Gardner, H. (1983). *The theory of multiple intelligences*. New York: Basic Books.

Gawain, S. (1978). *Creative visualization*. Berkeley: Whatever.

Goldberg, N. (1986). *Writing down the bones*. Boston: Shambhala.

Goleman, D. (1995). *Emotional intelligence*. New York: Bantam. College English.

Harris, M. (1986). *Teaching one-to-one: The writing conference.* Urbana, IL: National Council of Teachers of English.

Harris, M. (1995). Talking in the middle way: Why writers need writing tutors. *College English 57*, 27–42. [Abstract in the Bedford online bibliography for teachers of writing: www.bedfordbooks.com/bb/writ2.html]

King, J. A. (1979). *Teachers' comments on students' writing: A conceptual analysis and empirical study.* Unpublished doctoral dissertation, Cornell University.

King, S. (1980, October). Imagery and the third eye. *Writer,* pp. 11–13, 44.

Kolb, D. A. (1981). Learning styles and disciplinary differences. In A. W. Chickering & Associates (Eds.), *The modern American college* (pp. 232–255). San Francisco: Jossey-Bass.

Murray, D. (1979). The listening eye: Reflections on the writing conference. In G. Tate and E. P. J. Corbett (Eds.), *The writing teacher's sourcebook* (2d ed., pp. 232–237). New York: Oxford University Press.

Murray, D. (1989). *Expecting the unexpected.* Portsmouth, NH: Boynton-Cook/Heinemann.

Paull, M., & Kligerman, J. (1972). Invention, composition, and the urban college. In R. Ohmann and W. B. Coley (Eds.), *Ideas for English 101* (pp. 141–158). Urbana, IL: National Council of Teachers of English.

Planning (invention). Owl Online Writing Lab. (n.d.). [Online] Available: owl.english.purdue.edu/handouts/generalgl_plan1.html [Retrieved May 2, 2001.]

Responding to student texts. Composition Center. (n.d.). [Online] Available: www.dartmouth.edu/~compose/faculty/methods/responding.html [Retrieved May 2, 2001.]

Rico, G. L. (1983). *Writing the natural way: Using right-brain techniques to release your expressive powers.* Los Angeles: Tarcher.

Silver, W. (1993, October 21). *Teachers' written comments on students' essays—How much do they help?* Break-out session presentation at the Annual Conference of the English Council of California Two-Year Colleges, San Jose, California.

Stewart, D. (1988). Some history lessons for composition teachers. In G. Tate and E.P.J. Corbett (Eds.), *The writing teacher's sourcebook* (2d ed., pp. 16–23). New York: Oxford University Press.

Stiff, R. (1967). The effect upon student composition of particular correction techniques. *Research in the teaching of English, 2* (Spring), 54–75.

Traci's fourth list of ten: Ten ways to respond to student drafts. (1998, August 1). [Online] Available: www.daedalus.com/teach/tens/08_01_98.html [Retrieved May 2, 2001.]

Tutor stories. National Writing Centers Association: An NCTE Assembly. (n.d.). [Online] Available: nwca.syr.edu/NWCAStories.html [Retrieved May 5, 2001.]

WAC faculty handbook 2000–2001. (n.d.). [Online] Available: www.wright.edu/academics/wac/facguide.htm [Retrieved May 2, 2001.]

What is "help" with writing? A look at three sources. (1995). Word works: Learning through writing at Boise State University, 73. [Online] Available: www.boisestate.edu/wcenter/ww73.htm [Retrieved May 8, 2001.]

When tutoring becomes counseling. (1997). Word works: Learning through writing at Boise State University, 89. [Online] Available: www.boisestate.edu/wcenter/ww89.htm [Retrieved May 8, 2001.]

Writing matters #2. Responding to student writing. (n.d.). Manoa Writing Program. [Online] Available: http://mwp01.mwp.hawaii.edu/wm2.htm [Retrieved May 2, 2001.]

PART III

MATH AND SCIENCE CURRICULA

Chapter 7

The Role of Technology in Individualizing Instruction in Linear Algebra

Ananda Gunawardena

SETTING AND PERSONAL BACKGROUND

The University of Houston–Downtown is a four-year undergraduate institution, enrolling more than 10,000 students. The university's ethnic makeup directly mirrors that of the city of Houston. One of the university's primary missions has been to prepare students for direct entry into the job market upon receipt of their bachelor's degrees. For this reason our degree programs have generally been oriented to applications. The university is one of the most ethnically diverse universities in the western United States. This brings the challenge of meeting the needs of every student when they come from varied backgrounds. Despite students returning to urban universities and colleges in record numbers, many drop out in their freshman year, mainly because they are unable to receive individual guidance or cannot keep up with college demands or finances.

The Department of Computer and Mathematical Sciences (CMS), housed in the College of Sciences and Technology, offers a curriculum leading to degrees in applied mathematics, computer science, and quantitative methods. Linear algebra is required of all sophomore science, engineering, and mathematics majors. It is a course where the beauty and elegance of mathematical theories blends with applications, and students get a firsthand experience of the utility of mathematics in real life. Many disciplines have benefited from the tools of linear algebra. Aerospace engineers analyze the integrity of a structure using a mesh and compute the forces acting at the mesh points using the techniques in numerical linear algebra. Epidemiologists can measure the spread of an epidemic incorporating a mathematical model consisting of matrices. Despite its importance, attrition rate in this course is as high as 40 percent, and fewer than 30 percent of the students pass the course with C or better. Our experience in teaching the course reflects the concerns in the delivery of mathematics instruction nationally (National Research Council, 1989). The state of mathematics education in United States is currently in a crisis. Students who enter college are often underprepared and lack the background and motivation to succeed at college-level mathematics. The origin of the problems in college mathematics education can be attributed to poor high school foundations. The lack of bridge programs between high school and college mathematics make the situation worse. As a result, most students who enter college lack adequate preparation. The large classes and ineffective teaching techniques in freshman college classes have made the situation even worse. Therefore, the dropout rate for freshman and sophomore mathematics courses is alarmingly high. Most students repeat freshman math courses several times before they finally succeed or simply drop out of college unable to meet their basic math requirement. Another problem facing math education today is the negative attitude toward the discipline by the student and sometimes by the parents. The math instructors (including those in higher education) who are refusing to adopt new instructional techniques and still try teach math the old-fashioned way do not help a diverse student body needing alternative methods to succeed. Unfortunately many math teachers still insist that paper and pencil manipulation ("drill and kill") as it was done in the past is all that is needed for learning mathematics (Waits & Demana, 1996). The traditional approach of teaching to the middle of the class no longer works. With such a diverse and underprepared student body, it is inevitable that we must look for alternative ways to deliver math instruction. The answer to higher retention and better passing rate is an effective instructional system that supports the needs of every student. The task is especially challenging in an environment where resources are scarce.

The University of Houston–Downtown has encouraged and supported the innovation in instructional technology through internal and external grants. The author teaches undergraduate courses at the university in computer science such as object-oriented programming, data structures, and computer graphics and computational mathematics courses such as linear algebra and numerical analysis. The instructional system described in this chapter is designed for a course in linear algebra. Correct blend in theory and applications in linear algebra makes it possible to design experimental systems for individualizing instructions and measure their effectiveness.

GUIDING ASSUMPTIONS ABOUT LEARNING AND TEACHING

Role of the Teacher and of the Student

Traditional mathematics courses are well structured and cover a standard curriculum. The mode of delivery has remained, to a great extent, the traditional approach of definition, theorem, and proof and exercise. However, with the mathematics reform movement that is sweeping the country today, some mathematics teachers have begun to utilize new techniques for communicating mathematical knowledge. Greater use of technology, high emphasis on communal or collaborative learning such as group projects, and alternative assessment techniques are few of the new approaches adopted by modern math teachers. The new techniques encourage active mathematical exploration and discovery rather than a passive theorem–proof–exercise approach. Students learn specifics of mathematical theories before trying to generalize the results. This approach is in sharp contrast to the traditional approach where generalizations were introduced before specifics. The new model reflects the way some humans learn by processing specific information before trying to generalize. While the highly structured traditional approach may help less skilled students pass the course and highly skilled students ace the course, we can debate whether such instructional techniques produce students who are able to do only what they are told, rather than developing skills that are sustainable and extendible. The rote memorization of formulas and learning how to plug numbers into a formula does not constitute proper learning. Real learning takes place when instructors motivate students to explore mathematical results and conjecture theories. Real learning takes place when students are presented mathematical theories in the context of real problems. As noted in Chapters 2, 3, and 4 of this volume, the role of the student in modern education must change from that of a passive listener to that of an active participant. Traditionally, mathematics instruction has provided only limited opportunities for active participation by the student. Today math instructors must create informal classroom settings that encourage active participation. Students who actively participate in classroom discussions set the foundation for their own mathematical explorations. The discipline of linear algebra is rich with examples that require deep investigations. These explorations eventually lead to solid mathematical theories. Students who follow this model of learning appreciate the abstract mathematical theories and their utility. In this setting, students view instructor more as a facilitator than as a lecturer.

APPROACHES AND TECHNIQUES FOR INDIVIDUALIZING INSTRUCTION

The structure and the content of the new linear algebra curriculum developed at the University of Houston–Downtown are designed to be dynamic, adapting to the skill level of the learner. The course is taught in a computer lab environment using an innovative instructional method based on interactive electronic notebooks (iNote). The iNotes are interactive computer documents specifically programmed to combine elegant word-processing capabilities with the algebraic, graphical, and computational powers of a mathematical software engine built to support experimentation. The software engine behind iNote is a powerful program that uses automated learning functions to demonstrate concepts for learners. We shall discuss later the role of automated learning functions in more detail. The students are able to conjecture, experiment, and explain their mathematical theories, observations, and conclusions all within the iNote. The dynamic nature of iNote allows students to change problem parameters and perform mathematical investigations and seamlessly integrate the results into the iNote. Examples and exploratory activities in iNote can be changed by the instructor or student to meet a specific learning objective. The concept of iNote developed as a result of the recognition that standard classroom lecture notes are static and leave no room for the individual student to fit the lesson to his or her learning needs. Unlike the fixed lecture notes in a traditional teaching and learning environment, iNotes encourage student participation at every level in real time. Students using iNotes regard the instructor as a facilitator who would help them create an individualized set of notes by choosing appropriate examples for exploration and discovery. iNotes is built on the notion of learning by doing. The expert database behind iNote helps students experiment with a variety of lesson scenarios and get instant feedback. The strongest feature of iNote is its high adaptability to individual needs. Within this interactive environment, students are also assessed on a combination of continuous classroom activities.

General Classroom Approaches

The general classroom approaches for supporting individual learners can range from creating a more relaxed and informal learning environment to a set of individualized instructional and assessment tools. An informal classroom tone encourages active student participation and increases interaction among individual students. Frequent supervised laboratories also increase opportunities for individual students to interact with the instructor and their colleagues. Since the effectiveness of an individualized instructional system depends on strong instructor and student commitment to the system, instructors must strongly emphasize the necessity to use all features of the system in the classroom. The system supporting an individualized approach must be designed so as to accommodate a variety of activities such as individual lessons, supervised laboratories, and projects supported by a continuous assessment system while respecting the final course objectives, which are designed to meet the standard curriculum guidelines accepted by the linear algebra community.

Factors Supporting the Academic Success of Individual Students

It is important to make students feel that their needs are met in the classroom. In any traditional lecture setting, only a handful of students actively participate in classroom discussions. Often the instructor generates the questions and few choose to answer them. The great majority are reluctant to speak up even when they know the answer. This makes it harder to know the competency level of any individual student. We have created an electronic learning environment that effectively encourages the participation of each student. The learning environment is a combination of a limited instructional model and a hands-on lab environment. The instructional model, based on a dynamic response analysis model (DRAM), uses concept tests for providing instant feedback on student responses. In this model, the instructor takes the students through a learning path defined in the iNote. A concept test is a continuous assessment technique that provides just-in-time questions to measure the understanding of a particular concept that was just discussed using the iNote. The concept tests are provided during the lecture at designated points, but students are allowed to answer questions at any point of the lecture. Students get immediate feedback on their performance, including a comparison to the entire class. This model allows all students to participate in the on-going class discussion in a virtual setting, making each student feel as if he or she is part of the discussion. The instant feedback from DRAM also allows instructors to adjust learning paths, identify individual students who are having trouble with a particular concept, and design activities that will effectively address the deficiencies. The model has also been tested using handheld computers in a chemistry class at Carnegie Mellon University (Chen, Myers, & Yaron 2000). DRAM is an example of a computer-based system that effectively addresses active student participation in classroom activities. While technology helps us create a system that assures a virtual participation of each student, we cannot underestimate the role of the instructor who helps create a real class environment where student participation is an important factor in a successful learning environment. In linear algebra, the set of iNotes encourage active student participation. While the instructor acts as a facilitator who chooses the appropriate examples for exploration, each student will be able to create a customized notebook to meet his or her learning style and goals. The loosely defined order of activities in the iNote, from worked examples to projects to reference material and problem sets, also allow individual students to complete the activities in an iNote, perhaps taking different learning paths. The networked classroom environment allows the instructor to bring any individual student's exploratory activities to the attention of the entire class in an instant. Over time, students develop self-confidence that is critical to their success. Although the iNote approach seems to represent a more intense use of resources, as we shall discuss later, the technology plays a major role in creating this individualized system.

An Effective System for Supporting Student Learning

How does an instructor know whether the individualized techniques employed are effective? A highly enthusiastic and motivated student body with a passion for learning is an indication of an effective system. You know your system works when students no longer ask whether the topic you just covered is going to be on the final exam. You know the system works when students are willing to do whatever it takes to complete the task and enjoy its rewards. The system works when students view learning as a fun activity. Instructional techniques that fail to make every student feel as if he or she is part of the complete learning process are often not successful in creating an effective learning environment. We are convinced that technology can create such an environment.

It is important to recognize the learning differences among beginning and advanced students. Advanced students are usually self-motivated, self-starters, and are mathematically matured, while most beginning students need constant guidance and advice to succeed. Most beginning students lack the proper discipline to maintain their concentration during a problem solving process in a generic learning environment. Although customized lesson and activity plans for each individual student seems to be the ideal, it is unrealistic to assume that instructors have the time to manually prepare such plans with increasing teaching, service and professional demands. Instructors in four-year colleges regularly teach four courses per semester and have many service obligations and constant pressure to maintain scholarly activities. The sheer size of beginning undergraduate classes is also an obstacle to individualized instruction. In a typical semester, an instructor might be dealing with over one hundred students on the average. This makes it impossible to pay individual attention to each and every student in a traditional lecture setting. Therefore our approach is to create a "digital assistant" to the instructor who will help the instructor with routine tasks leaving critical decision making to the instructor.

Specific Instructional Techniques

Individual skills can be exploited by identifying strengths and weaknesses of each student. For example, while one student may do well in constructing a proof for an abstract theory, another may be skilled in accurately modeling a real-world problem. Instructors must recognize these differences and find ways to reward each skill, emphasizing the importance of all. Instructional techniques that regard only the students who can prove theorems to be mathematically competent fail to discover useful skills hidden in others. Therefore a varied set of evaluation measures aimed at these different skills must be implemented to evaluate the skill level of each student. In the beginning of the course each student takes a pretest that accurately determines a student's background knowledge and helps the instructor devise a study plan. All students are given the opportunity to take a pretest to assess their preparedness to take the course. A metric based on number of attempts and the difficulty level of each concept is applied to test results for initial evaluation of each student's competency level. The student scores are automatically registered into the instructor database, which can be retrieved for evaluation. Based on the pretest results, each student is assigned an initial competency rank and meets with the instructor to devise an individual study plan. The automated system can also generate an ambitious study plan geared more toward the well-prepared students. The study plan is flexible and is subjected to constant evaluation by the student and the instructor or teaching assistant. Each student must continuously work with the automated learning functions within the context of iNotes. The automated learning functions are computer programs that are capable of teaching important concepts. The programs allow users to select their own examples and show how the problem is solved in a step-by-step manner. The system collects user data and the statistics on student performance and writes the data to the instructor database for frequent evaluations. The statistics contain the number of concepts attempted, the number of tasks completed, and the updated competency ranking for each student.

Instructional Problem Solving

The experience of the instructor plays a major role in successfully implementing an effective instructional strategy. An experienced instructor is capable of immediately recognizing the individual learning differences. In mathematics, it is easy to distinguish students who enjoy the abstract nature of the discipline from students who appreciate its utility, students who need many examples to learn a concept from students who can conjecture a mathematical theory from a few observations. The individualized plan for each student depends on his or her mathematical background, major, level of exposure to technology-based instructional techniques, and strengths and weaknesses in understanding mathematical concepts and their utility. The interactive notebooks (iNotes), supervised laboratories, application projects, and automated learning functions create the comprehensive classroom approach that is required for assessment in an individualized learning environment. As we will describe later, an automated assessment system can help instructors choose activities that are appropriate for a particular student while maintaining course goals and standards. The iNotes support the general structure of a standard linear algebra course. The activities in iNotes utilize a set of automated learning functions that are designed to be highly interactive at all stages of the lesson. We shall discuss later the role of automated learning functions in more detail.

Technology-Based Individualized System

So what is the role of technology in helping us create lesson plans that addresses individual student needs rather than a mythical class norm? Today we are seeing a revolution in information technology. Interactive multimedia facilities are driving the development of computer-based learning. Knowledge can be presented in many forms, and the needs of the individual students can be met through effective use of technology (Anandan, 1989). But before delving blindly into integrating technology into a course, one must carefully analyze the resources at hand and advantages and disadvantages of using technology. A well-thought-out plan for integrating technology is indeed essential for successful implementation of an individualized curriculum. A technology can be an obstacle to learning, rather than a useful partner, if not adopted properly. A basic requirement for successfully integrating technology into a course is an adequate computer lab supported by a well-managed long-term maintenance plan. A poorly equipped or poorly maintained computer laboratory often can hinder students from getting the full benefits of a technology-based learning environment and may make them frustrated in learning activities rather than encouraged. Given a well-equipped and well-maintained lab, how can the instructor successfully utilize the equipment to create the individualized learning system? An effective individualized system must have good recordkeeping utilities that can immediately report the competency measures of a particular student. The instructor can draw on experience to advise students on how to reach or exceed minimum competency. For example, a student who lacks competency in a certain concept can be referred to the relevant automated learning function. Instructors can set learning objectives and adjust study plans if goals are not met at the end of the assigned time period. Frequent individual meetings and advice based on computer records can create an individualized lesson plan for each student. In the sections to follow, we will elaborate more on how such a system can be utilized in individualized instructions.

A fundamental requirement for any technology-based learning environment is a fully functional laboratory. Most entering freshmen students may not possess computer skills beyond simple word-processing skills. Such students are inadequately prepared to meet the high technical demands that are needed in computer-based instructions in mathematics. The answer to such deficiencies may be a technology track (Waller, Gunawardena, Becerra, Deeba, & Xie 1995). Examples of the sort of technology track we mean are those that fully utilize state-of-the-art computers assisted by powerful computer algebra system (CAS) such as Maple (Waterloo Maple, 2001), Mathematica (Wolfram Research, 2001) and Matlab (MathWorks, 2001). These systems are capable of displaying the output in text and graphical formats and are very useful in visualizing abstract mathematical concepts. The courses in the technology track range from beginning college algebra to upper-level courses such as linear algebra and differential equations. A student who follows the technology track becomes comfortable with the new technology-based interactive learning environment early and minimizes the overhead of learning a new technology in upper-level courses. Perhaps the biggest obstacle to individualizing instruction is the lack of human resources. However, a well-designed software system that takes over some of the laborious tasks in individualizing instruction and assessing students can relieve the burden on the instructor. An added benefit of instructing students with technology may be a future workforce who is equipped with advanced technological tools to function in a highly computerized world. For many years, instructors have made limited use of technology in their classrooms. This has included, for example, using PowerPoint® lecture notes in the classroom and placing all course resources on the World Wide Web. These techniques may have improved the method of delivery, but they have failed to exploit technology's full capability of improving pedagogical effectiveness, whose increase is well documented in recent literature (Eisenhower National Clearinghouse, 1999).

Our effort to individualize instruction using technology began as a result of three major grants, Interactive Math Text Project (IMTP) and two National Science Foundation (NSF–ILI grants (Sirisaengtaskin, Gunawardena, &

Waller 1992; Waller et al., 1995). These grants brought the University of Houston-Downtown three well-equipped computer labs to be utilized in technology-based instructional methods. We also secured funds from other sources to maintain and upgrade the equipment to make sure they operate in their highest condition. This initial work laid the groundwork for a fully technology-based curriculum. Although individualizing instruction was not the primary goal of integrating technology in a linear algebra curriculum, as we became experts in managing the technology-based environment we realized its enormous potential for doing so. We started to view technology not as a mere tool to enhance instruction, but as a significant partner in creating the customized educational environment that provides each individual with the increased chance to succeed in the course. We envisioned a system capable of (1) detecting deficient areas and learning habits of an individual student, (2) advising the instructor and the student on a proper study plan and assessment techniques, and (3) efficiently keeping track of the student progress and informing the student and the instructor of the competency level each student had reached at any stage of the course. Interactive Linear Algebra Text (ILAT) (Deeba & Gunawardena, 1998) is the result of this vision of a comprehensive computer-based system. ILAT is an electronic customized courseware system that evolved from simple computer-aided drill activities to a comprehensive software package using the latest software techniques and theories from disciplines such as artificial intelligence. The software package consists of interactive lessons, supervised laboratories, projects dealing with real applications, automated learning functions, an adaptive testing system and theory, and help screens supported by a multimedia user interface. While advanced students experiment in iNotes with more complex examples, novice students often use prepared examples or their own simple examples. However, regardless of the level of interaction, the final objective is learning the concept. A library of automated learning functions supports the interactive lessons. The purpose of the learning functions is to show the students the step-by-step process of solving a problem or learning a concept. Automated learning functions are computer programs written in the programming language of the symbolic algebra system Maple (Waterloo Maple, 2001). Learning functions serve in three capacities: demonstration, interactive, and no-step mode.

The demonstration mode of the learning functions allow students to see a step-by-step approach to learning a concept using their favorite example. The demonstration mode highlights important steps of the process. It is important to point out that mathematics is an ideal discipline to be supported by such automated learning functions, as concepts discussed in mathematics often have well-defined algorithms. Therefore, instructors who are designing and coding these automated learning functions can rely heavily on the well-defined algorithms to make the functions easier to program and more robust against user errors. The demonstration mode of the automated learning functions can be used by instructors to demonstrate learning by discovery techniques. Learning by discovery is a concept that encourages students to experiment with specific examples and try to generalize results before being introduced into the general theorem. For example, students learn by discovery with specific cases that unlike real numbers, two matrices A and B do not always commute (i.e., AB/BA). This helps students understand the concept in its context rather than being told it as a fact. The automated learning functions and their help system provide extensive learning support whenever student needs them.

The interactive mode is an automated menu-driven program that checks mastery after learning a concept in the demonstration mode. Programming the interactive mode is more involved, since it needs to accommodate various levels of student interaction and preparation. It must address the various learning paths the student may have taken to achieve the lesson goals. The program is capable of detecting knowledge gaps in student understanding based on student responses. The program keeps track of how well students answer certain questions. Questions are categorized according to the degree of difficulty and their membership in a particular class of concepts. For example, the questions that deal with the inverse of a matrix may belong to the class of "Gauss elimination." Therefore a failure in this question may mean a lack in understanding the Gauss elimination process. At the end of the execution of the interactive mode, the program provides a posttask assessment report. From this report the instructor can identify deficient areas and direct the student to various learning strategies. The effective learning strategies include, but are not limited to, retaking an interactive lesson, working exclusively with the demonstration mode of the automated linear algebra function, and redoing a lab activity, or any combination of the above.

The no-step mode provides an answer to a query without providing an explanation of how the answer was obtained. Although no-step mode does not provide any pedagogical value to the user on its own, its results can be used in a larger context such as a project situation to reach important conclusions. In many ways, this mode resembles the case of a user typing a formula on a calculator and getting an answer without any explanation.

ILAT also consists of supervised laboratories that are to be completed under close instructor supervision. Labs are small-group projects that emphasize the utility of the concepts and encourage collaborative work. Labs provide an opportunity for students to learn how to work in a group environment and interact with the instructor one-on-one. This is also an opportunity for the instructor to observe the performance of individual students or the group. Students alternate in taking responsibility for control of the group activities.

This encourages equal opportunity for learning leadership skills for each individual.

The ILAT system also consists of an adaptive testing system (ATS) that provides the student and the instructor with a flexible and adaptive testing environment that accurately measures the student performance. The ATS software automatically adjusts to the individual student's knowledge level and provides student with the questions at the appropriate level. The ATS software, backed by a complex categorization algorithm, groups the questions by membership in a concept class, by their degree of difficulty as assigned by the creator of the test, by their topical relation to sections of the course content, and by the test taker's performance history. The software has a user-centered approach and may change some of its predefined categorization as a result of user responses. For example, if many users easily answer a question ranked as difficult by the creator of the test, the system will automatically readjust its degree of difficulty ranking within its concept group. ATS is designed with the philosophy that users should eventually determine how the adaptive testing system should behave. ATS provides a competency report and a summary of the sections mastered. These statistics are very important to the individual student as they try to meet the course objectives. ATS provides statistics on deficiency areas and shows where to seek help. ILAT also has a comprehensive help system for immediate assistance to the student. The software comes with a built-in theory section that provides mathematical proofs for those who need them. All the components in the ILAT package are connected by a multimedia graphical user interface that provides easy access to the content through a well-designed navigational system. The design of the interface was enhanced by the human computer interaction project directed by the author at Carnegie Mellon University. The interface provides the user with multimedia features such as concept animation and sound.

A well-designed software system like ILAT can support individualized instruction and allow student–machine interaction through automated learning functions and adaptive lessons and tests. Although a machine can never replace the human's ability to make important decisions about an individual, it can greatly enhance the process. Besides, there is plenty of opportunity for student–instructor interaction through supervised laboratories and application projects. The automated learning functions provide students with a user-friendly learning system that keeps track of each one's mastery of concepts. ILAT allows linear algebra and all other courses in the technology track to be taught in a highly computerized environment. The method of delivery, user adaptability, assessment, and adjustment of plans are key components of an individualized system. The other factors such as small class sizes, access to open labs, and well-functioning equipment also play a major role in creating this effective environment. We only have anecdotal evidence at this point to share on the effectiveness of the ILAT individualized system. We have been using the ILAT system in the classroom since 1994 and have observed a greater rate of completion of the course, a more positive attitude on the part of students toward the course, and what is more important, student self-confidence in learning new material on their own. Students seem to enjoy and appreciate team activities. We have also noticed that the immediate-feedback mechanism using the dynamic response analysis model (DRAM) makes a significant difference in student participation and performance. However, continuous refinement to the system and more data is needed to validate the effectiveness of the system.

CONCLUSION

With increased class sizes and decreased funding for college education, it is not easy to find resources for individualized instruction. Reform movements in mathematics, however, have encouraged the use of technology in the classroom and a record number of technology initiatives to enhance instruction are funded by the federal government and local funding agencies. Through these grants many four-year universities and community colleges have been able to acquire equipment to support a technology-based curriculum. When used properly, technology can be a great asset in our quest to support individualized instruction that is demanded by a diverse body of modern college students. Using modern technology, instructors can make a genuine effort to satisfy more than the middle of the class. Each student deserves and must be provided with the tools and opportunity to succeed. The importance of technology-based instruction and its role in higher education is well documented (Anandan, 1989). In addition to the ILAT system described in this chapter, many other technological approaches to individualizing instructions are available. In particular, the Advanced Computer Tutoring (ACT) system developed at Carnegie Mellon University (Corbett, Koedinger, & Anderson, 1997) deserves special mention. The ACT Project uses artificial intelligence techniques to develop computer-based tutors for mathematics and programming that assists students in problem solving. Its cognitive tutor technology provides a unique and powerful approach to the creation of adaptive educational software. Based on a computational theory of thought, ACT tutors can generate and follow the multiple possible solutions a student might attempt on any given problem and dynamically tailor instructions to each student and problem. Like a personal human tutor or coach, computer-based cognitive tutors observe each student's performance, identify strengths and weaknesses, and provide individualized, just-in-time instruction. The comprehensive individualized systems such as ACT and ILAT have been developed through support from external agencies like the Mathematical Association of America (MAA), IBM Corporation, and the National Science Foundation (NSF) and from local support from the universities. Developing technology with the individual student in mind is a very time-consuming project that requires long-term commitment from the developers. Support both from university administration for technology-based instruction and from instructors who believe in alternative instructional methods is essential to the success of any such project. We believe technology should play an increasingly important role in individualizing instruction, and so far the technology-based tools have been underutilized in improving it.

The ideas implemented in linear algebra can be modified for any mathematics course and for courses in other disciplines where the concepts taught have well-defined algorithms. The author is in the process of designing a similar system for computer science courses at Carnegie Mellon University. The new system extends the ILAT capabilities by adding data-mining capabilities to the system. As more and more students begin to learn with computers, it becomes possible to automatically analyze performance data and create collaborative workspaces that allow learners to form learning communities. Learning communities share their educational experiences on-line and add another dimension to the individualized learning experience that was not possible before. The new data-mining algorithms under development may also identify nonintuitive relationships among learning variables, thereby giving instructors another tool to be effective. Other examples of individualizing instruction in English education through computers also are documented in literature (Kitao, 1994). Digital technology and its impact on education have just begun. It is certain to change the way each of us learns (Hardin & Ziebarth, 2001). It seems that technology can play a vital role in realizing the dream of one teacher for every student, an ideal that can be true only in a learning environment where instructors, computers, and students share responsibility.

REFERENCES

Anandan, K. (1989). *Transforming teaching with technology.* EDUCOM Academic Computing Publications.

Bowers, D. (1996). Customized study ware in mathematics. In B. Waits & F. Demian, (Eds.). *Proceedings of the International Conference on Technology in Collegiate Mathematics* (pp. 51–55). Reading, MA: Addison-Wesley.

Chen, F., Myers, B., & Yaron, D. (2000). *Using handheld devices for tests in classes.* School of Computer Science Technical Report no. CMU-CS-00–152. Human Computer Interaction Institute Technical Report. CMU–HCII–00–101. Pittsburgh, PA: Carnegie Mellon University

Corbett, A., Koedinger, K. R., & Anderson, J. R. (1997). Intelligent tutoring systems. In M. G. Helander, T. K. Landauer, & P. V. Prabhu (Eds.), *Handbook of human–computer interaction* (pp. 849–874). New York: Elsevier.

Deeba E.Y., & Gunawardena, A. D. (1998). *Interactive linear algebra with MapleV*. New York: Springer-Verlag.

Eisenhower National Clearinghouse. (1999). *Impact of information technologies implementation on education*. [Online]. Available: www.enc.org.

Hardin, J., & Ziebarth, J. (2001). *Digital technology and its impact on education*. Champaign, IL: National Center for Supercomputing Applications (NCSA). [Online] Available: www.ed.gov/Technology/Futures/hardin.html

Kitao, K. (1994). *Individualizing English instruction using computers*. Doshisha studies in English No 62. [Online] Available: ilc2.doshisha.ac.jp/users/kkitao/library/article/call/individualizing.htm

MathWorks. (2001). *Matlab*. [Computer software]. Natick, MA: MathWorks.

National Research Council. (1989) *Everybody counts: A report on the future of mathematics education*. Washington, DC: National Research Council.

Sirisaengtaskin, O., Gunawardena, A. D., Waller, W. (1992). *An object oriented framework for design and use of interactive laboratories*. Instrumentation and Laboratory Improvement Grant. Arlington, VA: National Science Foundation.

Waller, W., Gunawardena, A. D., Becerra, L., Deeba, E., Xie, S. (1995). *Creating an alternative technology track*. Arlington, VA: National Science Foundation.

Waterloo Maple. (2001). Maple software. [Computer software]. Ontario, Canada: Waterloo Maple.

Wolfram Research. (2001). *Mathematica*. [Computer software]. Champaign, IL: Wolfram Research.

Chapter 8

Helping Students Find Their Chemistry Voices

Keith Kester

SETTING AND PERSONAL BACKGROUND

The Colorado College is a highly selective private liberal arts and sciences coeducational college with 1,900–2,000 undergraduates, 2.6% of whom are international students and 15.5% of whom are minority students (African American, Hispanic, and Native American). There are 44 majors available (including three tracks in the English major, and a chemistry and biochemistry major). The college offers a B.A. degree and three M.A.T. degrees.

Colorado College's academic calendar is in modular form and consists of 81/2 sequential blocks of time, during each of which students take only one course. One block is 31/2 weeks long, and is worth four semester hours of credit. The half block comes at the beginning of the second semester. In addition, there are extended-format courses that extend over an entire semester, earning the student a half block's worth of credit. The transition metal chemistry course mentioned below is an extended-format course.

Recently I have been teaching both halves of the general chemistry course (entry level), inorganic chemistry, and transition metal chemistry (the latter two are advanced courses); a first-year experience course (Scientific and Religious Strategies for Ordering Chaos, team-taught with a professor of religion); and two intermediate women studies courses (Gender and Science and

Race, Class, and Gender). I also teach in the college's Integrated Science MAT program for in-service K–12 science teachers (with approximately thirty students). The college has a general class-size limit of twenty-five students, and that is the typical enrollment in the general chemistry courses, the first-year experience course, and the Race, Class. and Gender course. Inorganic Chemistry has ten to twelve students, and Gender and Science around eight students. My experiences with individualized instruction in chemistry are drawn from both the first two chemistry courses at Colorado College: General Chemistry I and II and the senior capstone course, Inorganic Chemistry.

GUIDING ASSUMPTIONS ABOUT LEARNING AND TEACHING

Chemistry is a material science. All the matter undergoing change around us falls within its purview. Part of my fascination with chemistry is that I and my students have to function at three levels:

First, at that experienceable, macroscopic level encountered in everyday life, in the laboratory, and in chemical demonstrations that are presented in the classroom

Second, at the submicroscopic level of electrons, atoms, molecules, ions, etc., not accessible to our senses even with the aid of the most sophisticated instrumentation (We chemists work with and think in terms of these entities. To aid us in this process we have physical models and mental images of the entities.)

Third, at the abstract symbolic level as represented, for example, by chemical equations such as that representing the burning of natural gas:

$$CH_4(g) + 2\ O_2(g)\ ?\ CO_2(g) + 2\ H_2O(g) + ?Hrxn$$

One of my most important tasks as an instructor in a chemistry course is to facilitate each student's ability to relate the three different levels in meaningful and understandable ways.

I need to provide the students in my chemistry courses with a rich array of supportive learning options in order to facilitate their going back and forth among the three levels. The learning options include:

- access to hands-on physical models
- opportunities to work with chemicals and chemical reactions in the laboratory
- computer manipulation of three-dimensional representations of atomic and molecular orbitals, molecules, and crystal lattices
- opportunities and encouragement for drawing their own mental images

- promoting awareness of and conversations about the level they are operating on
- collaborative work with their peers and their instructor at each of the three levels, including moving back and forth among levels

The most engaging learning tasks are likely to be at the macroscopic level. Then I can assist the students in making connections to the submicroscopic and symbolic levels.

The necessity of getting to and working at the second and third levels significantly contributes to the justifiable reputation that chemistry is a difficult subject to learn. The majority of students planning to take the beginning courses in chemistry see them as formidable. Consequently they typically approach the learning tasks I give them as a continuing series of challenges. As noted in Chapter 2, it is important therefore to frame learning failures (in assigned learning tasks or on assessment instruments) as temporary rather than terminal; and as possibly reflecting lack of effort, or more likely, lack of an effective learning strategy. Effective learning strategies need to be found and developed by teacher and student working together.

I assume that each of the students coming into my beginning chemistry courses has the potential to master at a satisfactory level the knowledge, skills, and conceptual frameworks that make up the curricular goals of the course. If that potential is to be realized, the student and I, working together, must find the effective combination of the student's learning strategies and my teaching strategies that will enable it to happen. I believe it is crucial for me to begin each course with this assumption if I am to maximize the possibility that all the students in the course will achieve at least a satisfactory level of mastery.

Because so much of the chemistry to be learned is at the second and third levels, students often also experience it as being pretty abstract and often irrelevant. How then can I facilitate my students finding or generating personal meaning and relevance in the material to be learned? I can go a long way toward this goal by presenting the chemistry in real-world contexts in the form of questions that I hope they would be interested in finding the answers to. In the first half of general chemistry I have three such questions:

1. What is causing global warming and how do humans contribute to it?
2. How could we manufacture an effective and safe automobile air bag?
3. Why should I take vitamin C?

I have another set of three such questions for the second half of general chemistry:

1. How did life arise on earth?

2. What substances are in natural water and how can I treat it to make it safe for human use?

3. How do I see?

With these questions I am framing both the content of the course and, in part, the type of learning I want to be taking place.

Of the three types of learning—accumulating factual information, developing procedural skills, and creating conceptual ways of organizing and understanding knowledge (Guskin 1994)—the latter two are the ones I focus on in both the laboratory and the classroom. For developing both procedural skills and a scientific conceptual frame of reference, I want the learning tasks to include those that have the students "doing" science, which means:

- designing experiments to test hypotheses they've generated
- conducting the experiments
- analyzing the results
- drawing appropriate conclusions
- reporting the results to the broader scientific community, which in most cases at the undergraduate level will be the learning community of the classroom

In addition to the chemical conceptual frameworks that I'm intending that they construct (or reconstruct, since high school chemistry is a prerequisite to my general chemistry course), I have a number of ways of organizing, understanding, and communicating knowledge that I want them to develop further:

- analytical, critical, and creative thinking
- oral and written communication skills
- problem solving
- the ability to reflect
- being able to see and consider things from alternative perspectives and make a reasoned choice of actions to take
- working collaboratively

I also seek to have my students pay attention to how they learn and what modes of learning are most effective for each of them. I want them to work at increasing their repertoire of learning and study skills.

For me, learning is sense making in a social context. Chapter 2 emphasizes that individuals construct understandings of their surrounding environments so that the world makes sense to them. They do not do this in isolation but in social environments such as the classroom and the laboratory. That is to say, knowledge is socially constructed and reconstructed. Learning most effectively begins with active involvement and concrete experience. It continues with reflection on that experience and abstract interpretation of it, essential components of sense making in chemistry.

As a chemistry and science teacher, I see myself as a facilitator of learning. I demonstrate chemical phenomena. I structure the learning situation to provide both hands-on and minds-on tasks (in both laboratory and classroom). I seek to build bridges between the knowledge and skills individual students bring to the learning tasks and the knowledge and skills I expect them to develop in successfully completing the tasks. I try to model for them how to learn, study, trouble-shoot, and solve problems. I am a guide for student inquiry and investigation and a resource person.

I also engage in pedagogical research. For example, I have investigated (1) what makes for effective cooperative groups (where each member of the group benefits from the group work), looking at such variables as the pace at which students work, the grade they hope to achieve, the intended major, chemistry background, preferred learning style, etc.; (2) what types of Gregorc learning styles (Gregorc, 1984) perform best on my exams; and (3) what learning aids students with differing learning styles find most useful.

My job as a teacher is to help each student progress to understandings that are more sophisticated and complete and closer to the way the world is. I try to structure the classroom environment so that it includes material new to the students yet relatable to the prior knowledge they bring to the classroom and to the world outside. Introduction of new material to be learned and skills to be developed is often enhanced by the intentional presentation of anomalies that generate a sense of disequilibrium in the students, causing them to question the prior knowledge and assumptions they've brought to the topic or skill at hand. Too much disequilibrium can have the consequence of unduly discouraging the student and should be avoided.

In addition to the prior knowledge students bring to the learning event, they bring diverse habitual ways of acquiring and processing new knowledge and relating it to the prior knowledge they have already constructed. They also bring diverse motivational dispositions that need to be drawn upon wherever possible. Their diverse habitual ways and motivational dispositions necessitate individualizing instruction as much as possible in order to meet the students where they are. Most students in my general chemistry course are there because it is a required course in their major or preprofessional program. This requirement serves as an external source of motivation to at least pass the course and often to obtain a good grade. Ideally, I'd like to find a way to foster an internal source of motivation in each student who is either externally motivated or unmotivated. To that end I solicit from each student, at the beginning of the course, their reasons for taking the course and what they want to take away from it, that is, what are their objectives in the course? Knowing what their objectives are, I may be able to assist them in meeting at least some of them.

The students' role is an active one. They are not passive recipients of knowledge, because while information can be gained that way, knowledge cannot. The knowledge they gain they have to construct themselves. It becomes their own. They take ownership of it when they realize they have constructed it themselves, that they've "got it!" which means that they can provide their own explanation(s), they can perform the skill(s), and after a lapse of time they can pick it up again without having to relearn it all over again.

Students should also be reflecting on their own thought processes, on how they learn, and on how effective the learning strategy they have chosen is. They also need to pay attention to how they can maintain, and what will help in maintaining, their motivation for learning. If they are to take responsibility for how and what they learn, and ownership of what they have learned, they need to be enabled to do these things in their own individual ways.

In the process of constructing new knowledge, they need to articulate their current knowledge and test it in the new learning environment. They proceed in the construction of new knowledge by asking questions about the material presented, making sense of it, relating it to their prior knowledge on the subject, and reconceptualizing (or reconstructing) the prior knowledge to accommodate their new understandings. This may necessitate some unlearning (deconstructing) of the prior knowledge, which can be a struggle for some students.

Learners work at different paces. Ideally one would want to accommodate each individual's pace. The constraints imposed by the academic calendar that we teachers and students work within make that accommodation difficult. I struggle to find ways to best structure the learning environment to accommodate the significant range of paces at which my students work in their effort to master the material I present to them. I relate some of the things I have tried in this struggle in the next section of this chapter.

The responsibility for learning, as noted in Chapter 4, is shared between student and teacher. Learning is most effectively accomplished when there is mutual cooperation and respect between, and mutual investment by, student and teacher. Together, the students and I become a learning community in which we learn from each other.

In this learning community it is important that I communicate expectations and standards to my students, from the beginning of the course and throughout it. It is also important that I give them regular group and individual feedback on how they are doing in meeting my expectations and achieving the standards I've set before them.

In evaluating the quality of the learning that has occurred, I look for the care, thought, and discipline the students put into their sense-making activities. I expect them to be on task most of the time. I ask for precision in their use of terms and in their experimental work. I am more interested in the reasoning processes that lead to their conclusions than in the "correctness" of the conclusions.

In communicating my expectations of my students, and in evaluating their work, I try to be consistent in teaching both beginning and advanced undergraduate students. There are two areas where the teaching approaches I use with beginning level students differ in degree only from the teaching approaches I use with senior chemistry majors. First, I feel that I need to work harder at engaging and interesting the students in the course material in beginning courses than in advanced courses in my discipline of chemistry. I have to think in the broader context of the natural sciences in relating the chemistry in beginning courses to the interests of students who are intending to major not in chemistry, but in biology, environmental science, geology, or psychology, or who are premedicine, prelaw, or preengineering students. Second, I have higher expectations for the sophistication, comprehensiveness, clarity, and closeness to current scientific understandings of the knowledge of students in the senior chemistry course than I do for students in the beginning chemistry courses. Sometimes I am fortunate enough to have the same student in both the first chemistry course at Colorado College and the last chemistry course. It is fascinating to see how those students have developed during the four undergraduate years. It also causes me to ponder what effect I have had on that student's intellectual development—and whether there are ways (as undoubtedly there are) that I could have more effectively contributed to that development.

APPROACHES AND TECHNIQUES FOR INDIVIDUALIZING INSTRUCTION

If instruction is to be individualized, it is essential that I and the students get to know one another. At the beginning of each course I have activities in which the students and I get to know one another by name and in which they share some of their concerns and interests. I try to address their concerns and enable them to pursue their interests during the course, in part by giving them open-ended options as part of the course assignments. We also engage in team-building activities where open, honest communication is of primary importance, since much of the course work will be done in teams of three or four.

I use the syllabus to present my objectives for the course, to explain to the students how I am structuring the course, how I am trying to teach in ways that will enable real learning and knowledge construction to take place. I have learned that addressing these issues once, and only in writing, is not enough. I have to reiterate my objectives for the course and why I am structuring it the way I am throughout the course, both in writing and orally. I have learned to call this "sign posting" (Seymour, Pedersen-Gallegos, Lewis, & Gutwill 1997). In sign-posting I address questions like "What have we accomplished?" "Where are we going?" "Why are we doing this?" "How is this related to what we have studied or what we are going to study?"

Another aspect of sign posting is communicating to the students my openness to and encouragement of alternative approaches to assignments and alternative problem-representation techniques, problem-solving strategies, and solutions to assigned problems. My way is not the only way. Rather than wanting my students to appropriate my way, I want them to find their own ways and to share that with me. In so doing the learning strategies of all of us become enriched. This is true whether it has to do with the strategy used to solve a problem in stoichiometry (using dimensional analysis, the factor-label method, direct proportions, etc.) or how to represent a plausible electronic structure for a molecular species. In this latter case I have improved upon my own ways of arriving at and representing plausible electronic structures by observing the different ways my students approach the task.

From the beginning of a course and throughout it I seek to elicit each student's prior knowledge vis-à-vis the topic at hand. I do this primarily by asking the students questions and asking them to write down their responses, which they then hand in, and by listening to conversations among students in their class groups as they work together on learning tasks. I structure almost every class session so that students are engaged in conversation with one another in groups of 3 or 4. Within this structure, I move from conversation to conversation, listening in. In this way, a significant portion of my time with the students is spent observing and listening to them, being an active listener as they share their ideas, thoughts, and explanations with me and with their peers. I have developed the habit of taking into class with me a journal in which to note down in situ observations, which I can then draw upon in my course reflections. Here are some of the things I look and listen for in gauging the learning of individual students:

- Whether the student is engaged and interested in the material
- Whether, over time, a student's understandings and explanations become more sophisticated, more comprehensive, clearer, and closer to the current scientific understanding(s) of the way things work in the world

- Whether each individual student is on task most of the time
- Whether students are struggling individually and together to make sense of the material at hand
- Whether I'm receiving lots of questions from the students, and on occasion witnessing a student's sudden insight, breakthrough, or "Aha!" experience
- Whether, when I'm working with a student, we identify and resolve a stumbling block to learning a specific concept
- Whether students realize that they have come up with their own explanations of observed phenomena that work for them and then take pride in and ownership of the knowledge they have constructed

My journal notes and reflections from these observations of my students at work become part of my course portfolio. The portfolio also includes (1) my objectives for the course, (2) my students' objectives for the course that they have written out (and modified as the course progresses), (3) prior knowledge assessments used in the course, (4) the course syllabus, (5) written exams/quizzes I give, and the corresponding answers/solutions, (6) rubrics I use, and (7) the progression of learning tasks in the course.

By analyzing my reflections, the students' statements of objectives, the prior knowledge assessments, the students' performance on problem sets and exams, and the evaluation forms and student reflections on their experience in the course, I devise and implement course modifications from semester to semester. I'm almost always trying something new each time I offer a course—this, after having been teaching chemistry for thirty-three years.

In planning the course, I seek to provide a diverse range of aids to learning (in as many different modes as possible: kinesthetic, visual, audio, acting out, individual, and group): aids such as computer software, programmed study texts, hands-on physical models, class demonstrations, reflective journaling, and laboratory experiments directly related to course content and designed to develop their experimental skills. I let students use the learning aid(s) with which they are most comfortable while encouraging them to try ones they haven't tried before. If using specific learning aids (such as the computer or particular laboratory equipment) will enable them to develop skills that I believe they should have, then I require them to use that particular learning aid.

I try to design manageable learning tasks, both in terms of the time they take and their degree of difficulty. As noted earlier, I allow for individual differences in the pace at which students proceed through the learning tasks, as much as I can. Students who finish the assigned learning tasks early can leave early or can proceed to available optional material of interest. I try to schedule within the time frame of the course an appropriate number of learning tasks as determined by two considerations: (1) ensuring that students working at a reasonable pace and putting in a reasonable amount of effort can successfully work their way through the essential, required tasks, and (2) ensuring that I can give both individuals and small groups feedback on their performance on the tasks early, often, and promptly in the course. This frequent feedback is probably the most important component of teacher–student interaction in enhancing the learning that occurs.

I seek to increase student awareness of different possible learning styles, of those with which they are most comfortable, and of those that are most appropriate to the learning task at hand. I identify and assess learning-style differences among individual students in the following way. At the beginning of the course I have the students complete a learning-style inventory. (I have experimented with the Canfield Learning Styles Inventory [Canfield, 1988], the Gregorc Style Delineator [Gregorc, 1984], the Max Learning Style Inventory [Ferman, 1991], and the Productivity Environmental Preference Survey [Dunn, Dunn, & Price, 1996]. The last is the one I currently use because it is the most informative for my purposes.) I show them or have them tabulate their own results and discuss the results with them both individually and collectively, so that both I and they become cognizant of their own preferred learning styles. With this knowledge I can more effectively support the learning of each of my students. I also want each of them to increase the number of learning styles with which they are comfortable and grow in their ability to learn in different ways. Thus I select learning tasks that are designed to facilitate this growth and encourage the students to try different approaches to learning.

Here are some of the instructional and assessment techniques I have used to individualize my instruction to better meet the diversity of backgrounds, learning styles, and goals the students bring to the course.

1. I have students create their own study guide to a specific course topic, rather than giving them a generic study guide on that topic. In so doing I'm asking them to consider how they study and to tailor their study guides to their own needs. In reviewing their study guides I gain valuable insight into how each student studies.

2. I have students keep working journals (i.e., where they do their course work, including taking notes from class or from assigned reading materials). To give them incentive to do their course work in their journals, I have made the journals authorized aids on the course exams. (Colorado College has an honor system in which, among other things, exams are unsupervised by faculty.) I also want them to learn how to take notes that are more useful to them. I believe that the process of writing things down for their own use on exams and finding how useful they are not only helps them learn the course material but also helps them improve their note-taking learning strategy. (This is an area I intend to include in my pedagogical research in the future.)

3. I give each student (typically working in groups of two to four) enough time to process material I have presented.

4. I give both written and oral exams, the latter only in the senior course. I have the oral exams videotaped and ask each student to view the videotape and give me one-page critiques of their performances.

5. In both beginning and senior courses I give both individual and group exams. In group exams I ask that each team turn in each member's exam but label one of them the master copy (which is the one I am to grade). Each team member receives the same grade on the exam. I reserve the right to rearrange teams until I get teams in which each member of the team demonstrates success in learning in the group, as shown by her or his performance on the individual exams they take over the same material, using related, but different questions or problems. As a result, each exam over a given body of material in the general chemistry courses has both an individual component and a group component. The team takes the group component first because the students and I have found that the group exam is more effective as a learning task than an individual exam is. Often the team does better on the team part of the exam than any of the individuals do on the individual part of the exam. As long as the individual team members' performances on the individual part of the exam are not too disparate, and not too far below the score on the team part, I know that the group work is benefiting all members of the team.

   I have found that groups that are relatively homogeneous in their background in chemistry, in their ability to satisfactorily complete the learning tasks, and in the pace at which they work are the most effective in enabling each member to learn. In groups heterogeneous in these characteristics, students with weaker backgrounds in chemistry who do less well on assessment instruments and who work at a slower pace have a strong tendency to rely on better-prepared and faster-working students in their group. The weaker students rely on the better-prepared students to take the lead in working on learning tasks and provide the explanations and solutions while remaining passive learners themselves. On the other hand, students in groups homogeneous in these areas are either eager to pitch in and contribute or more readily perceive that they are going to have to do so in order for the group to be successful on the group learning tasks and assessment instruments in the course. This allows them to learn to share with their peers the responsibility for their own learning, rather than relying on the strength of better-prepared and faster-working peers. In so doing they become, of necessity, more active as learners and, I hope, more proficient in the content and in skills. If, with my assistance, they assume a significant measure of responsibility for what they learn, they become more self-reliant. With perceivable progress in their mastery they become more confident in their ability to succeed.

6. Since I want my exams to be learning tasks, I will sometimes ask students who have done poorly on an exam to resubmit it, reworking those problems I have indicated are wrong. The students can receive extra credit for doing so. If a sufficiently large portion of a class has done poorly on an exam, I will give everyone the opportunity

of resubmitting the exam for reevaluation while still abiding by the honor code (in terms of authorized aids) mentioned above in item 2. On some exams I am an authorized aid. Students can come to me with their questions. I help them fully articulate the questions and then help them generate their own answers.

7. In the senior Inorganic Chemistry course I have the students maintain a portfolio showing the development of their skills and understanding. In particular, I have them keep records of their growing ability to describe the bonding and three-dimensional structure of a variety of substances, some of which are assigned and some of which they choose as specific examples from several designated categories.

8. In the same course I assign a creative writing learning task: to write a tale of an atom or element inspired by the tale of a carbon atom in the chapter Carbon in Primo Levi's *The Periodic Table* (Levi, 1984). In response I have received not only tales, but epic poems, haiku, songs, children's stories, and even a moral essay on lessons imparted by the element boron.

9. In the general chemistry course I present class demonstrations during which I ask the students to compare with one another their observations and explanations of what happened. I then solicit from the class all the different explanations, and we work together to achieve a consensus explanation.

10. I ask students to draw their mental images of chemical phenomena at the atomic and molecular level and share them with their classmates and me.

11. I have the students role-play electrons, nuclei, atoms, molecules, and so on, as a way of modeling chemical phenomena at a molecular, atomic, and subatomic level. I have even gone so far as to include some use of creative dance/movement in these activities.

12. I urge students to speak up when they don't know what is meant by a term or concept that I or one of their peers uses in a class lecture or discussion. In one class the metaphor we used for this was: "A 747 just went over my head [and I need to have it defined]."

13. I join a group working together on a learning task, mainly listening, but sometimes asking a question and sometimes participating as a group member.

14. I pay attention to the social dynamics of the class and work with students on team building. (For example: The class and I together go through a low ropes—challenge—course, or I take the class through activities that have the dual goals of developing good habits in working effectively as a team member and learning some chemistry content.)

15. We hold a class poster session in which teams of three or four students report the results of a particular research problem they have investigated in the course.

For me, a primary goal of education is for each student to become able to learn on his or her own, to find his or her own best ways of learning. To further this goal, more and more of the responsibility for student learning should shift from the teacher to the student as the students progress through their formal education. The further along my students are in the discipline of chemistry, the more they should be constructing their own explanations of chemical phenomena, taking pride in their ability to do so, and assuming ownership of the knowledge they have constructed. In enabling individual learners to become more responsible for their learning and take ownership of it I do the following:

1. Move from being the "sage on the stage" to being the "guide at the side."

2. Provide students with assignments and activities at which they can succeed.

3. Do regular sign posting, indicating what I intend for them to accomplish by completing an assignment or group of assignments.

4. Work with students to develop their skills in asking questions and formulating and testing hypotheses (For example, when I lecture, I do so for approximately ten minutes. I then ask neighboring students to compare notes on the ten-minute lecture for two or three minutes, and then invite the groups of neighboring students to ask me clarification questions.

5. Have students keep (electronic) journals throughout the course, in which they reflect on their learning experiences in the course and on how they have been aided or hindered in learning the skills and content of the course by the way the course is structured. I ask for comments in their journals on the usefulness of any of the course materials in learning chemistry and on the relevancy of the course content to their interests and to real-world issues.

6. Work with individual students or small student groups of three or four to figure out what learning strategies are best suited to the learning task they are engaged in. In so doing I am seeking to help them develop their metacognitive skills in thinking about how they learn and assessing the effectiveness of the learning strategies they've chosen.

7. Role-model thinking and study skills and then ask them to try their hand at practicing the skills.

8. Include the goal of taking responsibility for what they learn among the goals of the team-building exercises I engage the students in.

9. Make it clear that I am most interested in knowing how they got to their conclusion(s), and secondarily interested in the conclusion(s) they reached.

10. Emphasize the importance of students supporting their claims with evidence and the importance of being able to judge the reasonableness of their own answers and conclusions.

11. Use demonstrations in which the students do the telling, rather than I, in explaining what has occurred, and try out their explanation of the phenomenon with their peers and with me. (This helps both them and me become aware of their underlying assumptions.)

12. Discipline myself to allow sufficient first and second "wait times" (five- to ten-second pauses) after I have asked a question and before I ask another question or fol-

low up with the request to "tell me more!" The second pause or wait time is after a student responds, to see whether with further thought she has more to say. By observing wait times I'm indicating to the students that the responses I'm after will typically take some thought.

13. Allow students to pursue their own questions.

14. Value students' contributions, and on occasion appropriate them for future use, giving the student(s) credit (for example, "Debbie Schafner's Rules for Obtaining the Electronic Structure for a Molecule").

I have found the computer and computer software to be helpful in individualizing my instruction in several ways. Ideally computer-based instruction is one-on-one in that it is one student at one computer, and in many cases I have easily transferable records of what the student did while working at the computer, which I can analyze and do diagnostic work on in order to learn strengths and weaknesses. I have the students in both the beginning and senior courses do their journal reflections and formative as well as summative evaluations at the computer. Then, using software such as Ethnograph (Seidel, Friese, & Leonard, 1995), I can do an ethnographic analysis of their reflections and comments, looking for themes, repetitions, and the like.

I use computer software that allows manipulation of three-dimensional representations of atomic and molecular orbitals and crystal lattices in each of my chemistry courses. I have found that as the instructor I have to be very familiar with the software I am having the students use so that I can assist them in their interaction with it and troubleshoot problems they inevitably encounter. The first introduction of the students to the computer software should be carefully structured, notifying the students of specific desired outcomes but also allowing time to explore, experiment, and even play. I try not to let a computer software program be the only approach to the topic or the only means of completing an assignment, because there are some students who are either not motivated to learn that way or have significant difficulty in doing so. For those reasons, when I assign the software dealing with atomic and molecular orbitals and crystal lattices, I also provide physical, tactile models for the students to manipulate with their hands.

In my general chemistry course I use the *Daedalus Integrated Writing Environment* (Daedalus Group, 1993) software to have my students carry on a discussion (in groups of four to six) of the reality of global warming and what we could or should do about it. The students find it a little strange to be sitting in the same computer lab (where the software is available), and instead of talking to one another orally, sitting at a computer and typing in one's thoughts and therefore contributions to the discussion. They have the advantage (though they don't sufficiently use it) of editing their own thoughts before sending them to the on-screen conference. I don't preclude them from also talking to one another. I get a complete record of the discussion on the computers, which is much easier to carefully evaluate than listening to or tape recording an oral discussion would be. The software also enables me to sort the discussion by each participant's contributions to the discussion, so that I can also carefully and easily evaluate each participant's contribution.

I also encourage my students to use the Internet as a resource in getting the latest information on a topic such as global warming. One of the issues in having them do so is the reliability of the Web resource they hit upon. To help both them and me with this issue we refer to Chapter 5: "Evaluating Web Sources" in Robert Harris's *A Guidebook to the Web* (Harris, 2000). In addition the interactive CD–ROM, Conserving Earth's Biodiversity (Wilson & Perlman, 2000) that I use in one of my courses, encourages users to do further research on the Web and provides them with an essay on evaluating Web sources.

More and more interactive CD-ROMs are becoming available. They are worth investigating and often less expensive than texts. With serious investigation one can find CD-ROMs that are very well suited to individualized instruction and interactive learning. Conserving Earth's Biodiversity is one that is.

The approaches and techniques I use for individualizing instruction are the same for both beginning and advanced undergraduate students. They would not be the same for classes that differ in size. Thus, for example, I am more likely to use the ten- to fifteen-minute lecture followed by neighboring students comparing notes on the lecture in large classes, and the student portfolio in small classes. Whatever the class size, individualizing my instruction as much as I can is a primary goal.

CONCLUSION

I am always on the lookout at professional meetings, in faculty development workshops, and in the literature for approaches and instructional techniques to use in teaching for learning success of individual students. Because I am a scientist, it seems rather natural to experiment with the various approaches and instructional techniques I find. Each time I teach a course, I'm trying something new in supporting the learning of individual students. In 1991 I attended a conference called "Women and Men on Campus: Inequality and Its Remedies" at the Harvard Graduate School of Education. At the conference it became clear to me how important it was to give students in my courses a voice so that they could grow in their ability to articulate their ideas about the subject matter of the course and the discipline, and about how they best learn. Each student should have that opportunity; and each student's voice will be unique. In order to accomplish this I have to structure the course so that much of the time the students are engaged in conversation about the subject matter of the course with each other and with me. Communication is both vocal and written (whether via writing assignments or e-mail). I have to make it clear that I am interested in hearing them and hearing from them. This goal of giving my students voice is a significant motivation in my incorporating as much group work into my courses as I do.

The more communication there is between me and each of the students, the more I can tailor my instruction to their individual abilities, learning styles and strategies, sources of motivation, and goals. As trust grows between us through this communication, I become more effective in getting them to take responsibility for their own productive learning. With taking responsibility for their own learning comes ownership of what they have learned, pride in their accomplishments, and a growing confidence in their ability to master the discipline of chemistry and speak about it in their own voices.

REFERENCES

Canfield, A. A. (1988). *Learning styles inventory* (LSI). Los Angeles: Western Psychological Services.

Daedalus Group. (1993). *Daedalus integrated writing environment*, Version 1.3. [Computer software]. Austin, TX: Author.

Dunn, R., Dunn, K., & Price, G. E. (1996). *Productivity environmental preference survey* (PEP). Lawrence, KS: Price Systems, Inc.

Ferman, M. C. (1991). *The Max inventory of learning styles.* Santa Barbara, CA: Intellimation Library for the Macintosh.

Gregorc, A. F. (1985). *Gregorc style delineator.* Columbia, CT: Gregorc Associates, Inc.

Guskin, A. E. (1994, September/October). Restructuring the role of the faculty. *Change, 26*(5), 16–25.

Harris, R. (2000). *A guidebook to the Web.* Guilford, CT: Dushkin/McGraw-Hill

Levi, P. (1984). *The periodic table.* (R. Rosenthal, Trans.). New York: Schocken Books. (Original work published 1975).

Seidel, J., Friese, S., & Leonard, D. C. (1995). *The Ethnograph V4.0: A User's Guide.* Amherst, MA: Qualis Research Associates.

Seymour, E., Pedersen-Gallegos, L., Lewis, E., & Gutwill, J. (1997, April). *Evaluating together—Undergraduate chemistry reform in two NSF consortia*; Part 1: *Formative evaluation of student and faculty change.* Paper presented at the 213th American Chemical Society National Meeting. San Francisco.

Wilson, E. O., & Perlman, D. L. (2000). *Conserving earth's biodiversity with E. O. Wilson.* [CD-ROM]. Washington, DC: Island Press.

Chapter 9

Second Teaching: Small Groups As Mentors for Individuals in Physics Learning

Lisa Novemsky and Ronald Gautreau

SETTING AND PERSONAL BACKGROUND

In the downtown area of Newark, the New Jersey Institute of Technology (NJIT) evolved from a technical trade school. It progressed to become Newark College of Engineering, a conservative white male enclave near Newark's diverse downtown. The college of engineering merged with New Jersey's School of Architecture to become NJIT. Other areas of technological study were added gradually. There was a strong emphasis at the institution for traditional and tough teaching. This is the story of metamorphosis in one small area of that school.

One of the programs that facilitated the recent highly diverse nature of the institution was the state-funded Educational Opportunity Program (EOP) that helped prepare and assist "nontraditional students" to succeed in rigorous technological programs offered at the campus. EOP admits 125–130 nontraditional learners each year, from cities and towns throughout New Jersey. African American, Latina and Latino, Asian, and Arab students are among the rich mix that represents the minority populations of a highly diverse state. In preparation for their upcoming college experience, entering EOP students are required to participate in an intensive residential summer program, with instruction in physics, math, English, computers, and other subjects. Ronald

Gautreau, professor of physics, served as the summer EOP physics instructor for more than twenty-five years. Lisa Novemsky, a former special lecturer in humanities and social sciences, conducted a study of student learning in the context of this pedagogical reform effort.

Guiding Assumptions About Learning and Teaching

The first and major idea introduced in this chapter is "second teaching" (Novemsky, 1994, 1998), an idea that was developed from watching successful small groups at work. Second teaching is based on Vygotsky's (1978, 1986) idea that language serves as a tool and cultural means for developing logical and analytic thinking and learning. Vygotsky emphasized highly complex dynamic relations between developmental and learning processes. He argued that learning is converted into individual internal developmental processes in a "zone of proximal development," which is

the distance between the actual developmental level as determined by independent problem solving and the level of potential development as determined through problem solving under adult guidance or in collaboration with more capable peers. (Vygotsky, 1978, p. 86)

A second idea is appropriately couched in a physics metaphor. A problem in electrical engineering involves the use of a transformer to deliver power to a circuit. Each individual element in the circuit has a certain impedance. The maximum power to a given element is attained when the transformer is tuned to the characteristic impedance of the element. An analogous situation exists in education (Van Heuvelen, 1991b, 1991c). Each learner can be thought of as having an individual impedance. In our role as educators, we would like our students to become conversant in the wisdom and knowledge of a particular subject matter while developing analytic thinking skills that pave the way for lifelong learning. This can be accomplished by choosing pedagogies that meet the needs of individual students.

The physics metaphor can be useful in understanding education. A pedagogical system can be thought of as an educational transformer. If the educational transformer does not match the impedance of the individual learner, as is often the case with traditional teaching, very little learning will take place. On the other hand, if the educational transformer is tuned or tunable to the impedance of the individual learner, much more learning is likely to occur. Pedagogical approaches have been developed that emphasize addressing the impedance of individual learners. In this chapter we will discuss such pedagogical and curricular approaches specific to learning physics but generalizable to other domains.

Why Do They Just Sit There?

Dean Zollman (1996), upon receiving the prestigious Robert A Millikan Medal for excellence in physics teaching, told the following story: Twenty years earlier, he had taken his daughter Kim, then about eight years old, to visit his university. As they walked down a hallway, Kim looked into a lecture hall and saw a common scene that many physics instructors regard as the norm, but which she found somewhat unusual— more than a hundred students sitting silently, watching one person talking. Kim turned to her father and asked, "What are all those people doing?" Zollman came up with what he thought was an excellent answer: "They're learning physics." Kim's innocent but revealing response to her father was, "Do they just sit there?"

At her young impressionable age, Kim instinctively knew that learning does not take place by just sitting passively in uniform rows facing a leader, attempting to transcribe each utterance of the instructor and markings on the board. No matter how ebullient and enthusiastic the instructor, eyes glaze as students succumb to a tendency to fade off.

Traditional Physics Teaching

What Kim observed was traditional passive instruction in physics. A physics instructor, a fountain of knowledge, a purveyor of truths, stands in front of a class and "covers" the "material." A factory model of education is thus implied as if the material could be placed on a conveyor belt to be delivered to the student customer. In a mass-production model of introductory physics education, students in large numbers are programmed to arrive at the physics port of the assembly line. The nature of learning and individual student characteristics are of minimal concern in traditional physics teaching methods. In this model, little or no attention is paid to individual characteristics or needs of students. Even if the lecture includes some interactive activities, the structure is usually tightly controlled and aimed at covering the material.

APPROACHES AND TECHNIQUES FOR INDIVIDUALIZING INSTRUCTION

Second Teaching: Individualized Active Learning in Small Groups

Second teaching is a pedagogical construct, a model of structured small-group activity, designed to follow initial instruction, or first teaching, to facilitate individual learning processes in a diversity of students who find a new academic domain foreign. In the process of second teaching, learning of physics is effectively an induction into a new culture, with its unique way of seeing, body of knowledge, and specialized language. As they participate in the culture of physics, students are encouraged to become responsible active learners. Participatory learning, with students at the center, is driven by individual characteristics, strengths, and needs. As stated by Porter in Chapter 2 of this volume, this type of learning addresses higher types of learning, developing skills, creating conceptual frames of reference, and learning to learn.

With this approach, a first teaching may be a traditional lesson by the teacher; a reading, a laboratory experience, or a demonstration. Regardless of the format, new material is presented. Students then move into small groups. Their learning shifts to problem solving that requires them to apply the new concepts. As problem solvers, they are now teaching each other.

In informal small groups of three or four, students describe, explain, elaborate, test, and defend ideas in their own individual familiar vernacular as they collaborate in solving problems. Students practice new language usage in a natural context of learning new concepts and applying new skills. Gradually common vernacular is transformed into more formal physics discourse.

Learning to think as a physicist entails new patterns of language usage. Physics communication involves a very precise set of lexical items and linguistic structures that are particular to physicists and those in closely related disciplines. There is a significant gap between the formal and precise language of physics education and informal vernacular of nontraditional physics learners. Novemsky (1998) conducted a study of second teaching with forty-four nontraditional physics learners. The variables were development of clarity of (written) language of physics explanations as judged by independent language-knowledgeable judges and gains in physics knowledge as rated by independent physics-knowledgeable judges. A significant positive correlation was found between the development of clarity of language of physics explanation and gains in physics knowledge.

Language is the medium of this exploration; individual linguistic differences are accommodated in the small group process, and the zone of proximal development is expanded, since the collective wisdom of the group is likely to exceed an individual's expertise. Students speak to each other in their individual familiar vernacular, which becomes increasingly speckled with precise formal physics parlance. In small steps, each student gains elements of precise formal discourse that characterize communication in physics communities.

Note the progression in the following series of one student's statements. Each statement refers to the same observed phenomenon; together, they show the transformation or translation from initial attempts in the student's more habitual verbiage to a second attempt that includes more specific descriptors to a third attempt that produced accurately the technical language of physics.

It's reducing.

It's actually decelerating when it starts goin' down.

It's acceleration in the positive direction.

Second teaching occurs when the collective wisdom of a collaborative group, somewhat beyond the level of each individual member, but within the zone of proximal development of individual group members, is created and then recreated through self-correction. Since such self-correction is imperfect, a professor or teaching assistants are constantly moving from group to group, listening to student discourse and intervening with clarifying questions or pointers when needed (Novemsky, 1998).

As students interact with each other in small groups, differences in individual learning strategies and styles become evident. A spirit of inquiry is established in which each student is engaged in individual exploration through experimenting, drawing, questioning, and discussing. In a comfortable pleasurable small-group peer environment, individual learning strategies are nurtured by repeated self-correcting interactions within a group, guided by materials structured for small-group interactions to make implicit problem-solving steps explicit. Explicit stepwise moves from concrete observations to more formal physics representations are the hallmark of Van Heuvelen's materials (Van Heuvelen, 1991a, 1991b, 1991c).

As students work together in the comfort of peer culture, through multiple representations of a problem provided by the step-sequenced materials, increasing cognitive sophistication develops. The guided materials lead them from pictorial diagrams through simple qualitative diagrams to formal quantitative diagrams to formal equations. Group process helps individual students become ready to take the next step.

OCS Curriculum: A Case Study

Over the last decade, many nontraditional "interactive engagement" curricula have emerged on the physics education scene. The concept of second teaching emerged from a study of one particular example called Overview: Case Study, Physics (OCS Physics), developed by Alan Van Heuvelen (1991b, 1991c), who built upon earlier work by Arthur Farmer (1985) at Gunn High School in Palo Alto, California.

OCS instruction is designed to address and confront scientific preconceptions of individual students through multiple representations as well as opportunities to examine one's preconceptions. At the beginning of each topic of physics, the student is introduced to new physics concepts qualitatively through kinesthetic, visual, print, and auditory representations while using little or no math. In the absence of "mathematical noise," full attention can be given to physics concepts. Only after the concepts are understood is the necessary math introduced.

Visual representations of physics concepts provide a direct path for visual learning and thinking. Physics as a discipline makes heavy demands on visual imagination. Basic physics ideas such as forces are invisible entities that come to life in visual imagination. For example, in the very first days of a mechanics course, students are introduced to concepts of motion through pictorial and motion diagrams and to concepts of forces through force diagrams. Learners actively participate in collaborating to construct schematic motion diagrams to learn difficult distinctions between directions of velocity and acceleration. Further on, they use similar visual representations to identify various forces that act on bodies (weight force, tension force, friction force, normal force, and the like). Students discover that forces are related to acceleration— not velocities, in defiance of their intuitive preconceptions that tend to link force with velocity.

There are no hot equations to plug into, because there are no equations. When underlying concepts are understood, math is introduced at the appropriate level in a second round in the spiraling effort toward a more complete understanding of physics concepts. Students are frequently champing at the bit to show off recently acquired mathematical prowess learned in their accompanying mathematics course. This nontraditional presentation of physics is accomplished in large part by using print materials from a nontraditional unpublished textbook, written by Van Heuvelen and Gautreau (1997), titled *Active Physics: A Physics Learning System.*

As new topics are introduced within a subject area, the interrelationships between new topics and previous topics are stressed. Too frequently, students view a new topic as a new entity in itself to be treated separately with no connection to previous work. OCS instruction includes overviews of interrelationships between building blocks of various domains of physics knowledge, stressing a hierarchical overview as various chunks of knowledge are encountered.

One aspect of the OCS methodology that helps in matching impedance of individual learners is small-group work or second teaching. In recitations of about thirty that follow large-hall physics lectures, students work in small groups of three or four on assignments from Van Heuvelen's Active Learning Problem Sheets (ALPS) (Van Heuvelen, 1991a). These problems, designed specifically for small-group work, are quite different from typical end of the chapter problems. After a brief introduction, perhaps with some sample prob-lems, an instructor relinquishes the stage and becomes a wandering facilitator. From the sideline, the instructor listens to the groups, coaching and occasion-ally entering into group dialogue. Directive discourse is replaced by informal inquiry-driven communication.

A small-group setting differs markedly from a traditional classroom. Young people scattered in small groups are actively engaged in their learning. Objects fly through the air. Aha! Projectile motion. While working out the pulls to de-termine the directions of forces and accelerations, individual members of the group throw out their ideas in volleys of raw physics explanations. The expla-nations undergo dynamic transformations as they are challenged and refined by group members. This engaging process appears to lead to a reflective and deep learning. A physics instructor, moving among the groups, becomes pe-ripheral to the centrality of individual interactions within the group.

A common example of first teaching at NJIT occurs in large lecture situa-tions. Interspersed into within this seemingly traditional physics lecture set-ting are short spurts of small-group work on specially designed concept-based problems. These provide miniversions of second teaching. This technique was adapted from Eric Mazur of Harvard University (Mazur, 1997). After work-ing in small groups on a short problem, students vote for answers and explana-tions. Individuals raise their hands in agreement with a particular answer or explanation. Results of a vote provide immediate feedback to both students and instructor about the various states of student thinking about the problem. If the vote indicates understanding, the course moves forward. The student who raises his or her hand for the wrong answer or an incomplete explanation has invited the professor to engage in a dialogue of clarification.

We have described a particular type of interactive physics curriculum. There are other interactive methods that appear to be effective in physics learning (Workshop Physics, Laws, 1997; RealTime Physics, Sokoloff, Thornton, & Laws, 1999; Physics by Inquiry, McDermott, 1996). Some of these as well as some recent updates are based on recent instructional technology, wherein in-dividual learners work collaboratively in small groups on special problems through a variety of representations that rely on instantaneous and flashy pre-sentations on modern computers.

Studies Supporting Individual Engagement

In physics education research literature, many papers suggest that interac-tive methods are superior to traditional methods. We describe several such studies.

The Hake Study

Richard Hake (1998), professor of physics at Indiana University, has published results of a massive four-year study comparing physics learning in traditionally taught introductory physics courses (even when taught by the most talented and popular instructors) with physics learning in courses that used nontraditional interactive engagement methods. Hake's study surveyed precourse with postcourse data from 62 introductory physics courses enrolling 6,542 students. For pretest/posttest comparisons, Hake used the Mechanics Diagnostic Test and Force Concept Inventory developed by Hestenes, Wells, and Swackhamer (1992) and a problem-solving mechanics baseline test developed by Hestenes and Wells (1992). Fourteen courses with 2,084 students who were taught by passive lecture and problem-solving methods were compared with 48 courses involving 4,458 students who were taught with various interactive engagement methods.

The average normalized gain of students taught with interactive engagement methods was more than twice the gain achieved by students taught in a traditional manner. Hake's study seems to show that classroom use of interactive engagement methods increases physics understanding of mechanics well beyond that obtained with traditional passive methods.

The NJIT Study

Inspired by the idea of teaching physics conceptually after seeing a presentation by Alan Van Heuvelen, Ronald Gautreau decided in the fall 1991 semester to change from traditional lecture and problem-solving physics instruction to the OCS pedagogy. An educational experiment was designed to compare the new OCS method with traditional instruction. Two professors teaching six traditional sections in NJIT's standard first-semester physics course (each section had about thirty students) wrote the last two common exams and the common final exam. (The first exam was different because the OCS and traditional students were on different tracks.) To avoid bias, exam problems were commonly graded, with one professor grading a problem across all sections. The two traditional instructors also determined criteria for grades at the end of the semester. Gautreau, who taught three sections, intentionally abstained from participating in writing questions, grading, and determining final grade distributions. Thus, with the exception of the first exam, all the evaluations of the course were determined by the two traditional instructors.

The final result was quite dramatic (Gautreau & Novemsky, 1997). Interactive-engagement OCS students far outperformed passive traditionally taught students on every criterion established by the traditional instructors. OCS students had much higher averages on the common exams. While traditional students had standard bell-shaped distributions, OCS distributions were highly skewed toward higher grades, showing that not just weak students, but all students, performed better with OCS instruction.

The distribution of final grades was determined by the two traditional instructors. OCS students scored significantly better than traditionally taught students. Of the OCS students, 75% earned a grade of C or better, compared with 60% of the traditionally taught students. More than 50% of OCS students attained a grade of B or better, with 25% earning an A grade. This would be an unusually high distribution for traditionally taught students.

The educational experiment at NJIT provided strong evidence that interactive OCS instruction, that appeared to accommodate the widely diverse learning styles of individual learners, was significantly more successful than traditional instruction that treated students as a passive homogeneous group. One might think, therefore, that the traditional instructors would embrace the new OCS methodology as a far better way for students to learn introductory physics. Just the opposite reaction occurred with traditional instructors. They ignored the findings, refusing to discuss them at department meetings and refusing to cooperate in any further comparative experiments. One instructor suggested that the OCS roster should be checked for a possible overabundance of Asian students!

NJIT's Educational Opportunity Program (EOP)

The OCS approach to physics has proved highly effective with nontraditional learners at NJIT (Gautreau & Novemsky, 1997). In past summers, Gautreau used traditional teaching methods to introduce EOP students to as many of the physics topics that they would see in their fall physics courses as possible. The pedagogical philosophy seemed reasonable: Preliminary exposure to new subject matter would provide initial familiarity to promote effective learning upon a repeated exposure; when students recognized the same material in the fall, Gautreau expected that they would be able to comprehend it in the second repetition and do well in their physics courses. The pedagogical philosophy did not work in practice, however. Year after year, EOP students were barely able to survive their fall physics course.

In 1991, Gautreau changed his teaching method in summer EOP physics instruction to the OCS approach. Since then, EOP students have significantly outperformed non-EOP students in their fall physics courses. EOP students who studied OCS physics in the previous summer consistently scored significantly higher than non-EOP students who had no physics instruction in the previous summer: 19%–34% more EOP than non-EOP students earned a grade of C or better.

The superior performance of EOP has been a welcome outcome of the interactive OCS physics instruction.

CONCLUSION

A major goal in traditional physics teaching is to cover the material. However, an instructor's covering a given topic does not guarantee individual student understanding. Indeed, a major goal of education is not to cover material but to uncover material. Many studies, such as the ones cited above, show that far too many students taught by traditional one-way lectures and plug-and-chug problem-solving methods gain only a superficial temporary understanding of physics, which is soon forgotten after the course is over.

The nonmath concepts-first OCS approach toward introducing physics, together with second teaching that occurs in an active small-group learning environment, provides for matching the impedance of individual learners. A deeper understanding of physics tends to remain with individual learners. It may be true that with this approach less material is covered, but more solid learning is achieved. A salient point presented in this chapter is that learning happens when individuals become actively engaged in their own ways of learning. And learning can also be alive and enjoyable!

REFERENCES

Farmer, A. (1985). A new approach to physics teaching. *Physics Teacher, 23*, 338–343.

Gautreau, R., & Novemsky, L. (1997). Concepts first—A small group approach to physics learning. *American Journal of Physics, 65*(5), 418–428.

Hake, R. R. (1998). Interactive-engagement vs. traditional methods: A six-thousand-student survey of mechanics test data for introductory physics courses. *American Journal of Physics, 66*, 64–74.

Hestenes, D., Wells, M., and Swackhamer, G. (1992). Force concept inventory. *Physics Teacher, 30*, 141–158.

Hestenes, D., and Wells, M. (1992). A mechanics baseline test. *Physics Teacher 30*, 159–166.

Laws, P. (1997). *Workshop physics activity guide*. New York: John Wiley.

Mazur, E. (1997). *Peer instruction*. Englewood Cliffs, NJ: Prentice-Hall.

McDermott, L. (1996). *Physics by inquiry*. New York: John Wiley.

Novemsky, L. (1994). *The second teaching: Exploring a new pedagogy*. Paper presented at the Northeastern Section Meeting of the American Association of Physics Teachers, Ogoontz, PA.

Novemsky, L. (1998). *Second teaching: Cognitive factors in small group physics learning.* Unpublished doctoral dissertation, Rutgers University.

Sokoloff, D. R., Thornton, R. K., and Laws (1999). *Real-Time Physics*, New York: John Wiley.

Van Heuvelen, A. (1991a). *Active Learning Problem Sheets (ALPS) Kit.* Unpublished manuscript.

Van Heuvelen, A. (1991b). Learning to think like a physicist: A review of research-based instructional strategies. *American Journal of Physics, 59*, 891–897.

Van Heuvelen, A. (1991c). Overview, case study physics. *American Journal of Physics 59*, 898–907.

Van Heuvelen, A. (1997). *Active Physics 1.* Reading, MA: Addison-Wesley.

Van Heuvelen, A., & Gautreau, R. *Active Physics: A Physics Learning System.* Unpublished manuscript.

Vygotsky, L. S. (1978). Interaction between learning and development. In M. Cole, V. John-Steiner, S. Scribner, and E. Souberman (Eds.), *Mind in society: The development of higher psychological processes* (pp. 79–92). Cambridge, MA: Harvard University Press. (Original work published in 1935)

Vygotsky, L. S. (1986). *Thought and language.* (E. Hanfmann & G. Vakar, Eds. & Trans.). Cambridge, MA: MIT Press. (Original work published in 1934)

Zollman, D. (1996). Millikan lecture 1995: Do they just sit there? Reflections on helping students learn physics. *American Journal of Physics, 64*(2), 114–119.

PART IV

PROFESSIONAL PREPARATION CURRICULA

Chapter 10

Developing Individual Talent in Future Teachers Through Self-Regulated Learning

Randall Isaacson

SETTING AND PERSONAL BACKGROUND

The university setting in which I teach presents a challenge that is common in many postsecondary institutions—a diverse student body of both traditional and nontraditional students. Over the past decade our commuter campus has evolved from a campus of older nontraditional students who were highly motivated with extensive real-world experiences into a campus that includes many traditional 18- to 22-year-old students who have just graduated from high school and live at home. This new diversity offers many pedagogical hurdles to developing the individual skills and talents of all the students and challenges university teachers to address a myriad of learning styles, motivations, and individual needs.

Indiana University–South Bend is an urban campus that offers almost a hundred degrees to more than 7,000 students. The School of Education offers graduate and undergraduate programs in early childhood, elementary, and secondary education, special education, school leadership, and counseling and human services. I teach undergraduate and graduate courses in educational psychology, educational motivation, sport psychology, and interpersonal communication skills. The focus of this chapter will be on an educational psychology course I teach each semester.

GUIDING ASSUMPTIONS ABOUT LEARNING AND TEACHING

Individualized instruction is frequently associated with elementary class-rooms, with one teacher working with one child. This picture of individualized instruction is likely to come to mind because of the association of individual and solitude. Individualization is taken to mean working with one student, and since postsecondary education typically cannot afford the luxury of exten-sive one-to-one instruction, few educators think of individualization as a viable approach to university teaching. As a teacher of teachers with an interest in motivation, I have a different perception of individualized instruction. I see an individualized approach to instruction as having not only a micro component (teachers dealing one-on-one with students) but also a macro component in which large classes are structured with many individual choices that invite and encourage individual students to maximize their own learning.

I teach future teachers of elementary, secondary, and special education stu-dents their first course in education, and this affords me the opportunity to model many of the concepts I teach in educational psychology. Teaching lec-ture classes of fifty to sixty students that vary dramatically in age, race, and eth-nicity, educational background, socioeconomic level, and motivation presents the challenge of individualization at both a micro and a macro level. (See Chapter 3.) Since I teach the importance of individualization in elementary and secondary school classrooms it is imperative that I model individualization in my instruction. Individualized instruction is a basic cornerstone of the cur-ricular concepts I teach in my class and a guiding belief for the instructional ap-proaches I present to assist students in learning the class material.

The Teaching of Teachers—How Teachers Teach

There are five guiding beliefs about teaching that have become the template for the structure of my educational psychology classes and the individualiza-tion I model and encourage in my courses. I believe that teachers and learners must be reflective and metacognitively aware of their thinking and decisions if they are to be successful; at most grade levels (including college) students will benefit from assistance in learning how to learn; when teachers believe that ability and talent are modifiable states, their students are more likely to learn; teachers should create an environment that emphasizes the real learning that goes beyond a focus primarily on grades; and teachers should strive to maxi-mize the motivation of all students and not just successful students.

My students are studying to become teachers, and so the notion of reflec-tive teaching is important for them to understand and see in action. I believe that to grow as teachers we must take time to reflect on the structure of the learning environments we create, the daily instructional decisions we enact, and how these environments and decisions are consistent—or not—with our personal beliefs about the nature of learning and the roles of students and teachers. As a teacher of teachers, I model reflective teaching by verbalizing my instructional decisions and the rationale for those decisions.

Since the content of my class is teaching, it is useful for me to think out loud about my decision-making processes almost daily. To encourage students to apply class concepts to their own lives and make them real, I invite students into my life. I view my lectures as an opportunity to build a bridge from the textbook to their lives. My bridge-building strategy is to present enough examples, from a variety of situations from my own life (e.g., student, husband, father, coach, teacher) that I will spark a memory of an example from each of their lives. I take every opportunity possible to explain to students why I make the professional decisions that I make, whether it is grading, curriculum choices, questions I ask in class, or activities I develop for them to use. I ground all these ruminations with the notion that there is no one way to understand an idea, solve a problem, teach a concept, or learn for this class. They need to be actively involved in their own learning and take responsibility to learn what works best for them. To encourage prospective teachers to begin to become reflective teachers, I introduce them to a closely related skill—I invite them to become reflective learners.

My second guiding belief comes from my observation that most college students are not expert learners. Teaching students learning-to-learn strategies is a natural step on the road to becoming a teacher; to be an effective teacher one must not only be an expert teacher but also an expert learner. Because so many of my students have never examined how they learn most effectively, the first steps in helping them become expert teachers is to assist them in becoming expert students. In educational psychology we call the application of this knowledge self-regulated learning, and I have found that students benefit greatly from a classroom environment that encourages, even teaches, self-regulated learning. Education professors teach preservice teachers skills that those future teachers can use to improve the learning of their students, but it is also possible to ask those potential teachers to first be reflective and teach the skills to themselves.

The talent development model of excellence discussed in Chapter 1 assumes that talent, or ability, can be developed—this is consistent with my third guiding principle. I view talent as a modifiable state, not a static trait, and I believe the best way to give students the opportunity to realize their potential talent is to present a variety of tasks to invite them to stretch their present abilities. Research by Dweck (1999) has demonstrated that nurturing an incremental view of ability (i.e., talent as modifiable) encourages students to view mistakes as a natural part of the learning process, increases their willingness to invest effort into learning, and stimulates their interest in learning as opposed to simply performing what is necessary for a grade. Holding an incremental view of learning will be valuable to my students in their future roles as teachers, but it will also enhance their ability to learn in my class.

Today many educated people in our society believe that learning is a function of innate ability. My teaching experiences, and the research on multiple and learnable intelligence (Gardner, 1983, 1993; Perkins, 1995) have convinced me that intellectual ability is modifiable and a student's ability to learn can be enhanced by a classroom teacher's behavior. When ability is viewed as a modifiable state, learning-to-learn is a powerful tool that enhances one's ability and motivates student efforts. This is consistent with the talent development model of excellence. Many, if not most, college students can learn how to learn, but these learning-to-learn skills will not evolve without reflection and guidance.

The fourth guiding belief that informs my instructional and curricular decisions is the importance of nurturing a mastery/learning orientation and encouraging an intrinsic motivation to learn. This principle is the most difficult to realize, since many, if not most, students enter my class motivated primarily, if not solely, by grades and test performance. It is important for future teachers to move from a performance orientation (where grades are the primary focus) to a mastery/learning orientation (where grades become secondary to understanding) if they are to engender a love of learning in their students (Stipek, 1998). How I structure my class effects how reflective they become, how effectively they learn to learn, how much of their potential they realize, and their future orientation to learning.

My fifth guiding belief is directed by my own research and is the basis of many of my curricular decisions. My goal for my classes is not performance equity—I realize that there are too many individual differences that exist when students enter class the first day—but I do believe in pursuing what Covington (1992) describes as motivational equity. I aspire to create a classroom environment in which all students strive to do their best a majority of the time. It is relatively easy to motivate highly successful students: give them a challenging task, explain the requirements for an A, and they will usually persist at the task. When teaching students who have not experienced extensive academic success, on the other hand, the challenging task is in the teacher's court: How can I increase the motivation of all students at every level?

I am constantly tinkering with the variable of the curriculum to squeeze a little more out of each student: to teach each student that academic ability can be increased with effort; to help students realize that their failures can be attributable to a lack of effort or inefficient study strategies rather than a lack of ability; to convince students that different types of learning demand different study strategies; to show them that they can apply learning to real-life problems; and, most important, to create an environment where effort and the application of a variety of study strategies will lead to increases in learning and success. I try to assure all my students that even though everyone is at a different performance level at the start, everyone can improve and learn meaningful skills and knowledge that will help him or her to be a better teacher. My theme is encouraging excellence by maximizing their individual talent and encouraging them to learn teaching skills that will allow them to create their own talent development model of excellence once they become a teacher.

On the first day of class, I ask the students to discuss whether teaching is an art or a science. I believe it is important for students to consider that the teaching-learning process can be studied through scientific principles. For many students, viewing teaching as science is a paradigm shift that can dramatically change how they view teaching and how they will teach. I explain how important it is for teachers to examine the hypotheses they hold about their students and learning, to constantly question those hypotheses, and to carefully examine the evidence they use in supporting those hypotheses. On the first day of class a majority of students respond by saying that teaching is an art; I have fifteen weeks to present evidence that teaching can be a science as well as an art.

Teaching is a craft that combines science and art. To be an expert practitioner one must learn to think like an expert decision maker and behave like a master craftsman. I believe that active engagement in real experiences affords students the best opportunities for learning these characteristics. The best way to teach anatomy to medical students is to use a cadaver to demonstrate the concepts and structures of the body. The best way to teach preservice teachers how to teach is to create an open environment where students are encouraged to dissect the structure, content, and approaches to teaching and study these relationships to their own learning. My classroom is both a lecture hall and a laboratory—my students are both learners and teachers. My goal as a teacher of teachers is to encourage the first steps in the scholarship of teaching and learning—to begin to nurture pedagogical researchers.

As a teacher educator my focus is on the teaching-learning process and my credibility as a teacher depends on my ability to effectively model what I teach. To be successful in validating the content I am teaching, I must demonstrate the theories and principles I am teaching in how I structure my class, the daily strategies I use to facilitate learning, the interactions I have with my students, and the procedures I use to assess their learning. I am the prototype of the concepts I teach and the role model for the strategies I endorse.

The Teaching of Teachers—How Students Learn

As discussed in Chapter 2, learning is an active process; true learning does not come to passive individuals. Learning can be an intrinsically enjoyable activity; young children love to learn and need no reinforcement to engage in activities from which they will gain new knowledge and skills. Unfortunately, the longer students are in school the less motivated they are to learn, which results in college students having very different incentives for learning than young children. Adolescent and adult learners are different from young children: older learners have a higher need to be in control, but in a new learning environment they will also need assistance in managing and adapting how they learn.

In addition to the five guiding beliefs about the role of teachers in the teaching-learning process I also hold three basic premises about the learning process for older adolescent and adult learners. My first premise for adult learners is that students' motivation increases when they believe they have control over their own learning. The second premise is that students are more likely to regulate their learning when they are given frequent feedback on the progress of their learning. The third premise is that students respond more constructively and take more personal responsibility when they are given the appropriate strategies to learn and are held accountable both for assessing and making adjustments in how they learn and for the outcome of their learning. I believe all people are capable of learning and learn best when they are actively engaged in activities of their choosing in an environment that allows them to personally evaluate their growth.

Unfortunately, many classrooms seem to work against these premises. Many college classrooms do not encourage students to be active processors of knowledge. Many classrooms offer students few, if any, choices in what they learn, how they learn, or how their learning will be assessed. Likewise, many college classes give students very little feedback on their learning, and the feedback that is given typically is not about their mastery of knowledge or skill but rather normative feedback comparing them to their peers. I believe that to maximize the learning of college students we must create active, responsive learning environments that give support and scaffolding that enables students with a variety of strengths and weaknesses to succeed at their goals. While I am adamantly opposed to watering down a curriculum, I do believe it is the responsibility of teachers at all levels to create a support network in which students are responsible for their own learning.

My first premise about the learning of college students is that mature learners want to have personal control over their learning with choices related to their learning and the assessment of their learning (Deci & Ryan, 1985). I believe teachers should create an environment in which students have a variety of ways to engage in the learning process in class, and be motivated to continue that engagement outside class. Unfortunately, few students come to the university having been actively engaged in learning in school. Traditional students just out of high school typically have been passive recipients of facts with few choices in an environment that has encouraged them to regurgitate those facts back to their teacher exactly as they received them. Nontraditional students who are a number of years removed from high school are initially so worried that they will not know how to learn in their new environment that they ignore the real-world learning skills they have gained. This may in turn lead them to simply memorize information from the teacher without true understanding.

For students to understand any concept at a level at which they can apply it in the real world, it is imperative that they choose to integrate these concepts into their own understanding of the world. This cannot occur by simply memorizing the definitions from the textbook or lectures. Individual learners bring unique experiences to the classroom, and the challenge for teachers is to create an environment that sets the stage for each individual student to personally decide to actively apply theoretical concepts to their own life experiences. Effective teachers adapt their classrooms to allow for individual differences in experience but also invite students to change from a receptor of information to an active processor of knowledge and skills to their lives.

When students decide to change their learning orientation and become active processors of information, it is likely that they will have some initial adversities. My second premise is that frequent feedback is essential to promoting the learning of individual college students. College puts new demands on students, and they are unlikely to modify their approach to learning unless they are afforded the opportunity to assess whether those changes are effective. Many college courses still assess student learning using midterm and final exams that tempt students to continue with the same learning strategies they have used in high school. If the learning task demands more than rote memorization, the student is likely to fail. By the time the student realizes he or she is failing it is too late. The student who is given frequent feedback is more likely to realize his or her approach to learning is not adequate, which may encourage the student to take a new approach.

Once students recognize they are failing, they can increase their efforts under the same approach, they can adjust their approach, or they can simply become resigned to the fact that they do not have the ability to succeed. In many cases an increase in effort will not solve the problem: If the learning task requires more than memorization, an increase in time is not likely to change the course of events. Unfortunately, many able students take this approach and then abandon all hope for success after the next failure. My third premise is that students need to have the appropriate strategies to assess and adjust their approaches to learning. Giving college students control and responsibility for their own learning and making available frequent feedback on their learning is helpful, but only when students have assistance in identifying and choosing options that will lead to future success.

Students and learning requirements in postsecondary education are different from those in elementary and secondary schools. Older students have a greater need to control their learning, but they seldom possess the skills needed to take full responsibility for the new challenges of learning in college. The challenge typically includes higher-level thinking, but many students are unprepared for such challenges. Many college courses do not give students the needed feedback and assistance to judge their progress and change their approaches to learning. To encourage students to participate in real learning, we must raise the bar and create evaluations that include higher-level thinking skills, but we must also offer the resources that allow all students the possibility of learning at that level.

APPROACHES AND TECHNIQUES FOR INDIVIDUALIZING INSTRUCTION

My personal theory of undergraduate student learning is strongly influenced by my view of student motivation. Each student comes to my class with a different motivation for learning. The structure of a college classroom can mold that motivation in a way that facilitates or debilitates learning. There are five general areas in which I create a learning environment that supports the academic success of diverse student needs. First, when classroom structures advance performance on tests at the expense of learning for deep understanding, many individual students are lost or become misdirected in their motivation. Therefore, the teacher's goals and class structure should encourage students to learn deeply. Second, for individual students to take responsibility for their own learning and improve their strategies for learning, they must have frequent feedback on their progress. Feedback should encourage real learning as well as performance. Third, students who have difficulty need information beyond simply the summative evaluation of their learning; they need support in assessing why they are not succeeding. Failure must be framed as a natural part of the learning process that may require greater effort but may also need new and unknown learning strategies. Fourth, students must see their instructors as responsive to their needs. Teachers need to modify the variables of instruction in a systematic manner that increases real learning. Finally, students who are new to the type of independent learning that is required in college, or are failing in the college environment, may need personal contacts to keep them engaged. Let's begin with the first four strategies that can be applied on a large scale to an entire class—the macro strategies.

Macro Strategy 1: Encouraging Mastery Learning—Discouraging Interpersonal Competition

One of the basic premises to my personal theory of learning is that an emphasis on interpersonal competition can undermine our best intentions to individualize student learning. When students focus on performing better than other students instead of a focus on learning as much as possible, as deeply as possible, then student motivation and efforts may be misdirected and may become self-destructive (Covington, 1992). Students who are performing well will be encouraged by their grades, but because they are motivated to look good, they may create situations that embellish the perceived ability others ascribe to them (e.g., claim low effort so others attribute success to high ability), which may decrease future learning. Students who are performing poorly are embarrassed by their poor grades and attempt to create situations that attribute their failure to outside sources (e.g., blame the teacher or describe plausible handicaps such as illness or test anxiety), further exacerbating an already difficult situation. When the evaluation of a student's learning is based solely on interpersonal comparisons, it is likely that students will learn that performing (rather than learning) is the goal that will undermine the aim of individual improvement.

To reduce interpersonal competition and increase the focus on learning (as opposed to performing), it is important to create a grading system that is based on mastery, not competition, and clearly identify the learning task. To reduce competition, my classes are graded on a criterion-referenced point system in which everyone can receive an A (or an F). To reduce the guessing game, I have created a class Web site that includes a vast assortment of material to make the goals, objectives, and tasks of the course as clear as possible. The Web site consists of a set of material for each chapter, including an outline of the critical chapter concepts, all the class overheads, a self-grading practice test, an interactive graphic organizer, and examples of self-assessments.

Macro Strategy 2: Encouraging Self-Study Through Feedback

The second broad approach I use to create an environment that facilitates individual student learning is extensive feedback on their progress toward mastery. For students to identify mastery, see progress, and make strategy adjustments when they fall short of their goals, they need extensive, frequent, informative feedback. For a student who has had difficulty in school, there is no evaluative plan more demoralizing to motivation (and learning) than a course that is graded with a midterm and final; a poor grade at midterm with no other feedback is devastating. Successful learning environments give students many opportunities to measure their progress, see their improvements, and learn from their failures. When feedback is a yardstick to help assess mastery of skills and knowledge, rather than a judgment of personal competence, individual student motivation will thrive. One of the best ways to highlight an emphasis on mastery is to offer many assessment tools (e.g., practice tests, quizzes, short written assignments) from which students choose a limited number to be used to calculate their grade. Offering students a variety of assessment alternatives reduces test anxiety and shifts the focus from a single performance to the advantage of learning from mistakes.

To support the academic success of both the traditional and nontraditional students, it is important to offer students extensive feedback on their mastery of the course material and to offer this feedback in a variety of ways. A key ingredient in my courses is that I have many ways for students to assess their knowledge and skills. Many of these assessments are graded, but students are allowed to keep their best grades. The idea behind this strategy is that students are more likely to take academic risks and become learning-oriented and change their study strategies if they are not punished for trying new approaches to learning and can throw out their mistakes (Clifford, 1984). This also encourages students to learn from their mistakes and judge their abilities according to their improvements. Each assessment technique gives students feedback but is not necessarily part of their grade.

Individual choice of task difficulty in the context of receiving extensive feedback also encourages a more constructive individual motivation to learn. Some of the available assessment techniques are practice tests on the class Web site; weekly tests with variable-difficulty/variable-weight items (students take weekly tests with forty items worth 1, 2, or 3 points based on their difficulty and they choose thirty of the forty items); weekly quizzes in discussion groups (also variable-difficulty/variable-weight, where students choose five of ten items) can be used toward their grade if they do well but cannot hurt their grade; Immediate feedback on all tests and quizzes—most tests are objective tests that are graded immediately so that students can go over their results; challenge sheets—students are allowed to challenge, in writing, any test items that they miss and are given credit if they demonstrate understanding; self-assessment paper on self-regulated learning affords the students the opportunity to systematically analyze their study skills from the standpoint of self-regulated learning theory.

Macro Strategy 3: Encouraging Learning to Learn—Self-Regulated Learning

The third theoretical approach I use to support individual student progress is feedback beyond formative and summative evaluation. Simply knowing that you have done poorly, and that you do not understand the material, is not necessarily going to lead to improved learning. Students need to know why they succeeded or failed so that they can continue their success or change their strategies. Most students need a vehicle to help them monitor their progress in relation to the process of learning (i.e., what they did) in addition to the product of learning (i.e., the grade they received).

Self-regulated learners monitor their behavior, motivation, and cognition as they progress through a class and college. Self-regulated learning has become the template I use for most of the individualized instructional techniques I use in my teaching. Paul Pintrich's definition explains the philosophy behind many macro- and micro-level decisions I make in teaching: "Self-regulated learning involves the active, goal-directed, self-control of behavior, motivation, and cognition for academic tasks by an individual student." (1995, p. 5). By encouraging students to become more metacognitive about their learning and reflective about how they study, they can learn why they have succeeded or failed in my class and apply that to other classes.

One of the predominant themes in my class is the role self-regulated learning can play in assisting students from elementary school through college to learn more efficiently. Students are taught the theory of self-regulated learning as part of the content of the class and are asked to apply the theory to their own learning using data they have collected on themselves in a study journal and a variety of questionnaires taken during the semester. The students are required to write an extensive midsemester self-assessment paper on self-regulated learning including recommendations using the data they have collected in their study journal. This tool has been a very important learning device, which also helps me and their peer mentors to understand the learning difficulties of individual learners.

Macro Strategy 4: Teaching As a Work in Progress: Tinkering with Instruction

I seldom make wholesale revisions of my courses. My strategy is to tinker with one or two variables at a time in a very systematic manner. I view my curricular development as a steady refinement; my class is different every semester, but I rarely throw out the baby with the bath water. When I make a major change in the class structure, I usually plan an assessment of the consequences;

this may be a questionnaire for the students, class time to discuss their reaction, or a session to get feedback from the peer mentor discussion group leaders (see Micro Strategy 1).

I try to be very flexible and willing to make changes to procedures in class that students have found to be detrimental. However, I am careful to anticipate what effect midstream changes will have on the entire class before I make any changes. I have learned my lesson on making changes for the sake of a few vocal students only to have half the class be up in arms over the change. I try to anticipate how changes will affect groups of students: high versus low achievers; traditional versus nontraditional students; working students versus nonworking students; success-oriented students versus failure-avoiding students. I find it impossible to anticipate all the possible implications, but it is always prudent to enumerate as many possible effects as possible.

There are a number of macro-level strategies that I use to create a set that communicates that my focus is on individual success. Extensive feedback on their mastery of class material is an important first step in supporting the success of a diverse student body, but some students need more assistance. For students who lack study skills and test-taking skills, this product feedback may not be enough—they may need individual process feedback. I have found many students—particularly underachieving traditional students and anxious nontraditional students—have the ability to succeed in college but lack the study skills or test-taking skills to demonstrate their competence. For these students, individualization may have to be done on a micro level.

Individualization at the Micro Level Using Planned Strategies

The first four approaches outlined above can be implemented at the macro level. Since I teach many large (fifty- to sixty-student) lecture classes, I depend heavily on making these the foundation of my individualization. However, there is nothing that can take the place of the individual, one-on-one, contact to increase student involvement. I can structure my class for a learning orientation, I can give frequent personal feedback, I can create opportunities for students to learn about themselves, I can modify the classroom environment—but if a student fails a test, that student may need someone to be there to talk him or her through it. In class, and outside class, the instructor needs to be communicating a belief in each and every student just like a coach must do before the big game. In large lecture classes it is possible to create environments that lead students to believe that individual student efforts can lead to important learning, but many students need help at a micro level for them to believe learning is possible for them.

Micro Strategy 1: Peer Mentoring

To give students greater opportunities for individualized instruction, all students have the option to join peer-mentor discussion groups led by students who have successfully completed the course. This reduces the class size from sixty students to cohorts of six to twelve. The peer mentors are students who have successfully completed the course with a grade of B or better. Most of the peer mentors take a course on interpersonal communication with me as part of the training for teaching the discussion groups. The focus of the peer mentor groups reflects the macro strategies previously discussed: Students are encouraged by their peer mentors to study how they learn and become more effective at self-regulating their own learning. The peer mentors are encouraged to create discussions about what types of study strategies work for what types of learning. Instruction in these groups include quizzes and discussion of higher-level thinking questions; learning activities and games for higher-level thinking skills; lessons on study skills; emphasis on one-on-one assistance in learning and learning to learn; the use of study journals to examine each individual's study habits; and assistance in personal self-assessment of learning.

The peer-mentor study groups and study journals offer a valuable source of micro individualization. The reflective teaching and learning-to-learn themes of the class are carried out by requiring students to keep track of their study habits for the class during the entire semester. Students are asked to document the number of hours they study, where they study, whom they study with, the strategies they use to study for tests and discuss their findings with their peers. Students are also asked to set goals for each of their weekly tests and quizzes. In a class in which I am trying to encourage students to view teaching and learning as a science, this journal becomes valuable data in helping them test their personal hypotheses and analyze their personal self-assessment.

As part of our self-regulation program, students are asked to complete a number of assessment instruments on their study strategies and motivation to learn. The LASSI (Learning and Study Strategies Inventory; Weinstein, 1994) assesses students' attitude, anxiety, time management, and a number of other informative scales that allow the students, their peer mentors, and me to examine what might account for their learning difficulties. These assessment instruments are incorporated into the peer-mentor study groups through discussions and lessons on time management, test-taking strategies, and a variety of study techniques. Each week the peer mentors teach a short lesson on self-regulated learning. Early in the semester the peer mentors emphasize that the concepts they are teaching on self-regulated learning will be on their weekly tests, but the long-term goal of the lessons is to teach the students to assess their own learning and study habits. Students are asked to document the type of study strategies they use each week and explore the effects of any changes in their results. At midsemester the students are asked to write a self-assessment of their self-regulation that summarizes their strengths and weaknesses and develops an individual plan to increase their learning during the second half of the semester.

Micro Strategy 2: Individual Meetings with Students

The peer mentoring program offers students an opportunity to receive individualized instruction, but most students also benefit from developing a relationship with their professor. Despite the fact that most of my classes are large, I expect to establish a personal relationship with most of my students. In almost everything I do in teaching I am thinking, "What can I do to get each student more actively engaged and thinking in class?" In this large introductory class I have found technology to be an important bridge. Through our Web site the students have a connection to me and the materials I use in class (www.iusb.edu/~edp250). Through e-mail I can make a connection with them, even to the shy student who is hesitant to visit my office. After reading and grading their self-assessments, I have a good insight into most of the students. E-mail allows me to make contact with these students when they improve or are having problems. After each test I compare the student's present score to past scores and send an e-mail to students who have improved or have a sharp decline in their scores. I have been amazed at the response: Students who have never been to a professor's office often drop by to thank me or to discuss their poor test result.

Individualization Through Instructional Problem Solving

To promote the success of some learners, and of some types of learning, it is difficult to have a specific strategy planned; cookbook algorithms don't exist, and the most we can hope for is a general heuristic game plan. Some of this individualization occurs at the macro level when interacting with the entire class, and some of this occurs at the micro level while interacting with one student.

In small classes, such as my interpersonal communication class and honors class in educational motivation, I spend a great deal of time using micro level strategies to help individual learners. The majority of the students I teach are enrolled in large lecture classes, and I find these situations more challenging. My recent addition of the self-assessment paper on self-regulated learning has improved the breadth and depth of my understanding, but the task is still daunting. Assessing and facilitating the learning of students who are having difficulty in a large lecture class occurs at a number of levels in a variety of ways that are not easily solved with simple formulas.

No matter how well a teacher uses macro level individualization, there is no substitute for one-on-one analysis of a student's problems. I have found the more specific the data a student brings to the table the more effective I can be in analyzing and prescribing solutions for the problems. There are a number of approaches that I typically take, although I must admit I often fly by the seat of my pants. When students visit my office with a learning problem, I ask the students to bring their study journal. I begin by having the students walk through the problem: How did you study for the last test? Where did you study? With whom did you study? I try to collect data but at the same time have the student verbalize the facts. I have found that openly describing one's problem can be the best route to understanding it, and I try to encourage students to look to the data they have collected in their journals to help solve their problems.

I believe the most important skill a teacher can have in supporting individuals who are having difficulty learning is active listening. For most students, the biggest hurdles they have to overcome are their belief that they cannot succeed and rigid thinking in problem solving. When I ask students how they studied for the last test ("I read the textbook and used a yellow high-lighter") and then ask them what they plan to do differently next week, the most common response is "I'll read the chapter twice and highlight it in yellow and pink." When I respond, "If it didn't work the first time, why are you planning to do it again?" the most common response is "I don't know what else to do." Students need support to find alternatives, but simply giving them the solution will only make them more dependent on teachers for solutions to their next problem. We need to listen and help them find solutions that they will own as their solutions.

After our initial discussion of the problem, I will typically ask students for their explanation of their difficulties with a follow-up series of questions asking them what evidence they have to support their explanation. My next question is usually "Is there any other possible explanation?" I have found that many students have inappropriate attributions for their failure; they blame the wrong cause, and that only makes the problem more difficult to solve. Since students are likely to become defensive if I take an aggressive direct approach in an individual discussion in my office, I try to use examples in class that point out the problems when students use excuses rather than taking responsibility for their own learning. In a one-on-one discussion in my office I can refer to these examples: "Remember in class when I used the example of the high school student who blamed his failure on procrastination? Maybe you have a similar problem."

When I believe that students have misguided and self-handicapping attributions (Garcia, 1995) I try to create an "experiment" to introduce alternative explanations. For example, in an attempt to reduce the threat of failure, self-handicapping students create an excuse for failure prior to failure. Self-handicapping students are likely to procrastinate ("I could have done better but I ran out of time"); forget materials or assignments ("I would have done better on the test but I forgot my calculator"); or make a myriad of excuses for why they did poorly ("The fraternity had a party I just couldn't miss"). These excuses invariably guarantee failure—but with an explanation. For students for whom I see test anxiety as a potential explanation for their failure, I often suggest, "I think it might help if you studied earlier in the week and avoided studying right up to the final minutes before the test. Try relaxing the hour before this week's test and let's see what happens." These experiments are not always "the" solution, but they do encourage students to test out their own biases. I believe students need to come to the realization that they may be sabotaging their own success. We cannot force this pill on them, but we can give them opportunities to more objectively view the potential causes of their difficulties.

Unfortunately, most students enter college believing that mistakes are wrong; they equate mistakes with failure. I try in every way possible to teach students that the only way to make any progress is to take some risks and learn from your mistakes. I try to show them the value of this in a variety of ways: point out that they can throw out a number of poor tests; refer them to peer mentors who made dramatic improvements in their prior experience in this class; disclose my poor academic record prior to college; point out my own mistakes; and respond to their feedback in a positive manner inviting future feedback.

Given my goal of motivational equity, the guiding principles I use most often in instructional problem-solving come from the educational motivation literature, my twenty-five years of college teaching, and my personal reflection on what variables seem to affect which students in facilitative and debilitative ways. I do a lot of tinkering with one variable at a time and keep fairly systematic records of the results. I am very introspective about these changes, but I have found that it is always better to share my musings and hypotheses with others, especially the peer mentors.

I am familiar with the literature in the area of educational motivation and find myself turning to colleagues in this field more often as I begin to get actively involved in research on self-regulation and academic risk-taking. Past experience is very helpful in that I have a fairly good feel for the big picture. I can usually make an educated guess at how changes in my class structure will affect most of the students, but there are always surprises, since the most vocal students may not reflect the view of a class.

One other strategy that I use I cannot explain with any precision. I think in analogies. My students know me as a person who has an analogy for almost any concept we discuss in class. I also use these analogies in working with individual students, but I do not know where they come from, or how to teach someone how to think them up. In college classes, many of the theories we teach are so abstract that only experts in the field with broad conceptual backgrounds can visual the theory, identify examples, and imagine its implications. When I share my many analogies in class it's like firing a shotgun full of examples and hoping a piece of buckshot is close enough to the personal experiences of the learners that it will hit home and make an obscure theory explain their real-life experiences.

I believe that offering students options is important for a number of reasons. Students at every age have a need to be self-determined; being in control of your behavior increases an intrinsic motivation to learn. Giving students choices sends the message "I believe you are responsible for yourself and your learning." In class I try to offer students as many choices as possible and use their decisions to help me understand them. As a motivational psychologist, I am particularly interested in their motivation orientation as revealed by their academic risk taking. In my introductory educational psychology class, I examine, and discuss with them as part of my instructional problem-solving, which types of questions they choose for their tests and quizzes. I am interested in a number of dimensions that will help me to help them. Their choices help me assess whether the student is more success oriented or failure prone; a high achiever or a low achiever; high or low in test anxiety; mastery or performance oriented.

Frequently, instructional problem solving requires teachers to invite students to become partners in solving problems. This would include helping students to assess their own strengths and weaknesses by examining the choices they make. When prescribing courses of action for students, I try to emphasize that their success and failure have a great deal to do with the efforts they put forth and that these efforts are under their control. Extra effort is frequently the solution, but when honest effort does not solve the problem, it is important to consider changing strategy.

I believe an important goal of higher education should be the encouragement of lifelong learning and giving students the skills needed to be effective in this endeavor. In my field this goal is particularly important because future teachers need to be teaching their students how to pursue this very goal. Teaching students to be responsible for their own productive learning goes far beyond the classroom and will have an impact on work skills, parenting skills, community involvement, and general fulfillment. I believe the key to teaching responsibility is to hold students accountable by establishing clear guidelines and consequences.

Many of the techniques I have outlined are designed to increase student responsibility for their own learning. Weekly tests, quizzes, and practice tests, study journals, and self-monitoring are all attempts to hold up a mirror so that students can see the results of their behavior. I try to create a situation with a clear consequence for every step without making evaluative judgments of the person's worth. Students cannot be forced to become responsible; they can only be invited to take control of their own behavior, motivation, and cognition and offered support and strategies whereby they can become more successful at learning.

CONCLUSION

When I first began teaching in a university setting, I assumed that there was one, or maybe two, approaches that best facilitated student learning. I'm actually a bit embarrassed to admit that I thought I knew what those approaches were and that I could create a classroom setting that would take advantage of this knowledge. I now realize that there are many ways that students learn; in fact, students know more ways to learn than we know how to teach. My growth over the past twenty-five year from a novice to an experienced teacher has shown me that the key is to create an environment in which students make choices that have consequences and that these consequences are not perceived as fatal mistakes. Each individual learner must be given the opportunity to find their most effective learning strategies, but to discover these approaches we must give them the data they need in a supportive environment to assess their own learning.

As I begin planning for the new semester I look at my notes from the past year. My reflections lead me to new pedagogical questions and inspire me to consider potential solutions. Last semester the empirical data from my students, and anecdotal data from informal discussions, demonstrated to me a lack of metacognitive awareness in the lowest-achieving students. Students who received a C or less in the class could not predict the score they would receive on the weekly tests (i.e., their average prediction was almost five points more than they actually received on the tests) while A and B students were very close in their average prediction. If poor students overpredict how well they will do immediately before the test, it is very likely that they also assume they understand the material the night before the test—and therefore stop studying before they are ready for the test. What can we do to help individual learners assess how well they understand the content to be covered on the test prior to taking the test? Time to do some tinkering.

REFERENCES

Clifford, M. (1984). Thoughts on a theory of constructive failure. *Educational Psychologist, 19*, 108–120.

Covington, M. (1992). *Making the grade: A self-worth perspective on motivation and reform.* New York: Cambridge University Press.

Deci, E. L., & Ryan, R. M. (1985). *Intrinsic motivation and self-determination in human behavior.* New York: Plenum Press.

Dweck, C. (1999). *Self-theories: Their role in motivation, personality, and development.* Philadelphia: Psychology Press.

Garcia, T. (1995). The role of motivational strategies in self-regulated learning. In P. Pintrich (Ed.), *Understanding self-regulated learning* (pp. 29–42). San Francisco: Jossey-Bass.

Gardner, J. (1983). *Frames of mind: The theory of multiple intelligences.* New York: Basic Books.

Gardner, J. (1993). *Multiple intelligences: The theory in practice.* New York: Basic Books.

Perkins, D. (1995). *Outsmarting IQ: The emerging science of learnable intelligence.* New York: Free Press.

Pintrich, P. (1995). *Understanding self-regulated learning.* San Francisco: Jossey-Bass.

Stipek, D. (1998). *Motivation to learn: From theory to practice.* Boston: Allyn and Bacon.

Weinstein, C. (1994). Strategic learning/strategic teaching: Flip sides of a coin. In P. Pintrich, D. Brown, & C. Weinstein (Eds.), *Student motivation, cognition, and learning: Essays in honor of Wilbert J. McKeachie* (pp. 257–273). Hillsdale, NJ: Lawrence Erlbaum.

Chapter 11

The Use of Collaborative Learning to Individualize Instruction in Accounting

Carol Venable

SETTING AND PERSONAL BACKGROUND

San Diego State University enrolls more than 30,000 students and is the largest of the twenty-three campuses in the California State University (CSU) system. It is in a large and ethnically diverse metropolitan center bordering Mexico and the Pacific Ocean. There is much diversity in the student body; more than 55% of the students specify themselves as non-Caucasian on their records. The university encompasses seven colleges (Arts and Letters, Business Administration, Education, Engineering, Health and Human Services, Professional Studies and Fine Arts, and Sciences) and offers an extended studies program; the university awards both undergraduate and graduate degrees. It also collaborates with other institutions to offer joint doctoral degrees in several areas. In accordance with the state master plan for higher education, the CSU system provides access to higher education for students who are in the upper third of their high school graduating classes.

Professional accounting instruction is provided by the School of Accountancy, where I teach, in the College of Business Administration. The college is one of the largest undergraduate business schools in the country, with almost 6,000 students. My courses include advanced undergraduate and graduate topics. Of particular interest for this chapter is the team-taught course in communication for accountants offered in conjunction with a writing professor from the Information and Decision Systems Department. The course covers teamwork, leadership, and written and oral presentation skills as they apply to accounting. My other courses are accounting information systems, auditing, tax, ethics and professional responsibility, and tutorials in computer usage. Undergraduate business class sizes typically run from forty to sixty, but some have more than 120 students. There are typically forty students in the communication for accountants course.

GUIDING ASSUMPTIONS ABOUT LEARNING AND TEACHING

Students rely on faculty to create an appropriate environment where learning can take place. Learning occurs when students are actively engaged, when students are challenged, and when students feel safe to experiment. To create the appropriate atmosphere, one must continuously assess the responses of students in class, be open to the students' individualized ways of understanding the material, be willing to put control of the class in the hands of students, and allow time for flexibility and spontaneity in class sessions. In this type of environment, the role of the student is that of an active participant, rather than that of a passive recipient of information.

In the past, the classroom environment of many business classes was often a one-size-fits-all approach with standard lecture halls, assigned readings, and traditional homework assignments. Recently, however, educators have come to recognize that each student has unique needs. How should these needs be addressed? There are many ways to individualize instruction, but limitations, such as cost and time, make it hard for many instructors to do so regularly. In a large class with much diversity, it is a particular challenge to individualize instruction and maintain an active, engaged environment.

As noted in Chapter 1, today's campuses display diversity on a number of dimensions. Students who are economically disadvantaged, academically underprepared, challenged by disabilities, older, from other countries, or from diverse ethnic or cultural backgrounds (Hughes, Frances, & Lombardo, 1991; Landscape, 1993; Wagener, 1989) populate classrooms in large urban areas. In such environments, Wlodkowski and Ginsberg (1995) suggest using a culturally responsive teaching framework with four intersecting motivational goals or conditions that can "create compelling learning experiences through which learners are able to maintain their integrity as they attain relevant educational success" (p. 27). These four goals or conditions are establishing inclusion, developing attitude, enhancing meaning, and engendering competence.

They suggest that collaborative learning pedagogy fits into this teaching framework..

Collaborative learning practices and assignments (see, for example, Johnson, Johnson, & Smith, 1998; Millis & Cottell 1998; Putnam 1998; Slavin 1995) allow a diverse group of individual learners to observe peers who are learning and problem solving in alternate ways. It also provides students with the opportunity to practice new techniques in a supportive atmosphere. The ability to use a variety of problem solving techniques is important for students to learn and take into their post collegiate professional environment. In today's society, educators should not only teach facts and facilitate the intellectual and moral development of their students; they need to help students develop the ability to learn and survive in a variety of settings. As Porter notes in Chapter 1 of this volume, the challenges facing undergraduate educators are unprecedented, for they are called on to develop both individual growth and social utility.

Acknowledging and respecting diverse learning styles is at the heart of successful teaching. However, students need to be challenged to develop alternative learning techniques that will help them adapt to new situations. Often, they rely on their preferred learning style by seeking instructors who teach to that method. This does little to expand their ability to learn in new situations. Instructors, like students, also have a preferred learning mode, and this often influences instructional style. Instructors, however, need a backpack of pedagogy to pull out at the appropriate time and place. The role of the instructor is to meet the needs of individual learners and to help them develop to their full potential. The appropriateness of any pedagogy depends on various factors, including the topic being covered and the time available for the material, as well as individual student characteristics. Even outside events, such as sports or items of local or national interest, influence classroom atmosphere and interactions on a particular day. The instructor needs to be adaptable and have alternative ways of addressing the topic. Being alert and responsive to student demeanor and reactions is important. It is one way of knowing when to go into the pedagogy backpack. However, teaching to support learning is not about putting one's teaching bag of tricks on the floor and randomly picking one out to see if it works with a particular student. It is about the art and craft of expecting that this one should help that student reach a particular learning goal. Past experiences and even intuition come into play once one understands that individuals learn, remember, perform, and understand in different ways. Learning theories such as Gardner's (1993) multiple intelligence theory describe these differences and suggest that a topic or concept can be approached in various ways to accommodate individual learners. Thus, to reflectively solve the problem of which technique to use at a particular time requires some preplanning of alternative ways to present concepts.

Every day, I assess effectiveness in supporting student learning by listening and observing. To see and hear members of the class actively engaged in activity during a collective learning activity is like a barometer of learning. To an outside observer, some of the activity might be seen as positive and some as negative, especially when it comes to the difference between enthusiasm and frustration. However, some student frustration can be a positive sign that indicates that students are being challenged.

Collaborative learning techniques can be used successfully with all learners, but adaptations may need to be made to accommodate beginning undergraduates, advanced undergraduates, graduate students, and adult learners. An example of such an adaptation occurs with making team assignments. In some cases, as discussed later in this chapter, it is important to assign teams based on the traits of the individual learners. Students experienced in collaborative learning, however, may profit from self-selection of groups based on shared learning goals. As students become more sophisticated with group processes or with the subject matter, team assignments also can become less structured, requiring higher levels of thinking skills and more sophisticated team decision-making.

Overall, it is important to maintain an interdisciplinary perspective in teaching discipline-specific knowledge. Outside school, disciplines do not exist in a vacuum. By approaching problems from an interdisciplinary perspective, students are encouraged to see and think outside the box. Interaction with academic colleagues in other fields can provide an introduction to techniques that can be added to the backpack of pedagogy. Calculated risks and a willingness to experiment, combined with ongoing assessment, provides for effective learning. By making changes in small increments and constantly assessing what works, items can be added to the backpack while other items can be discarded when they are no longer useful.

APPROACHES AND TECHNIQUES FOR INDIVIDUALIZING INSTRUCTION

The communications course for accountants is the setting for most of the examples in this chapter. The course is continually revised to meet the needs of the changing student population, to reflect current technical material, and to respond to the needs of the professional accounting community. The course attempts not only to develop technical knowledge and abilities within the discipline and to apply them in the current professional environment, but also to develop interpersonal skills. A significant amount of time is spent on group dynamics (leadership and participation in small groups) with a text (Wilson, 1998) that students can use as a future reference for dealing with interpersonal or conflict situations. Practice responses are provided for a variety of settings. The techniques in the Wilson text apply across disciplines.

General Classroom Approaches

In Chapter 3 Porter discussed how individualization occurs on a macro level (Corno & Snow, 1986) as well as in one-on-one situations. The macro level includes creating the overall classroom climate that fosters the learning of individual students. To create this climate, one of my main objectives is to create an open environment that shows respect for diverse points of view but at the same time readily questions all points of view. The first day of the course is the most important in creating this climate of inquiry and encouragement for divergent views. The first day sets the tone and the expectations for the entire semester. The syllabus may set the framework covering course objectives with specifics on due dates, exams, and grading standards, and the syllabus provides a summary of major assignments, but much of the first day is devoted to developing a classroom culture.

Critical Thinking Model

One of the first topics to discuss is critical thinking, its role in the accounting profession, and its use as a method for looking at oneself to understand individual learning and behavior. Critical thinking is defined as the ability to participate in an "investigation whose purpose is to explore a situation, phenomenon, question, or problem to arrive at a hypothesis or conclusion about it that integrates all available information and that can therefore be convincingly justified" (Kurfiss, 1988)—in essence, the practice of applying professional judgment. This definition of critical thinking captures the responsibility of accounting professionals by acknowledging the need to distinguish between fact and personal beliefs that may influence observations and conclusions (Baker, Cunningham, Kimmel, & Venable, 1995). Students receive a handout describing a model of the critical thinking process and its affective, cognitive, and behavioral components (Huffman, Vernoy, & Vernoy, 1994). Discussion of each element in the model and how it applies to the profession occurs on the first day to highlight the importance of understanding personal biases and tolerating ambiguity. Students are encouraged to self-assess their critical thinking skills with the model and to use it to develop personal critical-thinking goals for the semester. Small-group discussion of the self-assessments exposes students to the range and diversity of responses within the classroom.

During the semester, students are reminded of elements in the critical-thinking model that apply to specific assignments or topics. An example of where reference is made to the critical-thinking model is in preparation of a budget for an event that is to be held by a not-for-profit organization. Although students do research on individually selected organizations and hold personal interviews, they often have difficulty in identifying all the budget items and in making estimates. Their own biases and experiences hold them back because they make global assumptions. Bringing the assumptions to the forefront improves their ability to complete the assignment. In preparation, one class session is used to develop a semester budget for a student. Individual differences and assumptions become readily apparent, providing the opportunity to focus on critical thinking elements. Thus, the components of the critical-thinking model serve as a student tool for individual learners to use for their own ongoing self-assessment in the course and as the teacher's analytical tool to apply to new content as it is introduced.

Simulation Assignments

The semester assignments also are discussed on the first day, and assignments where students have individual choices on topics or approaches are highlighted. Students are told that many assignments are designed to provide them with simulations of real-life experiences. An example is a team project to interview a local organization about its payroll system. The final output includes working papers and flowcharts to analyze the organization's internal controls and a class presentation with appropriate graphics detailing strengths and weaknesses, as well as recommended improvements.

The objective of simulation assignments is to prepare students for new situations after leaving school. Since work situations typically are not forgiving, the classroom and school-directed projects become ways to safely experiment with new techniques and behaviors. In this context, it is important to acknowledge particular challenges of the class that may be felt by some individual students by noting that "You may be uncomfortable in this class when you are doing new things. This is good, because it shows that you are taking advantage of increasing your abilities in new situations and developing your capacity to learn in unfamiliar settings after you leave school."

Open Environment

One way to generate an open and supportive environment for each student is to clearly announce the open boundaries:

This is the place to experiment. This is the place to make mistakes. This is the place to ask what you think may be a stupid question. If you have a question, there is a high probability that many others do too. Take the chance and ask it. I will always attempt to address it immediately. If, however, I can't because I don't know the answer or there isn't time at the moment, I will follow up—either in a later class or individually.

In creating this open climate, it is important to acknowledge the instructor's limitations: "I will admit when I do not know or when I am uncertain about the exact answer to your questions." Self-disclosure and role modeling of professional responses and appropriate follow-up can enhance a teacher's credibility and allow students to admit their own lack of understanding.

At the end of the first day as well as on regular class days, it is often useful for students to do a one-minute essay on what they learned in class and to note any concerns they might have (this is in addition to asking for feedback in class). Any concerns or questions are answered at the beginning of the next class or individually, if requested. This technique recognizes individual needs and aspects of learning.

Specific Instructional Techniques

A combination of individual and collaborative learning strategies is important for both in-class and out-of-class activities in the communications course. In addition, the use of technology allows individual students to not only perform traditional research tasks, but also to create and experiment with knowledge in various media, allowing for written words, sound, and graphical interfaces and thus supporting a variety of individual learning characteristics.

Collaborative Learning

Collaborative learning is a broad umbrella term for various types of cooperative and participative strategies involving team-based active learning (Smith & MacGregor, 1992). It provides a framework that fosters higher-level reasoning strategies and critical thinking skills (Johnson et al., 1998). It also provides an environment that assists in the development of communication and interpersonal skills.

In a collaborative learning classroom, the use of small groups for discussion, problem solving, and assignments gives the instructor time to observe how students differ in their learning characteristics and to respond to those differences to support individual academic success. Collaborative learning brings to the surface, through the structured tasks assigned by the instructor, individual differences such as prior knowledge, communication skills and technical abilities. It also allows individual students to expand their knowledge of process because it allows them to observe, learn, and practice other approaches to problem solving.

Cooperative learning typically is seen as a subset of collaborative learning that uses a more structured approach. Attributes common to all collaborative approaches are common tasks or learning activities suitable for group work, small-group learning, cooperative behaviors, interdependence, and individual accountability and responsibility (Davidson, 1994).

Johnson et al. (1998) describe three types of cooperative learning groups: formal groups in which instructors provide structured assignments lasting for a class session or even for a whole semester, informal, ad-hoc groups with interactions lasting from a few minutes to an entire class period in which students share information and develop responses to instructor-imposed questions, and cooperative base groups, such as ongoing study groups that support inclusion and development by providing an ongoing support base.

Nested Assignments

To structure individual and group work in the communications course, assignments are nested and students are assigned to formal cooperative learning groups. A nested assignment has two parts: an individual component done outside class, and a related team component. The team component is done partly in and partly outside class. Team meeting time in the classroom is important because the instructor is available to observe and respond. With a structured assignment in a facilitated setting, students are exposed to the rationale of other team members in the planning stages of a project. Traditional approaches to group work often put students in out-of-class groups with no class time allocated to team interaction, and often the result is a spotty success rate or an ineffective learning environment because students divide the work into parts on which each student works alone rather than work collaboratively.

An example of a nested assignment in the communications class is to have each student research and write a summary memo to an accounting audience on a professional journal article of their choice. This allows individual students to focus on a subdiscipline of accounting in which they have an interest or in which they have already developed some expertise from prior classes. Students then meet with their teams to select one member's article to revise in letter format for a different audience that is nontechnical, such as a client or community group. The team also must plan an oral presentation with appropriate visuals and handouts. They are to simulate a scenario, such as a meeting at which they are to provide information to the nontechnical audience and answer questions. During the presentation, the rest of the class plays the role of the nontechnical audience asking questions. Teams are free to structure the meeting and the roles of the team members as they like, the only requirement being that everyone must actively participate.

Collaborative learning activities and nested assignments are useful in supporting individuals to become more responsible for their own learning, since the instructor gives more control to the students. By sharing responsibility for learning and sharing control of the classroom, the instructor becomes free to observe and assess the individuals or groups that need additional attention. The instructor also can participate in more individual student–teacher exchanges. This allows more time for individuals with the greatest need for individualized attention.

Identifying and Assessing Learning Differences

As Porter notes in the opening chapters, assessment needs to be embedded in instruction. The communications course specifically includes assessment measures at the beginning and end of the semester, as well as continually during every class meeting.

Beginning of the Semester

An assessment of student skills and knowledge is needed on the first day of class to determine overall student performance levels. In addition, the use of cooperative learning groups requires an assessment of students in order to form heterogeneous groups. "Instructors should distribute students from team to team based on their academic preparation and ability, their gender, their ethnic background, and any other characteristics that might provide useful. The idea is to create teams that will build on students' varied strengths" (Millis & Cottell, 1998, p. 51).

On the first day of class, students complete an index card asking for information on their background. They are asked about completed accounting courses, work experience, gender, and first spoken language. The information is used to assess the class characteristics as a whole, and it can be used as a reference if an individual student is having difficulty with the material or projects. Differences in class makeup from semester to semester or even among sections of the same course can be dramatic—affecting the learning environment and in-class coverage of material. The overall assessment at the beginning of the semester provides an early warning of difficulties that may arise with students in understanding and applying the material.

The gathered information also is used to form teacher-assigned heterogeneous groups. The objective is to bring students together who can support and learn from each other. Students are told that there are several objectives in forming the groups. The first one is to create teams so that experienced students (either academically or from paid work) are distributed across groups, since work experience in accounting can be a surrogate for familiarity with accounting study. Second, students are told that in the rapidly growing multicultural workplace, it is important to become comfortable with and able to interact with students from other cultural and ethnic backgrounds. With a large number of foreign born students, the first spoken language is used to assign students to groups for collaborative assignments.

Although students have completed prerequisite writing courses, students in a class vary a great deal in their writing skills. To identify those who will need additional help or referral to appropriate campus resources, students prepare a writing sample for the second day of class. They are provided with individual feedback on the writing sample, suggesting areas that need improvement and recommending specific approaches to improve their writing skills. Information from the writing sample is also used for placement in cooperative learning groups.

Students also are provided with a means to assess their level of apprehension about communication in certain public speaking situations, which can be an early indicator of difficulties that could arise in the class. They receive a ten-item self-assessment handout that the Speech Communication Department adapted from McCroskey (1970). The assessment provides the student with a self-computed measure that may suggest they seek advice from the instructor. One option is for students to enroll in a one-unit informal class that teaches techniques to reduce speech apprehension.

During the Semester

It is important to assess student understanding and the classroom climate daily. Direct simple observation of student reaction can often be a good indicator of understanding. When some students appear lost during a lecture, it may be good to open the class up by saying, "I don't think I'm getting through what I wanted. Do I need to rephrase this or try something else?" This technique avoids the appearance of accusing students of not trying or not paying attention, and it may pull back those who for some reason have drifted from the material. If I ask for feedback on what I said, students are more willing to participate in a discussion, and it minimizes the risk of their misunderstanding my remarks.

Another form of assessment is to do postmortems on classroom activities. Postmortems work well for mini assignments at the beginning of the semester or for new and unfamiliar activities. For example, on the first group presentation day, the instructor can point out the group that had the good ending or highlight the use of a particularly effective visual-aid technique. The instructor can ask, "What did you see done by other groups that you would want to try in your next presentation? What impressed you?" The postmortem on a group presentation also is a good opportunity to mention people who had good posture or physical presence and those who stood still and moved their hands appropriately with nothing in them to distract the audience.

Another technique that can be used at random is to ask for a one-minute essay about an assignment asking students what they learned that day. The essay can be unstructured and anonymous. It also can be effective as a team-writing essay if the teams are allowed to discuss possible responses for several minutes. Another variation is to ask students to write down any questions they have on what was covered. At the beginning of the next class, the questions can be answered for the benefit of all students.

End of the Semester

In addition to the university's formal student assessment of the course at the end of the semester, students are asked to complete another anonymous questionnaire. The feedback is used to assess trends and characteristics of the general student population, as well as to make adjustments to course materials and to design assignments that address the needs of various learners with their individual learning characteristics and learning strategies. The questionnaire asks the student to identify which of the projects and assignments were the most beneficial, the least beneficial, and why. Students are also asked to make recommendations for improving the course. Often students note how particular assignments required them to branch out from their preferred way of learning and benefited them by developing new skills.

Another individualized assessment tool is the portfolio. With a portfolio, students select completed course items and prepare an assessment that demonstrates the learning that occurred during the semester. Students are encouraged to include both original and revised work, as well as descriptions of what they learned and how they would do assignments or tests differently.

Another useful assessment is to talk with former students at alumni events about school experiences that have been most helpful for them. Often their stories can be used in class to provide current students about the relevancy of the projects and materials.

Using Technological Tools for Individualizing Instruction

Technology is a tool that can enhance the learning environment and increase the interaction between all members of the class. It can be used to supplement in-class activity, and its ability to change the actual classroom space and to reconfigure in-class sessions grows constantly. Faculty can harness student interest in computers to create an interactive learning environment with on-line courses or at least on-line access to materials. There are various ways to promote student interaction, such as computer conferencing, Web page and computer graphics development, e-mail, and new, technology-enabled classrooms that promote hands-on learning.

Computer Conferencing

Computer conferencing with instructor-posted articles can meet the needs of learners who are hesitant to participate in class discussions by allowing them sufficient time to clearly think through material and write down their comments. In subsequent class sessions, these students often are able to participate in expanded discussions on the topic. Computer conferencing has been used in the communications course and is extensively used in the accounting curriculum as well as in other disciplines (Venable & Vik, 1998).

Web Pages and Presentation Graphics

Another method of individualizing the learning process with technology is to have students create Web pages or use presentation graphics programs to create presentations on topics that they select. Advances in technology make the technical tasks easy to master. Self-selected topics allow for individualized and self-directed tasks. Individualized learning also occurs because of the synthesis that students bring to creating the Web page or graphics. To provide a coherent synopsis, students must first gain a good understanding of the material.

E-mail

The most individualized form of technology is e-mail. Students who are reticent to speak in class will often use e-mail to ask questions of an instructor when encouraged to do so. Responding to individual questions is not the only way to use e-mail. Instructors can design assignments to follow a class session and then provide immediate feedback in the following class.

An example of an e-mail assignment with feedback in the subsequent class is a business ethics case. In the classroom, the discussion focuses on public cases of large businesses in which there has been fraudulent or unethical activity. Often fraudulent or unethical activity is the result of structure, policy, or reward systems that create a climate that fosters such behavior. To bring personal experiences into the assignment increases the relevance of the material. Students can be asked to do an essay describing the structure, policy, and reward system of their own workplace or a past school experience. They can then suggest changes to the structure, policy, or reward system either in an ideal format or a modified format that may be more likely to be adopted. As an assignment to be completed immediately after a class session with the results e-mailed to the instructor before the next class session, students have immediate reinforcement of the concepts in a personalized setting. The instructor can summarize e-mail responses to report in class and guide a discussion of the real-life experiences.

Students are exposed to new experiences, and some receive feedback about activities that they may not have openly discussed. This technique can be used for various assignments in which consolidated feedback can help the instructor guide the classroom discussion and share a variety of individual perspectives and experiences with the class.

There are many positive outcomes from using e-mail to evaluate assignments before the class meets for its next discussion session. It allows an instructor to incorporate minority views into the classroom and open up diversity issues, and it draws out quiet students. It also respects the privacy of individuals when dealing with sensitive topics bringing out new points of view and personal experiences without singling out individuals.

Computerized Classrooms

With the increase of network technology on campuses and the movement toward group learning (Shneiderman, Alavi, Norman, & Borkowski, 1995), many faculty members have sought more advanced classroom designs (Shapiro, Roskos, & Cartwright, 1995) that include placing technology at the fingertips of the individual students. One of the newer developments used for the accounting communications course is a collaborative learning technology classroom that integrates collaborative group work with technology (Venable, 1997). The room has six team workstations that allow up to six members to interact and gain access to on-line resources.

In specially planned sessions, the resources in the room support the learning of individual students who are visual or hands-on learners. The room provides access to library materials, Internet resources, and software tools. The disparity in technology skills between students is overcome in this environment, since individuals with limited exposure to computers are now collaborating with others who can immediately demonstrate search techniques to access new information. In this environment, students also work on developing presentations and using collaborative writing tools.

CONCLUSION

In large classrooms it is a challenge to individualize learning experiences to meet the needs of diverse learners. While many might argue the impossibility of customizing instruction in that environment, it is nonetheless a task that can be accomplished in various ways. This chapter has focused on the combined use of individual assignments, collaborative learning techniques, assessment strategies, and technology as tools to individualize instruction. Instructors with a backpack of pedagogy available can address individual differences in the normal course of their teaching. Knowledge of collaborative learning techniques provides the ability to quickly form impromptu classroom groups who examine an issue and report their findings. Access to technology provides immediate on-line access to information and the ability to demonstrate new developments. The importance of individualizing instruction with these tools will continue to grow. The number of diverse learners coming into our classroom is rapidly increasing, and classroom walls are expanding as technology provides opportunities to new students without regard to space or time constraints.

REFERENCES

Baker, R., Cunningham, B., Kimmel, P., & Venable, C. (1995). *A catalog of resource materials for teaching accounting students critical thinking.* Accounting Pedagogical Resource Series, Critical Thinking 1995–2001. St. Louis: Federation of Schools of Accountancy.

Corno L., & Snow, R. E. (1986). Adapting teaching to individual differences among learners. In M. C. Wittrock (Ed.), *Handbook of research on teaching* (3d ed.) (pp. 605–629). New York: Macmillan.

Davidson N. (1994). Cooperative and collaborative learning: An integrative perspective. In J. S. Thousand, R. A. Villa, and A. I. Nevin (Eds.), *Creativity and collaborative learning: A practical guide to empowering students and teachers.* Baltimore: Paul H. Brookes.

Gardner, H. (1993). *Multiple intelligences: The theory in practice.* New York: Basic Books.

Huffman, K., Vernoy, M., & Vernoy, J. (1994). *Psychology in action* (3d ed.). New York: John Wiley.

Hughes, K. S., Frances, C., & Lombardo, B. J. (1991). *Years of challenge: The impact of workforce and demographic trends on higher education in the 1990s.* Washington, DC: National Association of College and University Business Officers.

Johnson, D. W., Johnson, R. T., & Smith, K. A. (1998). *Active learning: Cooperation in the college classroom.* Edina, MN: Interaction Book.

Kurfiss, J. G. (1988). *Critical thinking: Theory, research, practice, and possibilities.* ASHE-ERIC higher education report no. 2. Washington, DC: Association for the Study of Higher Education.

Landscape. (1993). The changing face of the American college campus. *Change, 24*(4), 57–60.

McCroskey, J.C. (1970). Measures of communication-bound anxiety. *Speech Monographs, 37,* 269–273.

Millis, B. J., & Cottell, P.G., Jr. (1998). *Cooperative learning for higher education faculty.* Phoenix, AZ: American Council on Education and The Oryx Press.

Putnam, J. W. (1998). *Cooperative learning and strategies for inclusion.* Baltimore: Paul H. Brookes.

Shapiro W., Roskos, K., & Cartwright, G. (1995). Technology-enhanced learning environments. *Change, 27*(6), 67–69.

Shneiderman, B., Alavi, M. Norman, K., and Borkowski, E. (1995). Windows of opportunity in electronic classrooms. *Communications of the Association for Computing Machinery (ACM), 38*(11), 19–24.

Slavin, R. (1995). *Cooperative learning.* Englewood Cliffs, NJ: Prentice-Hall.

Smith, B. L., & MacGregor, J. T. (1992). What is collaborative learning? In A. S. Goodsell, M. R. Maher, V. Tinto, B. L. Smith, & J. Macgregor (Eds.), *Collaborative learning: A sourcebook for higher education.* University Park, PA: National Center on Postsecondary Teaching, Learning, and Assessment (NCTLA).

Venable, C. F. (1997). Design, development and implementation of a collaborative learning technology classroom. In *Preliminary case studies in information technology,* National Research Council, Committee on Undergraduate Science Education Meeting, Washington, DC, March 16.

Venable, C. F., & Vik, G. N. (1998). Computer-supported collaboration in an accounting class. In D. Reiss, D. Selfe, & A. Young (Eds.), *Electronic communication across the curriculum* (pp. 242–254). Urbana, IL: National Council of Teachers of English (NCTE).

Wagener, U. E. (1989). Quality and equity: The necessity for imagination. *Harvard Educational Review, 59*(2), 240–250.

Wilson, G. L. (1998). *Groups in context: Leadership and participation in small groups* (5th ed.). New York: McGraw-Hill.

Wlodkowski, R. J., & Ginsberg, M. G. (1995). *Diversity and motivation.* San Francisco: Jossey-Bass.

PART V

INTERDISCIPLINARY CURRICULA

Chapter 12

Einstein's Universe:
Focusing on Student Learning
in Interdisciplinary General
Education

Judith Patton

SETTING AND PERSONAL BACKGROUND

Portland State University (PSU) is a comprehensive urban public institution. The university has more than 17,000 students enrolled and serves a population of more than 40,000 individuals in credit or noncredit classes each year, including nearly one-third of the Oregon University System's enrolled graduate students. The location of the university in its urban setting provides the impetus for engaging with the community as part of the curriculum. Our motto, "Let Knowledge Serve the City," illustrates the importance of that connection. The faculty includes almost 600 full-time and several hundred part-time members. The major academic units of the university are the colleges of Engineering and Computer Sciences, Liberal Arts and Sciences, and Urban and Public Affairs; the schools of Business Administration and Fine and Performing Arts; and the graduate schools of Education and Social Work. Bachelor of arts and bachelor of science degrees are offered in a wide variety of fields from the academic colleges and professional schools. In addition, specialist certificate programs, minors, preprofessional programs, and secondary education programs supplement major studies and provide many diverse opportunities. Master's degrees are offered in numerous disciplines, and the university offers ten doctoral degrees, including degrees in civil engineering, computer science, engineering, education, mathematics education, social work, and social research and four interdisciplinary degrees in which approximately a dozen departments participate.

In 1994 University Studies, a new general education program, was initiated as part of the improvement of undergraduate education. It is required for the majority of students at PSU. University Studies is a four-year, interdisciplinary curriculum based on four goals: inquiry and critical thinking, communication, the diversity of human experience, and social responsibility and ethical issues. The foundational course, Freshman Inquiry, lasts one full year. Courses are designed by interdisciplinary teams of faculty and peer mentors to introduce students to all four goals of the program through thematic content. The middle portion of the program consists of twenty-six upper-division theme-based clusters that are introduced through one-term Sophomore Inquiry courses. Students choose three Sophomore Inquiry courses to expand their range of knowledge and then specialize in one area by taking three upper-division cluster courses in the chosen cluster. The final course is a Senior Capstone. Capstones are courses in which interdisciplinary groups of students work with a faculty facilitator and a community partner to address needs and issues in the metropolitan region or beyond. Each Senior Capstone course results in a final product that may be a report, a presentation, a technological product, or a performance. More information about the institution is available at www.pdx.edu, and www.ous.pdx.edu has information about University Studies.

GUIDING ASSUMPTIONS ABOUT LEARNING AND TEACHING

As stated above, Freshman Inquiry is the required, entry-level class in PSU's general education for most students. Teams of three to six faculty members from different disciplines develop curriculum for a one-year-long team-taught interdisciplinary course. Each of the Freshman Inquiry faculty members works with an undergraduate peer mentor as a teaching partner. The entire class (thirty-six students, faculty member, and peer mentor) meets twice weekly, and in addition, each student meets twice a week in smaller groups (twelve to fourteen) with the peer mentor. Peer mentor sessions take place in specially designed computer labs. A set of goals and objectives for student learning, designed around the four goals of the program and theme-based content, form the basis for the courses. The intention of the year-long courses is to lay the groundwork for successful student learning. Thus the focus is to help students learn how to learn and to make the transition to the university; to surface the process of successful learning through rich and challenging content. The theme for the freshman course varies from year to year and is determined by the faculty teams; mine was "Embracing Einstein's Universe: Language, Culture and Relativity."

As I reflect upon what I do, I find the attraction of being a university faculty member is that I am constantly learning and solving problems in new situations. There is a lot of variety in the work I do, and it is fun; there is real joy to seeking solutions, to planning, teaching, and doing research. We dismiss too easily the joy of learning, and it is critical to share the natural pleasure of discovery with our students. Working hard to understand a difficult concept, and getting it, is really satisfying. It is the satisfaction that, in the end, will entice our students into being lifelong learners. Creating a place where every student experiences the excitement of learning is the objective of education, and we need to see the university as that place where the natural learning process becomes part of every student's way of life.

Because of the focus on a student-centered learning environment, University Studies provides a variety of faculty development opportunities for those who teach in the program. Because I have had the opportunity to learn about collaborative teaching and student-centered classrooms, my teaching is now based on a learning community model. Faculty act as guides and colearners rather than as experts forever isolated at the front of the classroom. Each student is a singular and significant part of the community. Since moving into new subject areas of teaching, I have had to admit that I was not an expert in areas we needed to explore (physics, for instance), and that some of my students would know more than I would. It was uncomfortable at first and can still be so, but I have found that I enjoy working alongside the students, guiding, suggesting, and seeking resources. This way of working is much closer to my former teaching in dance, and comfortable in that respect. The most exciting thing about learning is discovery, and students need to participate actively in this process. We are partners in making meaning; however, as the teacher I need my knowledge and expertise to guide the students successfully. I have found it more difficult to plan a class in which I do not know exactly where the discussion will go than to give a lecture that I control in its entirety. It takes all my expertise to be able to ask the right questions at the right time.

A learning community in the classroom includes the professor who shares the authority of the classroom with students and other colleagues. I have found that this learning environment opens possibilities. Students learn better in a safe environment where ideas can be expressed freely in an atmosphere of mutual respect, one without fear of ridicule or rejection. My peer mentor and I use our own learning process to model for students. In class we validate asking questions, not knowing the answers, and clarifying understanding through class discussions; in other words, showing what effective students do in the classroom. The modeling strives to make it okay to not know and to work together to come to an understanding.

Part of my responsibility as a teacher is to create a place in which difference is appreciated, and I try to demonstrate through the curriculum how diversity enriches our lives. We are all different, and the differences add to what we can know and experience. Students come into our classrooms with diverse viewpoints, learning styles, and disciplinary perspectives. Learning begins when students question their assumptions and use new evidence to integrate former beliefs and understandings with new information. By expanding our definition of how to teach and to learn, we can take advantage of our students' talents and interests and share and build upon them by encouraging student growth and progress.

The classroom space itself and how it is used during the class has been an important aspect of a more individualized model. Configuring the space in a pattern that allows students to form small groups and to talk in the larger group facing each other transforms the work of the class. It also makes it easier for the instructor to become part of the class. Teaching in rooms with movable furniture and tables, seats that adjust to individual heights, and flexible lighting makes a significant impact on how students behave in the classroom and what they expect to happen there. Where the faculty and students sit in the room affects learning and the experience of the class.

I have learned that we as faculty can teach what we want students to be able to do and to know at the end of the course. I am sure this statement sounds self-evident, but a common understanding cannot be assumed. The difference is the focus on the students, not on the delivery of content. When the focus of the class is on covering content, the assumption is that if the professor delivers the content, then the students have gotten it. Our methods of checking to see whether that assumption holds true often do not get to the reality of student learning. Of those in the class who are earning grades of C or lower, it is presumed that there is something wrong with them. They were not well enough prepared for college or have not worked hard enough in the course. A student who gets high grades is assumed to know the material, but we often do not look closely enough to see whether students really understand and can use the material. Covering content is not enough. Surfacing the process, showing how to do the assignments, helps all students. Often even the students who are used to receiving high grades on research papers and other kinds of work do not really know how they got those grades nor trust that they will continue to do so. Often students think they have "lucked out" and fear getting unmasked. It is important to teach the things we expect students to be able to do if they do not already know it.

We need to use our assessment strategies (see Chapters 3 and 4) to find out what students have actually learned in class and then utilize the information to redesign our courses. Changing a class to focus on what students know and can do, rather than on what the instructor presents, involves giving students the opportunity to work with material when the professor is present, the opposite of traditional teaching activity. In the majority of classes the professor talks while students listen, and when students actually work with the material, they are alone, after class is dismissed, doing work with no one there to answer questions or help their thinking along. Organizing a class around active student involvement means more discussion, presentations by students, and assignments that are open ended and encourage student thinking and choice. Classroom work that allows the instructor to be present while students deal with the material gives the opportunity to know more accurately where each student is with the coursework and with her or his learning.

When we change how we view the relationship between teaching and learning, we also change what we expect from students. We all know how easy it is to sit at the back of a class and take notes and sit for an occasional test. When we begin to ask students to participate in class, to think, to evaluate, to share, and to risk learning together, we are asking a lot. We are asking students to take responsibility for their learning. In the beginning it can be a tough sell, but the rewards from perseverance are well worth the trouble. As students gain confidence and trust in their faculty and in their peers, their progress can be rapid and impressive. Validating the student voice in class and fostering discussion that allows for divergent views brings students to learning in powerful and active ways. Often students you never thought were doing anything in class begin to bring the most compelling arguments to discussions.

All students benefit from individual faculty attention, and all students need to be challenged and supported where they are in their learning. I need to find out how my various students learn most comfortably and then stretch them into strengthening and using less familiar ways of operating. My process involves getting to know my students, using that knowledge to plan the course, giving students multiple ways to engage with the material, discussing why we are doing what we are doing and helping students to become active learners and to take more control of their education. It means I have to be willing to change my plans and accommodate student needs. Often I find I have not planned enough time in the syllabus for discussion of material or for some of the assignments. I have changed due dates on occasion and, with the class's input, have eliminated some projects in order to give more time to develop others.

Helping students make connections and apply successful learning strategies in such a way that they can continue themselves when they are no longer in the class is real success. I want students to be able to remember and use what they have learned during their time with me. To that end, all reading, class plans, and assignments are aimed at a final result: helping students become self-directed learners, who think critically and communicate their own ideas in multiple mediums and who value and respect others. I cannot claim to having succeeded totally in realizing my vision of learning and teaching, but I have seen positive results. Students report using skills learned in Freshman Inquiry in other courses and being able to make connections between content areas and aspects of their lives beyond college because of our work.

APPROACHES AND TECHNIQUES FOR INDIVIDUALIZING INSTRUCTION

My overarching strategy for individualizing instruction is to create a series of class activities and assignments designed to offer several learning opportunities and assessments for each major unit we are to study. As students identify how they learn, they write and talk about their process. Students identify how they learn most successfully and then are encouraged to strengthen areas that are not so comfortable for them. I also learn how best to work with each student to maximize her or his time in class. A parallel goal is to foster student–student and student–faculty relationships within the class structure. As a part of the relationship work, we strive in class to understand and to value the various learning styles and strengths of each student. This support helps to create an environment of trust and comfort for everyone. In more practical terms, teaching communication, group process, and problem solving respond to major skills currently sought in other areas of the college curriculum and most career areas.

Building into the curriculum ways to maximize students' working with other students is central to building community in the classroom. In journal reflections students talk about ways in which they participate more fully in class because they feel an obligation to other students. I believe this increase in self-reported motivation is a result of feeling responsible to a community. One student wrote about reading a novel fully for the first time because the discussion in class was so lively and exciting. He wanted to experience what the other students were so engaged in through the complex structure and relationships in the book. To allow ways for students to become more active in class, I rely on small-group discussion and informal, as well as formal, group presentations. As an example, we begin studying special relativity by reading and talking. Providing more than one way into the material is important. Our students read both an ingenious and witty text, *Einstein for Beginners*, by Schwartz and McGuinness (1979), and then tackle the more complex work, *Physics: Concepts and Connections*, by Hobson (1999), a text oriented to a conceptual study of science. Using segments from the video series "Mechanical Universe" offers yet another view of the concepts through animated graphics and cartoons. For many, this visual version is the cement, the final brick that brings it together. We use the concepts in physics to write creative stories and read *Einstein's Dreams*, by Alan Lightman, as part of our exploration. As this illustrates, our learning proceeds through a series of diverse activities that call for a variety of learning styles and experiences.

As we cover both video and reading materials, class is broken into small discussion groups. We share reading and note-taking strategies and report how different ways worked for different students. One note-taking assignment is to ask students to write a summary of the chapter reflecting on how the material is hitting the student and a list of questions and surprises. In class groups of three to five, students take ten to fifteen minutes to compare notes and create a group report for the rest of the class. Each group member takes on a role, leader (makes sure everyone contributes, guides the discussion, and keeps the group on task), recorder (takes notes of what is said), voice (reports to the class), encourager (gives positive feedback), or observer (watches and notes the group process). The roles are rotated for every discussion, giving each student experience in multiple capacities (see Karre, 1994). At the end of the group time each "voice" reports the results of the group's work and a full-class discussion follows. In the last part of the class discussion, each "observer" talks about the group process and engages in metacognition: How did the group think about the assignment? Was it a productive way of thinking? Was anything missed? Were the right questions asked? Was there a problem with how the group functioned? What really worked in the process? This technique allows students to experience their strengths in action, to see and value how others learn and operate, and by trying various roles, work in modalities that are not as familiar but become new resources.

Using small group discussions within the larger class and asking students to write thoughts and questions before discussion gives those students who take longer to think things through a chance to feel comfortable talking in class. For students who find speaking in class difficult, e-mail and free writing can provide an entryway. Reading a perceptive piece from a quiet student can validate a student's thoughts and encourage those students to share more as the class progresses. It is through class dialogue that learning takes place and watching and listening to students can show faculty where students actually are in relation to the course material. It can be very hard for faculty to refrain from talking and to allow silences, but giving the stage to the students means hearing what they know and understand.

Early in the course I use a series of surveys and questionnaires to determine a baseline for each student's strongest modality. We also discuss multiple intelligences and do some short personal inventories of our learning using Howard Gardner's work (Gardner, 1993). In the first weeks of class I spend time watching students during class assignments and look for indicators of comfort levels while they work on a range of activities from speaking and writing to visual design and use of numerical information. By midterm I have a fairly accurate portrait of each student as a learner and can help each student hone her or his strengths while pushing each into new skill areas. I place students in groups that demand the use of their strengths, and after we have established the strengths, move to asking students to work in less familiar roles. This work can take very simple forms. Using small groups to present sections of the physics text and assigning each person in the group a role shifts from lecture format to group presentation. Initially, we allow the most talkative students to report what the groups decide everyone needs to know about each section of the text. We continue the same groups but move roles to different students, eventually making sure that everyone takes a turn reporting to the class, keeping the discussion on track, and making sure all the key points are covered. If the class continues to rely on those with prior experience in physics, we create a group consisting entirely of those students but call on that group last. Students begin to see that they need to understand the concepts themselves. We have found that many students may understand the material but do not speak up. When they start to reveal their understanding, they gain confidence in their own ability to grasp physics. Once the discussion opens up to more than the identified "physics brains," discussions begin to be full-class discussions, and new issues and questions come up. It becomes okay to say "I'm lost," or "I don't get it." The discussions then address everyone's questions, and the class sessions are energetic and rich in dialogue. The payoff is that everyone in class demonstrates good understanding of relativity by the end of that unit of study.

The final stage in our exploration of relativity is a multiphase assignment, "Teaching Relativity to a Relative," that was part of a syllabus cocreated by Lois Becker and me. The assignment asks students to plan and design a lesson in special relativity to deliver, one on one, to a relative or friend. Students work in groups to decide on the set of concepts needed to explain special relativity. This part of the work integrates technology into the assignment and includes using PowerPoint®, Internet research, and importing graphics. It also draws on the student's design skills and aesthetic sense. Creativity in the design is encouraged and valued. The actual teaching uses oral presentation skills and rests on the idea that one of the best ways to learn is to teach. The assignment also allows students to share their educational experience with someone important to them. For the last phase of the assignment we set up a speakerphone to call those relatives who are available during class time to talk about how the teaching of relativity went and what the relative understands about it. The students respond well to the calls, particularly after the first one. It is fun, creates classroom camaraderie, and gives students confidence and pride in their mastery of this difficult material.

As illustrated above, I depend on variety in assignments to give students opportunities to access different ways of learning and to see where their strengths reside. Once a student has succeeded in class in some way, improvements in other areas often follow. When the classroom is set up to allow students to exhibit and know success on a broad spectrum of abilities, they become more confident and able to work in the traditional academic skill areas too. The arts represent a wide range of skills, and using the arts in assignments offers the opportunity for students to showcase talents often left out of the classroom. I use assignments that integrate choice in how students present and craft their work. We also work on writing and oral communication in a variety of ways as a regular part of class, thus giving students experience in the kinds of academic and career-related work that will be expected of them.

An example of incorporating the arts as a learning strategy, the "Box Assignment" requires students to collect objects that represent significant ideas, learning moments, and personal memories during the entire term. Students use the objects to create artistic boxes or just cigar boxes full of the things they have collected. They can decide what the box is as well as what goes into it. At the end of the term each student presents his or her box to the class. The presentations allow students to learn about each other in a completely different way than other kinds of discussions or presentations. Using art as communication, sharing humor and creativity, students and faculty gain a much fuller sense of who the people in class are and what each can expect from the others. These projects also introduce all students to the artistic perspective, a valuable and significant thinking and creating process in and of itself.

Creating the space for and encouraging the student voice is a powerful strategy for individualizing teaching. For learning to take place, every student needs to feel free to express ideas in a respectful environment. In an early class we talk about times each of us has experienced being put down in some way in a class. We share behaviors like eye rolling or sighing that can powerfully affect what we do as students. All generally agree that they would not want to be the person who made it difficult for another person to learn. We also share stories of successful and unsuccessful learning experiences. At the end of the discussions we design class ground rules. Students are more invested in class when they have a voice in the decision making. As a teacher, I have blind spots and assumptions that student involvement in the decision making can illuminate. Course goals and expectations remain high but become more encompassing. Students participate in decision making by having input on assignments, class pace, and group project development. We work together to formulate ground rules for class discussions and scoring rubrics that establish the class evaluations. I give students a lot of choice in topics for most major projects and papers. I have even given group essay tests. By spring term I have students help create the syllabus by giving a choice in topics and texts read for the term. The strategies I use stem from my belief in the need for students to be active in the class work. When they feel comfortable with their peers, have choice in how they participate and do assignments, and have multiple opportunities to discuss topics orally and on paper, they gain a better understanding of content. Their learning is more useable and lasting. When students work on subjects that they are genuinely interested in, the resulting work is deeper and shows their care and interest. Many times students have commented that they thought they could never write a fifteen-page research paper, but because they became so interested in their topic, it happened without their thinking about it. They report that the paper seemed to write itself. Students spend more time and effort on work that they have some say in formulating and evaluating.

Another way to include the student voice in class is using peer response groups for all major projects and papers. This strategy gives students the chance to learn how to form an academic support group for other classes. Students like to help each other and talk about their work together. They also learn more about their own writing by using a thoughtful process of response to each other's papers. It is through this close work that students get to know each other as colleagues in the academic realm and as friends. Students who find community at the university are more likely to finish their education and to care about how well they do. They also share their strengths and see who can be relied upon for what in different learning tasks.

Assessment is a faculty member's greatest tool for knowing what is really going on in the classroom. By thinking about what assessment is and how to use assignments and class time in different ways, faculty can shift from having a small amount of information about what students are really learning to having a great deal. It can take the form of faculty reflection, class assignments, daily class work, and end of the term projects or portfolios.

Every Freshman Inquiry class has a small-group instructional diagnostic (Angelo & Cross, 1993) given midway through the first term of the three-term course. We find out what is working in class, what barriers have been encountered, and what suggestions students have. This strategy can be used at any time in a course, but we feel that at the midpoint there is still time to do something about the issues the students express. Students are not often asked what they think, but they have important things to say about the classes they take and how their learning is progressing. There are scores of ideas for including classroom assessment techniques in classes. I have found those techniques to provide a clear idea of where each student is with the material.

Classroom assessments, free writing, and reflective assignments can show an instructor where the gaps are in each student's understanding, and instructors can plan the next class discussions and activities to fill in those gaps or give some students more individual attention. Reflection—asking students to think about what they have done and to evaluate their process—is a critical part of learning and of assessment. We use a year-long student portfolio to teach students reflection and to help them understand their own progress. It is easy for students to finish a paper, get the grade, and then put the paper away and never look at it again. If we ask students to look at that paper and think about how it could have been improved, we give them a chance to take a little step forward. They can see the habits that impede or support their own learning. With portfolios students are asked to think about what they have done and learned over an entire term, year, or educational experience. They look at the work they did, choose samples that show their progress, and make an argument for how the samples show progress. Portfolio assignments include reflective essays that ask students to discuss their strengths and weaknesses as learners and to set goals for the future. Those essays are some of the most compelling direct evidence of what is working and not working for individual students in class. They are the basis for thinking through the next term's syllabi to take advantage of a clearer understanding of each student's relationship to the class material.

If we want our students to improve, we need to think about how our courses are allowing improvement to happen. Getting a C on a paper on the surface is not a rich learning experience, but getting a C can be if the student is shown how the paper can be improved and then given an opportunity to rewrite it. I meet with students, one on one, for writing conferences. Working individually with students seems necessary to the writing process. Through the process of revision, they begin to recognize that they have gotten away with low-quality work before and that there has been a price to pay for it. Giving an answer on a multiple-choice test can be an exercise in guessing unless the student is asked to explain why that particular answer was chosen. If I want my classes to support inquiry and to stretch how students think, I need to see where the student is in her or his thinking process and use questions and give assignments that call for students to find answers that may not already exist.

To teach in an individualized manner we must know the students as individuals. No matter what kind of work the class is engaged in, I watch the students. Keeping aware of what is going on in the classroom is crucial. In any moment a breakthrough can occur, and the need to pick up on the breakthroughs is critical. I have to be willing to change, to slow down or speed up according to how things are going. I have had help in this, and I would recommend taking opportunities to have classroom observations or to participate in team teaching. I have had a research assistant, Cheryl Ramette, working with me on a class ethnography as one of our program assessment projects. I also have the other faculty on my team and my peer mentor in the class with me. Having another set of eyes and ears in class is invaluable. It is difficult to both keep on top of the class dynamic and track individual student behavior, but it is what is demanded of us. It is doubly difficult when at the same time we are trying new teaching methods and having to pay even closer attention to what we are saying and doing in class. Other people in class can validate your take on students and on what is really happening. After class, we discuss and share insights and suggestions for the next class and for working with particular students. In this way we can keep a closer watch on the informal exchanges that go on continually during classes that can help create a supportive environment for learning or totally undercut it.

As a constant check, I take time after each class to visualize the session and think through what happened. This time helps me record what I actually did that day and note things I should take advantage of or try to redirect. The habit also allows me to practice what I preach in terms of reflection and to show that these are, indeed, lifelong learning habits. I share my reflections with the students as part of the class review. We begin most classes with a summary or review of the work we have done in the previous class that needs to be brought forward. In the program we have found that doing what we ask our students to do is very helpful for understanding what the students are going through and for finding the pitfalls in assignments before they become class problems. Students react strongly and positively when we share our work with them too. I bring my writing into our writing response groups and work along with my students. At times both my mentor and I do the assignments and presentations along with our students.

Close contact with and knowing the students has changed what I do in class. I meet with students individually each term at least once, one on one, and in addition any time I sense a difficulty. The dynamic of the class as a whole is important. Providing an environment that supports each student's growth takes careful observation and strategizing. Specific behaviors I watch for are students who never talk in class, students who sit off to one side or behind the class, and groups of students who interact only within their own group. It is more difficult to work well with a fragmented group of students, and it is important to watch both the overt and the subtle classroom interactions. Strategies I have used to influence various behaviors are sitting in various places in the room, taking part in different small-group discussions, changing the seating in the room—the actual way the space is used and how the tables and chairs are arranged—asking individuals to sit in particular places, changing groups for discussion and group projects. The most important strategies, though, are the ones that are woven into the curriculum; and working together is integrated with learning the material.

Team meetings are our place to resolve teaching difficulties, share successes and good assignments, and vent frustrations. Much of the reward for working in the new program has come from the relationships among faculty members who would never have met or worked together if it had not been for the program. Having a place and the opportunity to talk with other faculty members about teaching has made a visible difference in how we teach and think about teaching at the university. Many of us have begun to research teaching and learning because of our involvement in University Studies, and the Freshman Inquiry faculty teams have become learning communities of their own. Our ability to stretch beyond our own disciplines has come through teaching each other in the team meetings and in each other's classes as well as through our individual research. This cross-teaching is important for our being able to deliver an interdisciplinary curriculum and to model individualized teaching. We are experiencing what we ask of the students and drawing from that experience to enrich our teaching.

Through this teaching process, students deal both with the content and with their own learning styles. There is a constant dance between specific content and the process of learning. Discussion about effective ways to read the material, to take notes, to write to understand, and to clarify thinking surfaces the learning process and opens it to speculation. The way each class member learns most effectively and how we exercise critical-thinking skills in various applications becomes the class content. In each step of the assessment, students are evaluated as individuals and participate actively in the process.

A key to the process of individualizing teaching is to give clear examples of what is expected for each assignment. The ambiguity of our current grading methods works against the majority of students, particularly those who are traditionally thought of as less skilled or motivated (Haycock, 1997). When students can see what is expected, they can produce it themselves. All students can learn, particularly if they are given challenging material and shown the level of expectation. We help this process by giving clear assignments that connect materials from class and by using grading rubrics to evaluate them. Showing students examples of good work helps increase a student's chance of success.

With a class of more advanced students I ask for a deeper level of analysis and discussion and spend less time on basic process steps and more on how to achieve the next level of accomplishment in each of the program objectives. I survey the class to locate areas of less confidence or experience and make sure to include work on those. I find I can move faster and carry on the discussion at a different level. The general class strategies, the active group and hands-on work does not change. The most difficult class situation is one with a broad range of preparation and motivation on the part of the students, the norm in our program. In that case, I ask advanced students to work with less experienced students. I often pair students who can work with each other in different areas, computer-knowledgeable with good writers, science majors with artists. Using and sharing different expertise enhances everyone's learning. Here, shared scoring rubrics and topic choice work to challenge but not overwhelm each student.

CONCLUSION

One of my touchstones is to ask myself how I would have liked my education to have been. Not how was it, but what kind of experience would have been ideal? Then I try to teach to that vision. One of the most difficult things I have had to learn is to stop doing something if it does not work. It may be my favorite assignment or text. Every group of students is different, and the same strategies do not necessarily work from one group to another. When you know your students, you also know how unique each one is. To create an environment that gives each student the best opportunity to learn, faculty need to use varied teaching and assessment practices and research to see whether their methods are actually making a difference. Am I really doing what I think I'm doing? How do I know? These two questions need to be constantly asked and the answers used to validate what is going well and to change what is not.

REFERENCES

Angelo, T., & Cross, K. P. (1993). *Classroom assessment techniques: A handbook for college teachers.* San Francisco: Jossey-Bass.

Gardner, Howard. (1993). *Multiple intelligences: The theory in practice.* New York, NY: Basic Books.

Haycock, K. (1996). *Speech to Portland State University faculty on the Education Watch Report.* Portland, OR.

Hobson, A. (1999). *Physics: Concepts and connections.* Englewood Cliffs, NJ: Prentice-Hall.

Karre, I. (1994). *Busy, noisy and powerfully effective: Cooperative learning tools in the college classroom.* Self-published.

Lightman, A. (1994). *Einstein's dreams.* New York: Pantheon.

Schwartz, J., & McGuinness, M. (1979). *Einstein for beginners.* New York: Pantheon.

PART VI

SUMMARY

Chapter 13

Individualizing Instruction: Insights and Implications

Jeffrey E. Porter

This culminating chapter highlights common insights, along with some related practices, expressed by the contributing authors. It goes on to explore the implications of these insights for the culture of undergraduate education in which we work and live and points to some needed changes. It begins with a recapitulation of the book's introductory framework, as detailed in the first four chapters.

RECAPITULATION

Efforts by undergraduate teachers to support the learning of individual students take place at the intersection of the talent development model of educational excellence (Astin, 1985) and the uniqueness of individual undergraduate learners. When the criterion of educational excellence is defined as the difference made in supporting progress by each and every student toward a course's target objectives (or a degree program's target outcomes), and when the reality of unique individual learners is accepted as overwhelming the myth of the average learner, the importance of undergraduate teachers striving to individualize effectively their instructional efforts with students comes front and center.

The willingness and ability of teachers to respond instructionally to unique learning differences among students is critical in determining an educational program's approximation of excellence. Progress toward learning outcomes and long-term curricular goals falters when incongruity exists between the learning characteristics and strategies of individual students and the instructional environments that teachers orchestrate.

Individualizing instruction involves crafting an array of alternative learning /teaching paths for diverse students leading to common curricular outcomes. Its goal is to foster learning success by individual students. Elements of individualizing instruction are designing the overall course structure and classroom procedures, translating curricular objectives and course materials into sequential learning tasks with expected outcomes, implementing learning tasks through teaching strategies that foster student engagement and support learning success, and revising learning tasks, learning outcomes, and teaching strategies through ongoing assessment of student learning. At its core, individualizing instruction involves reflective teaching, viewing instruction as an ongoing act of instructional problem solving.

Reflective teaching fuels the development of alternative instructional approaches for supporting individual learners. Reflective teaching requires teachers to make explicit their implicit theories and personal orientations regarding how learning happens, what is worth learning in the first place, the role and responsibilities of students, and their role and responsibilities as teachers. It entails constantly holding up such assumptions made explicit to experience, and revising them accordingly. It means using one's evolving assumptions-made-explicit as a frame of reference for interpreting ongoing interactions with individual students, considering formal pedagogical theory and research, rethinking past teaching and learning experiences, incorporating the insights and suggestions of students, picking the brains of colleagues, and sparking intuitive hunches—all with the aim of figuring out how best to support the engagement and learning of *this* student, with *this* learning task, given *this* curricular objective. There are no precise formulas, no guaranteed prescriptions for realizing this aim. Instructional problem solving of this sort is complex, elusive, and idiosyncratic. It depends ultimately on partnership among teachers and students committed to innovative experimentation and learning success.

Reflective teaching does not mean teachers practicing in contemplative isolation. Just the opposite, reflective teaching naturally relies on sustained and intense interactions between teacher and students, and among teaching colleagues. It is informed by assessing continuously the progress (or lack thereof) arising from the interaction between a student's learning characteristics and strategies and a teacher's instructional approach. Such assessment is embedded in the learning/teaching process and guides reflective teaching. It provides data that shapes the hypotheses and interventions of the reflective teacher as pedagogical researcher. Assessment as embedded in individualizing instruction is aimed not primarily at normative comparisons of finished learning products, but illuminating the process of learning and enhancing its productivity along the way.

Student learning is an active, constructive, and personal process. Students learn when they apply the cognitive processes of acquisition, integration, application, and refinement to the content of learning tasks. Learning, however, includes more than just cognitive processes. Like all human action, learning is unitary and holistic, entailing motivational, affective, and behavioral capabilities as well as the cognitive. The student, not anyone or anything else, generates new learning based directly on his or her existing set of knowledge, skills, and ways of conceptualizing resulting from past experiences, motivational orientations, and operative learning strategies. Learning depends ultimately on student engagement with the learning task. The student plays the determinative role regarding the extent and nature of such engagement and the resulting quality of learning.

It is clear that individual learners engage the same learning task with uniquely different learning strategies, strategies differing along affective, organizing, and self-monitoring dimensions. The daily experiences of teachers and students working together make it clear that such differences among learners are sufficiently rich to defy capture by contrived taxonomies of learning styles. They also are sufficiently rich to reveal the reality of the *individual learner* as opposed to the fiction of the *average learner*.

The role of teacher in individualizing instruction involves crafting alternative instructional approaches for helping diverse students accomplish the learning task at hand, in light of expected learning outcomes and established curricular goals. It involves as well helping students develop new learning strategies, becoming more versatile, lifelong learners. The effectiveness of any instructional approach can be gauged by its capacity for fostering student engagement and success. Engagement is fostered by tailoring instruction to support and extend those learning characteristics (e.g., current levels of knowledge and skills motivational orientation) and those learning strategies (e.g., ways acquiring, integrating, and applying new content) that students bring to and apply throughout the learning event. Different instructional approaches will be more or less effective with different students; an approach effectively fostering engagement for one student with a learning task will not do so for another.

Individualizing instruction should be understood not as an impossible challenge (though to do it effectively with all students all the time surely is), but an educational ideal. It is an ideal that defines educational excellence in terms of the difference made with every student. It also is an ideal that frames teachers and students as partners, working together toward learning success based on pedagogical innovation.

INSIGHTS AND RELATED PRACTICES

In addressing the challenge of supporting successful learning by individual learners from their respective disciplinary perspectives, the contributing authors offer numerous insights about individualizing instruction and a host of related practices. Their insights are compiled below, along with a sampling of practices. A few words about this compilation are in order.

The insights offered in this volume, generated by teachers from a wide spectrum of undergraduate disciplines, range from the philosophical to the practical. Some echo points raised in the four introductory chapters, others present additional considerations. The manner in which I group these insights and illustrate where possible with selected practices, like any effort to categorize, reflects conceptual and communication convenience rather than the way things are. Some of the noted practices reflect more than one insight and their inclusion under one insight rather than another is arbitrary. As well, dividing lines between insight and practice, and among practices themselves, can be artificial. Insights both arise from and are expressed through practice, assessment practices also can be teaching practices, and the act of instructional problem solving encompasses and does not stand separate from the act of instruction itself. The seamless realities of insight embedded in practice and single practices serving multiple purposes underlie the categorization that follows.

Finally, from the compilation that follows, it is clear that many if not most of the insights and practices apply across the undergraduate disciplines included in this book. There may be some exceptions to this. For example, math's precise algorithms seem to lend themselves particularly well to computer-based assessment systems that generate individualized sequences of prescribed instructional modules (see Gunawardena, Chapter 7). As well, English composition and literature benefit naturally from writing-intensive activities that encourage the personal backgrounds and thinking of individual students to come to the surface, as well as from the well-established cycle of student draft/teacher feedback/student revision that enables students and teachers to accommodate and extend individual ways of understanding and learning (see Coon, Chapter 5; Paine-Clemes, Chapter 6). But overall, it appears that the challenge of tailoring instruction to support and extend individual learning is discipline-neutral, with teachers across discipline lines having much to offer and learn from one another.

Learning

1. Learning is most meaningful when it is an act of creation rather than replication; when the student is an active agent rather than a passive participant. Learning is struggling to make personal sense of new content in light of past experiences, current ways of acquiring and processing information, and future goals. (See Coon, Chapter 5; Paine-Clemes, Chapter 6; Gunawardena, Chapter 7; Kester, Chapter 8; Novemsky and Gautreau, Chapter 9; Isaacson, Chapter 10; Venable, Chapter 11.)

2. As personal as learning is, it also is a social activity. Learning is sense making in a social context. It is richest when students and teachers are contributing to, and benefiting from, the learning of one another. (See Coon, Chapter 5; Kester, Chapter 8; Novemsky and Gautreau, Chapter 9; Venable, Chapter 11; Patton, Chapter 12.)

3. Individual learners bring unique configurations of personal experiences, learning characteristics, and learning strategies to the classroom. Students generate learning when they build bridges (either by themselves, with your support, or perhaps through working with other students). These bridges connect what the student brings with the specific content of the learning task at hand and related content in other domains, both curricular and real-life. (See Coon, Chapter 5; Kester, Chapter 8; Isaacson, Chapter 10.)

4. All students can learn; talent is modifiable. This does not imply equity among individual students in terms of the final level of learning outcome resulting from engagement in any particular learning event. Even when time of engagement, instructional approaches, and learning strategies are allowed to vary among individual students in order to maximize learning, some students always will learn more and more deeply than others. The complexity of learning and range of individual differences assures this. What it does mean is this: For any particular student able to qualify for admissions to an undergraduate program, any particular learning task and corresponding instructional approach can be designed and revised in ways that accommodate and extend that student's learning characteristics and learning strategies, such that the student engages the task and is able to realize a satisfactory level of learning outcome. (See Gunawardena, Chapter 7; Kester, Chapter 8; Isaacson, Chapter 10.)

Instruction

1. Effective learning by individual students is significantly influenced by your instructional skills, including your teaching and assessment expertise. Ul-

timately, however, it is a function of what individual students bring to the learning task, the nature of their existing knowledge and skills, their motivational deposition to engage and sustain effort, their metacognitive adroitness in monitoring and revising learning strategies to optimize performance, and their willingness to accept ultimate ownership and responsibility for learning success or failure. Progress in realizing learning outcomes and curricular objectives is best understood and accounted for in terms of this interaction between student and teacher factors, with student factors playing the determinative role. (See Paine-Clemes, Chapter 6; Gunawardena, Chapter 7; Kester, Chapter 8; Isaacson, Chapter 10; Venable; Chapter 11.)

2. Your creation of alternative teaching and assessment strategies for supporting the learning of individual students cannot come at the expense of established curricular goals and academic standards. This is an ongoing tension for teachers, arising from deep commitment both to the promise of individual learners and to the integrity of established goals and standards. (See Paine-Clemes, Chapter 6; Gunawardena, Chapter 7; Kester, Chapter 8; Isaacson, Chapter 10.)

3. Efforts to individualize instruction should aim not only at supporting existing learning strategies, but requiring students to experiment and practice new ones as well. Undergraduate education aspires to helping students develop new ways of learning, beyond learning new content. In acting on this aspiration, you need to ensure that expected outcomes of learning tasks and long-term curricular goals focus on ways of learning as well as content, and craft your instructional approaches for supporting individual students accordingly. (See Kester, Chapter 8; Isaacson, Chapter 10; Venable, Chapter 11.)

4. To identify and respond to diverse learning characteristics and strategies among individual students, you have to figure out how to conduct classes in ways that bring them to the surface. Strategies for doing so are many and varied, but their common thread is arranging classroom dynamics to call upon, liberate, and reveal personal stories and ways of processing and interpreting new learning among individual students. Once revealed, individual differences can be used to enrich already established learning tasks with the added implications and multiple perspectives that unique learners bring. Individual differences also can inform variation of your existing instructional approach in ways that better relate to the backgrounds and better support and expand the learning strategies of individual learners. Revealed individual differences are vital in guiding your ongoing instructional problem-solving. (See Coon, Chapter 5; Paine-Clemes, Chapter 6; Gunawardena, Chapter 7; Venable, Chapter 11; Patton, Chapter 12.)

5. The notion of individualizing instruction could conjure up images of solitary students confined to study carrels, immersed in self-paced learning mod-

ules and cabled to computers (released from their learning cells weekly perhaps to attend one-on-one tutorials). On the contrary, individualizing instruction not only *can* happen, but many times happens *best*, in group contexts with other students. You can orchestrate group activities to bring to the surface learning differences among students that make visible the endless diversity in how people learn. Diversity made visible helps students better understand their own ways of learning, provides new strategies to model, and lays the groundwork for ongoing emphasis throughout the course on the relative merits of alternative strategies. (See Coon, Chapter 5; Paine-Clemes, Chapter 6; Gunawardena, Chapter 7; Kester, Chapter 8; Novemsky and Gautreau, Chapter 9; Venable, Chapter 11; Patton, Chapter 12.)

Sample Practices:

- If possible, arrange the classroom so that all students easily can see, hear, and communicate with one another and are able to move between small-group and whole-group formats. (See Patton, Chapter 12.)

- Using a technique like "think/pair/share," ask teams of students to compare notes after ten minutes of lecture and generate questions for both teacher and classwide clarification. Such activities change the pace of a class and provide opportunities for *all* students to participate. (See Novemsky and Gautreau, Chapter 9.)

- During as many classes as possible throughout the course, structure learning tasks to require meaningful interaction among students in groups of three or four. Circulate among the groups, listening, participating, and coaching from the sidelines as appropriate. Such small-group learning activities can accommodate widely diverse learning characteristics and learning strategies among individual students, with students pushing and pulling each other's thinking and learning rather than passively listening to you lecture. (See Kester, Chapter 8; Novemsky and Gautreau, Chapter 9.)

- To make sure students are ready for engaging in such in-class learning tasks, create out-of-class assignments that require students to prepare beforehand (e.g., written assignments on scheduled class topics that are to be brought to class and discussed in small groups; see Coon, Chapter 5).

- Use group projects as long-term learning vehicles, requiring collaborative work among students in selecting, researching, and presenting on a topic. A group project brings to the surface individual learning differences, revealing student talents that might not otherwise surface. It provides opportunities to show group members that there is more than one way to solve problems and allows members to observe, interact with, and model diverse ways of learning among their peers. (See Patton, Chapter 12.)

- Use peer critique groups to discuss the formative status of individual or group projects. (See Patton, Chapter 12.)

6. It trivializes individualizing instruction to view it as merely rifling through a pedagogical bag of tricks until you find one that works for a particular student engaged in a particular learning task. The operative mentality for this kind of approach simply would be "the bigger the bag, the better." When you individualize instruction, it is not about how many pedagogical tricks you possess. It is not about randomly applying instructional techniques until you find one that works. In the end, it is about your guiding assumptions about learning and teaching, your orientation toward the roles of teacher and student, and your commitment to and belief in the promise of the individual learner. This is the realm that gives meaning to, and legitimizes, any particular instructional approach you choose. It is about framing your instructional efforts with some first beliefs: that the particular learning task at hand is worthwhile, that the students you work with have promise in generating significant learning for themselves, and that your role as teacher is to care about and invest in helping fulfill that promise. (See Paine-Clemes, Chapter 6; Isaacson, Chapter 10; Venable, Chapter 11.)

7. Effectively supporting individual learners requires providing students a rich array of learning tasks (supporting but also stretching existing learning strategies) that help build bridges between what a student brings to a learning event and the skills and knowledge defining expected learning outcomes. You need to reach out to individual learners with a variety of instructional approaches that support their task engagement and creation of personal meaning. (See Coon, Chapter 5; Gunawardena, Chapter 7; Kester, Chapter 8; Isaacson, Chapter 10; Venable, Chapter 11; Patton, Chapter 12.)

Sample Practices:

- Where appropriate, develop individual learning contracts representing student/teacher partnerships based on a student's personal interests or assessed strengths and weaknesses in relation to course objectives. Such contracts should be subject to periodic review and revision between you and the student. (See Paine-Clemes, Chapter 6.)

- Incorporate as many diverse learning tasks in your course as possible, while ensuring their relevance to established course objectives and standards. Such activities need to reflect a variety of formats and media (lectures, hands-on experiences, group discussion, computer simulation, 3–D models, video, text, collaborative activities, independent projects, etc.). They need to be manageable for students (in terms of the time required for task engagement and degree of difficulty) and, where possible, self-paced. Allow students to engage in learning tasks that are familiar and comfortable; also require students to experience novel learning tasks with unfamiliar requirements so that they gain practice with alternative ways of learning. (See Coon, Chapter 5; Gunawardena, Chapter 7; Kester, Chapter 8; Isaacson, Chapter 10; Venable, Chapter 11; Patton, Chapter 12.)

- Provide as many diverse examples and analogies as possible in building bridges between course content and individual learners. Emphasize the point that there is no one best way for every learner to understand an idea, solve a problem, or refine a skill; each learner needs to create his or her own best way. (See Isaacson, Chapter 10.)

8. Effective teachers radiate a variety of roles, depending on the individual learner, expected learning outcomes, and long-term curricular goals. These roles include teacher as senior partner, coresponsible with students for interweaving teaching, assessment, and learning strategies in supporting productive learning; teacher as expert, serving as the source of authoritative information; teacher as consultant/coach, providing advice and feedback to students on the learning strategies they are using in striving to achieve learning success; teacher as resource person for students to consult throughout their learning inquiries; and teacher as master learner, role modeling how to solve problems, conduct inquiry, experiment with new approaches, and savor learning within a particular disciplinary context. (See Coon, Chapter 5; Paine-Clemes, Chapter 6; Gunawardena, Chapter 7; Kester, Chapter 8; Novemsky and Gautreau, Chapter 9; Isaacson, Chapter 10; Venable, Chapter 11; Patton, Chapter 12.)

9. You enhance student learning when you create classroom environments that emphasize the joy of learning beyond earning a grade, encouraging in students a sense of confidence and control in their learning endeavors. (See Paine-Clemes, Chapter 6; Isaacson, Chapter 10; Patton, Chapter 12.)

10. You enhance student engagement with learning tasks when your instructional approaches enable individual students to (a) experience optimal disequilibrium between current abilities and expected learning outcomes. (See Kester, Chapter 8.) and (b) experience choice and control over what is learned, how learning happens, and how it is assessed. (See Coon, Chapter 5; Paine-Clemes, Chapter 6; Kester, Chapter 8; Isaacson, Chapter 10; Venable, Chapter 11; Patton, Chapter 12.)

Sample Practices:

- Give students a voice in designing and choosing among learning tasks and assessment strategies, so that they have opportunities to act on their interests and knowledge regarding course content, how best they learn, and how best they can demonstrate such learning. Provide open-ended in-class learning tasks, homework assignments, and long-range projects; encourage students to pursue their own questions. (See Coon, Chapter 5; Kester, Chapter 8; Isaacson, Chapter 10; Venable, Chapter 11; Patton, Chapter 12.)

- Give students guidelines for doing projects, but don't spell out project requirements to the point of imposing a cookie cutter template for turning out their finished products. Give students a role in shaping learning projects. (See Patton, Chapter 12.)

(c) have ongoing opportunities to assess their own learning progress and figure out how to improve through targeted feedback arranged by the teacher. (See Coon, Chapter 5; Paine-Clemes, Chapter 6; Gunawardena, Chapter 7; Kester, Chapter 8; Isaacson, Chapter 10; Venable, Chapter 11.)

Sample Practices:

- Ensure that your syllabus provides detailed course expectations about the what of expected learning outcomes and the when of learning assessments so that individual students will know the big picture and where they stand along the way. Conduct sign-posting sessions for students throughout the course (e.g., "This is what we have accomplished so far," "This is why we are doing this now," "This is how it is related to what we will do later." (See Kester, Chapter 8.)

- Establish vehicles for early, frequent, ongoing, prompt, and focused feedback for students on their learning progress. Feedback needs to inform students about their progress toward content mastery, and the appropriateness and productiveness of their learning strategies. (See Coon, Chapter 5; Kester, Chapter 8; Venable, Chapter 11.)

- Give feedback to students about learning that goes beyond simply how they are doing. Give feedback that explains *why* they are succeeding or failing in terms of the learning strategies they are using and what they can do differently to improve. (See Isaacson, Chapter 10.)

(d) assume personal responsibility for being the locus of their learning efforts and determiner of their learning outcomes. (See Paine-Clemes, Chapter 6; Kester, Chapter 8; Venable, Chapter 11.)

Sample Practice:

- Use nested assignments that incorporate both *individual* and *team* components and that can be worked on both in and out of class. Nested assignments promote individual and collective responsibility among students for both their own learning and the learning of their peers. They also can free you up during class to spend more time working with groups and individuals. (See Venable, Chapter10.)

(e) learn how to frame the meaning of learning success and failure in ways that foster sustained learning effort. (See Kester, Chapter 8; Isaacson, Chapter 10.)

11. In your efforts to individualize instruction, emphasize the importance of students paying attention to their own learning strategies and evaluating how best to learn in which situations. Whatever your discipline, this emphasis

can become part of your course content. Individualizing instruction entails not only supporting students' existing learning strategies but stretching students to practice and develop less familiar ways of learning. Promote among students an appreciation for the differential effectiveness of alternative ways of learning for different kinds of learning tasks, and encourage students to learn from one another in analyzing and experimenting with the learning strategies of classmates as potential strategies for themselves. (See Coon, Chapter 5; Paine-Clemes, Chapter 6; Kester, Chapter 8; Isaacson, Chapter 10; Venable, Chapter 11; Patton, Chapter 12.)

Sample Practices:

- Encourage students to identify the various ways they learn and their associated strengths and weakness. Make such analyses an ongoing aspect of your course. Encourage students to stretch in trying out new learning strategies by requiring engagement with a variety of learning tasks within a variety of instructional approaches. (See Patton, Chapter 12.)

- Select and administer a learning style inventory at the beginning of your course. Share and discuss critically, both individually and with the whole class as appropriate, how the results illuminate (or perhaps overlook) key individual learning characteristics and strategies. Refer to the results throughout your course when discussing learning successes and failures. (See Kester, Chapter 8; Isaacson, Chapter 10; Patton, Chapter 12.)

- Require students to keep study skills journals that help them examine their own learning and develop more ownership for it. Ask students to voluntarily share their entries occasionally with the class so as a group they can learn to understand and value the diversity of individual learning approaches. Encourage students to analyze where and why a particular learning strategy is working for them and where and why it isn't. Encourage students to evaluate for themselves what they have learned about their learning strategies and outcomes along the way and what they have to do differently to improve learning productivity. (See Kester, Chapter 8; Isaacson, Chapter 10.)

- Role-model your own reflective teaching publicly, in front of your students. Create an open environment in which students are encouraged to dissect your own process of instructional problem solving, the learning tasks you create, and the teaching and assessment strategies you use; ask them relate this to their own learning strategies (reflective learning and reflective teaching, after all, being two sides of the same coin). (See Isaacson, Chapter 10.)

12. Teachers aiming to support and extend student learning need to get to know their students. Instructional problem-solving is informed and refined by this knowledge. Improved instructional problem-solving, however, is only part of the goal. A more fundamental reason for teachers and students creating

ways to know each other more deeply is the cultivation of genuine caring, re-spect, and mutual commitment among partners in the learning/teaching en-terprise. This is the stuff, more than pedagogical techniques, that sparks and sustains student learning. (See Coon, Chapter 5; Gunawardena, Chapter 7; Kester, Chapter 8; Isaacson, Chapter 10; Venable, Chapter 11; Patton, Chap-ter 12.)

Sample Practices:

- Collect information from individual students at the beginning of the course on such issues as reasons for taking the course, personal interests, prior coursework, work ex-periences, and first spoken language. Information like this gives you a flavor for the class and helps to inform your instructional problem solving throughout the course. (See Coon, Chapter 5; Kester, Chapter 8; Isaacson, Chapter 10; Venable, Chapter 11.)

- Maximize opportunities for personal contact between yourself and your students throughout the course. Get to know your students (using such vehicles as frequent mini writing assignments, individual conferences, e-mail correspondence, in-class observations of small-group discussions, and assignments that encourage students to share their personal histories and outlooks) so that you can become more familiar with their individual ways of learning, assess their learning progress, and forge com-mitted learning/teaching partnerships. Be as available as possible to students out-side class. (See Coon, Chapter 5; Paine-Clemes, Chapter 6; Kester, Chapter 8; Venable, Chapter 11.)

- To create as much personal contact for students as possible, recruit and train a pool of peer mentors to get to know and work with individual students beyond the times you are available. (See Isaacson, Chapter 10.)

13. Use the assessment information you generate throughout the course as a source for your instructional problem solving efforts to individualize instruc-tion, beyond evaluating the final learning outcomes of students at the end of the course.

Sample Practices:

- Create vehicles such as those noted below for monitoring and staying in touch with the ongoing learning experiences of individual students. (See all chapters.)
- eliciting students' prior knowledge regarding the topic being introduced
- requiring students to create and share their own course study guides
- requiring students to keep their own journals—on both course content and their metacognitive reflections about the effectiveness of their learning strategies
- using free writing by individual students or brief discussions among pairs or small groups of students on questions you insert throughout lectures (followed by classwide votes on alternative solutions and opportunities for resolving differences)

- conducting postmortems with students on their learning task experiences
- carefully observing, listening, and scanning the body language of individual students during small-group exercises
- using open-ended, extended assessment tools like course-long writing assignments and projects that allow for ongoing revisions and give and take between you and students, and that reveal the evolving learning refinements of individual students
- Develop and apply your own set of indicators that signal when students are engaging effectively with learning activities. Examples of indicators are students being able to provide their own correct explanations for new learning content and being able to reclaim and apply past content without significant relearning (see Kester, Chapter 8); students demonstrating greater investment of time and effort in learning tasks; students expressing and incorporating personal interests and abilities related to the learning task at hand, increased participation in class, and increased willingness to ask questions. (See Coon, Chapter 5.)

14. Be aware (and beware!) of the powerful link between the choices you make and the criteria you use in assessing learning outcomes to determine student grades and how students go about learning in response. (See Isaacson, Chapter 10.) Rhetoric affirming the value of diverse ways of learning does not have a chance against the gravitational pull of narrowly conceived evaluation systems that reward only one (of several possible) correct solutions, and only one (of several possible) ways of arriving there. Such evaluation systems, so much a part of undergraduate education, make the game all too clear: perform on the test however the teacher wants you to perform in order to get the highest grade possible. If, for example, you believe in the importance of students learning the skill of relating discrete incidents as examples of overarching conceptual principles, and you have spent time and effort with students illustrating and practicing this conceptual ability, don't then assess how well students have learned this expected outcome by asking them to merely list the memorized sequence of steps necessary for its execution! If you do this, know that students will depart your course more practiced in memorizing than conceptualizing. Whatever ways of learning and knowing stand out for you as most important for students to practice and develop in encountering the substance and nuances of your discipline, make sure they are reflected as genuinely as possible in the pragmatics of your assessment efforts.

15. Your assessment of how individual students are progressing over time is a natural means for informing your ongoing reflective instructional problem solving about how to support student learning as productively as possible. Assessment and reflective instructional problem solving are complementary activities carried out by teachers attempting to support effectively the learning of individual students.

Sample Practices:

- Take time after each class to think through and make notes in your course portfolio about what happened, speculations about why, and hypotheses about learning and teaching to test during upcoming class sessions. (See Kester, Chapter 8.)
- Instructional problem solving with individual students consists of collecting information from the student about current knowledge, skills, conceptual perspectives, learning strategies, personal interests, and motivational orientation in engaging the learning task at hand; helping the student overcome low confidence, make more appropriate attributions for failure, and move beyond rigid problem-solving approaches; reconsidering and redesigning your instructional approach in light of such collected information; and supporting the student in practicing alternative, more productive learning strategies. Successful reflective instructional problem solving requires considering a variety of factors (e.g., assumptions about how learning happens, the expected outcomes and curricular goals framing the learning task, learning task design, teaching and assessment strategies, time available, student learning characteristics and strategies) and relies on mutual commitment and ongoing adaptability between student and teacher. (See Coon, Chapter 5; Paine-Clemes, Chapter 6; Kester, Chapter 8; Isaacson, Chapter 10.)
- Constantly try out and evaluate new teaching and assessment strategies with students in the spirit of pedagogical research; seldom make wholesale changes in instructional approaches but instead tinker with one or two new initiatives at a time and systematically assess the impact. (See Kester, Chapter 8; Isaacson, Chapter 10; Venable, Chapter 11.)

16. Instructional problem solving is greatly enhanced by the wisdom and shared experiences of your fellow teachers. Reflective teaching is diminished when it happens in isolation, deprived of ongoing contact with colleagues working on learning/teaching challenges of their own and who are committed to supporting and learning from one another. Reflective teaching is nourished when it is embedded in such collegial relationships. Engage your colleagues in collective reflective teaching, share difficulties, test out insights, vent frustrations, celebrate successes. (See Isaacson, Chapter 10; Venable, Chapter 11; Patton, Chapter 12.)

17. Instructional technologies can be powerful tools for individualizing instruction. These technologies can enrich in-class learning activities, as well as extend learning/teaching interactions among students and teachers beyond classroom constraints of space and time. For all their potential power as tools for individualizing instruction, instructional technologies rely on the skills and experiences of you as reflective practitioner in applying them in ways that support the academic success of individual learners. Incorporating instructional technologies within your instructional approaches has to be well thought out,

implemented with sufficient budgeting and technical support, and evaluated along the way in terms of the difference made for student learning. If it is not, student learning can be hindered rather than helped. (See Coon, Chapter 5; Gunawardena, Chapter 7; Kester, Chapter 8; Isaacson, Chapter 10; Venable, Chapter 11.)

Sample Practices:

- Record-keeping utilities for tracking the changing performance status of individual learners (see Gunawardena, Chapter 7)

- Assessing the profile of competencies for individual students in terms of course placement and charting student mastery of learning outcomes throughout the course (see Gunawardena, Chapter 7)

- Self-paced student progression through sequential instructional modules (based on demonstrated mastery of learning outcomes along the way) (see Gunawardena, Chapter 7)

- Alternative multimedia modalities (text, audio, graphics) responding to diverse ways of learning (see Coon, Chapter 5; Kester, Chapter 8)

- Teacher preparation of instructional materials or student presentation of completed learning projects (e.g., through PowerPoint®, Web page editors) (see Coon, Chapter 5; Venable, Chapter 11)

- Reflections and journal writing by individual students, and use of thinking tools for brainstorming and organizing writing content through various software applications (see Kester, Chapter 8)

- Communications among teachers and students (e.g., using e-mail and discussion-group software applications) serving a variety of purposes: content clarification, recording and sharing of journal entries, involving students who might be reluctant to speak out in class, and the like (see Coon, Chapter 5; Kester, Chapter 8; Isaacson, Chapter 10; Venable, Chapter 11)

- Access to information and databases through the Internet (see Coon, Chapter 5; Kester, Chapter 8)

- Using course Web sites for posting course materials, reading assignments, and self-assessment quizzes (see Isaacson, Chapter 10; Venable, Chapter 11)

- Using computerized classrooms and laboratories (see Gunawardena, Chapter 7; Venable, Chapter 11)

IMPLICATIONS FOR NEW WAYS OF DOING BUSINESS

The preceding section summarizes insights and practices related to individualizing instruction, as generated by contributing authors representing a variety of undergraduate disciplines. Individualizing instruction represents a pedagogical ideal supporting a particular vision of educational excellence, the talent development model. Ideals and vision aside, however, undergraduate education's current dominant culture works against systematic efforts to support the learning of individual students, by even the most skilled and persistent teachers. Traditional student and faculty roles and expectations about learning and teaching are too ingrained, incentives for supporting the learning of individual students too weak, and focus on the learning/teaching enterprise too peripheral.

The point, of course, is not to set aside ideals and vision, not to be content with our current undergraduate culture. What matters is not our inevitable educational shortcomings in supporting the learning success of students as often as we would like. Practice is not supposed to be perfect. What does matter is which vision of educational excellence we choose to work toward and how we use this vision to transform our existing organizational culture and the roles, aims, and practices of teachers and students within the culture.

Below are some of the parameters and changes central to the needed transformation, if indeed we are to better approximate the ideal of supporting the success of every learner. The needed changes within these six parameters mutually reinforce one another; change in one area depends on changes in the others.

Mission Excellence

- View an undergraduate program's mission not as conducting teaching, but as helping students produce learning; not disseminating knowledge to students but creating educational environments responsive to individual students constructing learning for themselves (Barr & Tagg, 1995; Levine, 2000; Spence, 2001).

- Shift from defining educational excellence in terms of such criteria as institutional resources or ranked prestige to the talent development model, with excellence calibrated in terms of the difference made with individual students in supporting their engagement with learning and accomplishment of program outcomes (Astin, 1985; Barr & Tagg, 1995; Guskin, 1994; Kuh, 2001).

- Base the awarding of a college degree, symbolizing an individual student's fulfillment of the college's mission, not on satisfying a required number of total credit hours but on demonstrating achievement of those knowledge, skills, attitudes and ways of thinking established as the intended overall program outcomes (Barr & Tagg, 1995). The traditional approach for conceptualizing the nature and amount of student learning relies on the metric of number of academic courses taken and passed. This metric leaves murky the actual proficiencies realized by students as a result of their course experiences. A different unit of analysis is needed. This unit would make explicit that which has been left implicit, "demonstrated proficiencies as a result of learning" (Weingartner, 1994). Accrediting agencies throughout higher education more and more require this new metric. If undergraduate education doesn't respond, legislative and funding agencies will (Kuh, 2001).

- View student mastery of discipline-based subject matter not as an end, but as a powerful tool serving an even more powerful goal: students developing themselves as lifelong learners, dedicated to lifelong fulfillment of their human capabilities (Orr, 1994).

Faculty Role

- The traditional role of undergraduate teachers is not one of creating learning space for individual students to fill with their own learning, but creating teaching space to fill with their own teaching (Palmer, 1993). The role of teacher as discipline expert—imparting knowledge primarily if not exclusively through lecturing and standing apart from the strivings of individual students to master content and develop new ways of learning—needs to be replaced. It needs replacement by the more complete role of teacher as designer of responsive learning environments, supporting and investing in the learning success of diverse individual students through alternative instructional approaches (Barr & Tagg, 1995; Edgerton, 1993a; Spence, 2001).

- Teachers need to define themselves as coresponsible with the individual student for learning success (and failure) (Barr & Tagg, 1995). This coresponsible relationship is one in which students are fully responsible for their own learning, and teachers are fully responsible for supporting them.

- A vision of the personal orientation and attributes of teachers who effectively individualize instruction includes a passion for their discipline, a deep respect and liking for students, and an unfaltering commitment to find effective ways of helping individual students engage and learn from their discipline (Carson, 1996); a view of students as fellow travelers, with the teacher as actively involved in learning within the learning/teaching relationship as the students (Welker, 1991); and a view of teaching as not simply a matter of competency, but of investment in another (Palmer, 1997; Welker).

Aims of Instruction

- A traditional goal of undergraduate instruction is disseminating information to groups of students, with teachers as sources and students as receptacles. A new way of envisioning the goal of instruction is needed, one that strives to foster student engagement with learning in a rich context of reciprocal interaction between students and teacher and among students themselves. In such instructional contexts, all participants, students and teacher, become sources of learning (Edgerton, 1993b; Guskin, 1994).

- The aim of instruction needs to be supporting individual students in learning content for themselves, not covering content for students. Teachers' instructional approaches, whatever the disciplinary domain, need to have the goal of helping students make this shift from passive recording of information to active learning (Edgerton, 1993b).

- As much emphasis is as placed on helping students achieve mastery of discipline-based knowledge, equal emphasis is needed on helping students develop both discipline-based skills of inquiry and expanded learning strategies. Teachers, as master learners, need to model skills of lifelong learning (e.g., alternative ways of accessing and sifting through information, forging connections, generating hypothetical models, making reasoned judgments based on available evidence), and support such skill development in their students (Welker, 1991).

- Instruction needs to continue to explore the incorporation of various instructional technologies in supporting individual learners (Guskin, 1994). The benefit promised by these technologies is tremendously exciting; delivering content and providing access to endless information among fellow travelers engaged in a common learning/teaching enterprise and doing so in ways highly responsive to the diverse learning characteristics of individual students (Green & Gilbert, 1995). This promise can be realized, but only through the experience and guidance of teachers and students working together to experiment with and refine these technological tools.

- Instead of holding time, learning tasks, and teaching and assessment strategies constant while allowing outcome levels of learning to vary among individual students, the goal of instruction needs to be holding constant the expected levels of learning outcome and supporting students in achieving them by allowing everything else to vary (Astin, 1990, Barr & Tagg, 1995; Bloom, 1976).

- Rather than evaluating instructional quality in terms of the traditional constellation of criteria (teacher knows content, teacher is organized in delivering information, teacher shows enthusiasm about his/her discipline, etc.), instruction needs to be evaluated in terms of its defining goal; positive impact on the learning of individual students (Barr & Tagg, 1995).

Student Role

- Students need to shift from taking courses to making learning, from being passive receptacles of other people's learning to becoming their own sources of learning (Barr & Tagg, 1995; Ehrmann, 1999; Guskin, 1994; Welker, 1991).

- Students need to rely more on personal curiosity, a sense of competency, and growth toward personal goals as sources of motivation for their learning efforts and less on the teacher-controlled dispensation of points, grades and other extrinsic incentives (Guskin, 1994).

- Students need to see themselves in partnership with teachers for support and guidance throughout their learning efforts, but ultimately as responsible for their own learning outcomes (McKeachie, Pintrich, & Lin, 1985).

- Students need to focus on and value learning not only in terms of finished products (e.g., newly acquired knowledge, skills, or attitudes) but also in terms of the processes they use to generate those products (e.g., analyzing which learning strategies are more or less productive for which learning events). Students need to be open and committed to developing richer repertoires of alternative learning strategies. When colleges talk about helping students develop the skills of lifelong learning, and incorporate such talk in mission statements, this is precisely what is being described. Students need to hold themselves, and us as teachers, responsible for making real this rhetoric through the way we work together in the learning/teaching enterprise.

Organizational Support for Learning and Teaching

- Most undergraduate faculty members spend most of their time teaching. This reality, coupled with the reality that teaching generally is not the faculty activity most rewarded in the culture of undergraduate education, has been termed the great paradox of academic work (Clark, 1987). Fairweather (1993) has presented data illustrating this paradox, showing that among four-year institutions in general, the more time faculty spend teaching, the lower their pay; the more time spent on research, the greater the pay. Research activity is where the rewards are (Massy & Wilger, 1995). Efforts by undergraduate institutions to maximize their public prestige (given traditional ways of defining educational excellence) coupled with efforts by individual faculty to establish and advance their own careers (given the payoff value of research and publications) generally conspire against teaching being highly valued within undergraduate education (Winston, 1994).

- Paulsen and Feldman (1995) summarize various characteristics of those undergraduate communities where this traditional norm fails to prevail, and where instead teaching in support of student learning is highly prized. Such characteristics include support of senior administrators, shared values among community members, the existence of faculty development programs, and broadening the conception of traditional scholarship to include teaching and learning as suitable subject matter. These characteristics, taken together, describe institutions where substantive issues of learning and teaching are at the center of community life. Where "pedagogical solitude" (Shulman, 1993) and the "privatization of teaching" (Palmer, 1993) are abandoned in favor of ongoing discourse among teaching colleagues; discourse representing nothing less than collective reflective teaching, with teachers learning as much about themselves as about their pedagogy (Palmer, 1997; Roth, 1997). Where philosophical debates, practical critiques, interpretation of research findings and speculation over their practical significance, and daily frustrations and triumphs—all having to do with learning and teaching—are the stuff of sustained community focus. Where indeed teachers create learning communities not only with their students at the classroom level, but with one another all across the campus. Within such undergraduate institutions, learning and teaching become the community property of scholars (Edgerton, 1993a). Within such communities, teaching in support of learning is not just a high priority, it is the core value.

- Undergraduate programs, in their academic policies, pedagogical approaches, scheduling practices (for individual courses and the academic calendar), and organizational structures often reflect more concern for the convenience and preference of administrators and teachers than for enhancing the learning of individual students (Terenzini et al., 1994; Vorkink, 1995). The challenge for programs dedicated to supporting optimally the learning of individual students is to reverse this institutional priority. Decisions about organizational structure and practice need to flow from the focal point of the institution's mission and meaning: supporting the academic success of individual learners (Lidman, Smith, & Purce, 1995).

Defining Instructional Costs and Faculty Productivity

- Following Massey and Wilger (1995) and Barr and Tagg (1995), how an undergraduate institution calculates cost of instruction and faculty productivity in carrying out instruction comes down to how it defines its educational mission and the role of its teachers. The traditional mission of undergraduate institutions is to teach, operationally defined as transmitting knowledge to a large number of students. From this perspective, instructional costs are figured in terms of cost per unit of instruction per student. In such an equation, each teacher represents a cost center, with students serving to concentrate or thin out instructional costs, in proportion to their numbers. The way to increase teacher productivity from this perspective is to increase the number of students per course, or the number of courses constituting teachers' workloads. Both strategies clearly hinder teachers having the time, focus, and energy to work toward supporting the success of individual learners.

- From a different perspective, one reinforced throughout this book, the educational mission of undergraduate institutions, the path toward educational excellence, is not to teach, but to support effective student learning. The role of teachers is not transmitting knowledge, but creating alternative instructional environments responsive to supporting and extending the learning of individual students. This perspective calculates instructional costs in terms of cost per unit of learning per student. Teacher productivity in this perspective now can be increased by teachers helping more students learn, as well as helping students develop progressively more powerful learning strategies for themselves. What is important is that such means for increasing teacher productivity encourage, not hinder, the investment of teacher time, focus, and energy toward supporting the success of every learner. In the economics of teaching and learning within this alternative model, teachers still represent fixed cost centers, but now individual students become their own revenue streams based on their learning gains and their skill in developing more powerful learning strategies (Spence, 2001). The engine driving improvement in instructional productivity appropriately becomes student learning, with instructional efforts by teachers accounted for *not* in and of themselves, but in terms of how well they contribute to and enhance such learning.

CONCLUSION

Teachers who strive to support the success of individual learners make a substantial commitment. Direct costs—in terms of time, energy, focus, humbling self-scrutiny, and ceaseless problem solving—are considerable. The indirect costs include the time and energy not allocated to traditional research and publication activities because of the commitment to supporting student success (with such costs magnified by an organizational culture typically rewarding the former over the latter). Indirect costs also can include the personal toll of being out of step with your colleagues, your department, and the broader educational community about institutional focus and priority; about the bottom line and how we conceptualize and measure it. It is easy to appreciate why the virtues of individualizing instruction in undergraduate education are expressed more often in rhetoric than in practice (Pascarella & Terenzini, 1991).

The benefits of striving to individualize instruction, on the other hand, are considerable. In their comprehensive synthesis of research findings regarding on the impact of undergraduate education, Pascarella & Terenzini (1991, p. 646) conclude "Instructional approaches that accommodate variations in student learning styles and rates appear to produce greater subject matter mastery than do more conventional approaches." The costs of *not* striving to support the academic success of individual students also must be considered. The roughly 45% of first-time students who enroll in two- and four-year colleges without earning a degree (Gumport et al., 1997; Tinto, 1987) represent huge costs; not only narrowly in terms of lost institutional revenue but broadly, in terms of wasted individual potential and human capital. Effective efforts to individualize instruction would reduce substantially this unacceptable level of attrition.

In the end, do the benefits of efforts to support individual student learning keep pace with the costs? Ultimately, the issue of the costs and benefits of individualizing instruction is inseparable from the issue of which model of excellence should anchor undergraduate education. If the excellence of an undergraduate program depends on the scholarly reputation of its faculty, the SAT scores of the entering class, its endowment size, or the average starting salary of its graduates, the costs of individualizing instruction are difficult to justify. If, instead, approximating educational excellence depends on the talent development of each and every student in light of established program outcomes and standards, then efforts to individualize instruction not only become justified but define the role of teacher and the meaning of teaching.

REFERENCES

Astin, A. W. (1985). *Achieving educational excellence*. San Francisco: Jossey-Bass.

Astin, A. W. (1990). Educational assessment and educational equity. *American Journal of Education*, 98(4), 458–478.

Barr, R. B., & Tagg, J. (1995). From teaching to learning . . . a new paradigm for undergraduate education. *Change*, 27(6), 13–25.

Bloom, B. S. (1976). *Human characteristics and school learning.* New York: McGraw-Hill.

Carson, B. H. (1996). Thirty years of stories. *Change*, 28(6), 11–17.

Clark, B. (1987). *The academic life: Small worlds, different worlds.* Princeton, NJ: Carnegie Foundation for the Advancement of Teaching.

Edgerton, R. (1993a). The reexamination of faculty priorities. *Change*, 25(4), 10–25.

Edgerton, R. (1993b). The tasks faculty perform. *Change*, 25(4), 4–6.

Ehrmann, S. C. (1999, September/October). Technology's grand challenges. *ACADEME*, 85(5), 42–46.

Fairweather, J. S. (1993). Faculty rewards reconsidered: The nature of tradeoffs. *Change*, 25(4), 44–47.

Green, K. C., & Gilbert, S. W. (1995). Great expectations: Content communications, productivity, and the role of information technology in higher education. *Change*, 27(2), 8–18.

Gumport, P. J., Iannozzi, M., Sharman, S., & Zemsky, R. (1997). *Trends in United States higher education from massification to post massification.* Stanford, CA: National Center for Postsecondary Improvement.

Guskin, A. E. (1994, September/October). Restructuring the role of the faculty. *Change*, 26(5), 16–25.

Kuh, G. (2001, May/June). Assessing what really matters to student learning. *Change*, 33(3), 10–17, 66.

Levine, A. E. (2000, October 27). The future of colleges: 9 inevitable changes. *Chronicle of Higher Education*, B10–B11.

Lidman, R. M., Smith, B. L., & Purce, T. L. (1995). Good practice respects diverse talents and ways of learning. In S. R. Hatfield (Ed.), *The seven principles in action* (pp. 95–106). Bolton, MA: Anker.

Massey, W. F., & Wilger, A. K. (1995). Improving productivity: What faculty think about it and its effect on quality. *Change*, 27(4), 10–20.

McKeachie, W. J., Pintrich, P. R., & Lin, Y. G. (1985). Teaching learning strategies. *Educational Psychologist*, 20(3), 153–160.

Orr, D. W. (1994). *Earth in mind: On education, environment, and the human prospect.* Washington, DC: Island Press.

Palmer, Parker, J. (1993). Good talk about good teaching. *Change*, 25(6), 8–13.

Palmer, Parker, J. (1997). The heart of a teacher. *Change*, 29(6), 15–21.

Pascarella, E. T., & Terenzini, P. T. (1991). *How college affects students.* San Francisco: Jossey-Bass.

Paulsen, M. B., & Feldman, K. A. (1995). *Taking teaching seriously: Meeting the challenges of instructional improvement.* ASHE-ERIC Higher Education Higher Education Report No. 2. Washington, DC: George Washington University, Graduate School of Education and Human Development.

Roth, J. K. (1997). What this book teaches me. In J. K. Roth (Ed.), *Inspiring teaching: Carnegie professors of the year speak* (pp. 226–232). Bolton, MA: Anker.

Schulman, L. S. (1993, November/December). Teaching as community property. *Change, 25*(6), 6–7.

Spence, L. D. (2001, November/December). The case against teaching. *Change, 33*(6), 10–19.

Terenzini, P. T., Rendon, L. I., Upcraft, M. L., Millar, S. B., Allison, K. W., Gregg, P. L., & Jalomo, R. (1994). The transition to college: Diverse students, diverse stories. *Research in Higher Education, 35*(1), 57–73.

Tinto, V. (1987). Dropping out and other forms of withdrawal from college. In L. Noel, R. Levitz, D. Saluri, & Associates (Eds.), *Increasing student retention* (pp. 28–43). San Francisco: Jossey-Bass.

Vorkink, S. (1995). Time on task. In S. R. Halfield (Ed.), *The seven principles in action* (pp. 67–78). Bolton, MA: Anker.

Weingartner, R. H. (1994). Between cup and lip: Reconceptualizing education as student learning. *Educational Record, 75*(1), 13–19.

Welker, R. (1991). Expertise and the teacher as expert: Rethinking a questionable metaphor, *American Educational Research Journal, 28*(1), 19–35.

Winston, G. C. (1994). The decline in undergraduate teaching. *Change, 26*(5), 8–15.

Index

uniqueness of, 15–16, 32, 34, 35 (*see also* Learner diversity, uniqueness of individual learners). *See also* Learning strategies; Learning styles

Learning strategies: and adaptations as related to framework for individualizing instruction, 47–48; alternative conceptualizations, 34–35; development of, 35; related to assessment and instructional problem solving, 58, 63–64 (*see also* Assessment, related to individualizing instruction; Instructional problem solving, related to assessment for individualizing instruction); related to effective instruction, 41; related to individualizing instruction, 42; related to what student derives from new content, 31; uniqueness of, 15–16, 32, 34, 45, 209 (*see also* Learner diversity, uniqueness of individual learners). *See also* Learning characteristics; Learning styles

Learning styles: assessment of, 132 (*see also* Learning and Study Skills Inventory); beyond demographic variables, 15; definition of, 15; usefulness and limits of 16–17. *See also* Learner diversity, beyond demographic variables and learning styles; Learning characteristics; Learning strategies

Mathematics education in United States, state of, 108

Motivation: definition, 33; implications for student engagement and learning, 33–34, 125, 156, 158–159, 168–169, 174–175 (*see also* Learning, and student engagement); strategies for fostering student motivation and engagement, 76–77, 86–87, 93–94, 100, 161, 215–216; strategies for fostering student moti-

vation and engagement, at the level of designing specific learning tasks, 60–61 (*see also* Learning, and student engagement); strategies for fostering student motivation and engagement, at the level of overall instructional approach, 60

National Survey of Student Engagement, 33 (*see also* Learning, and student engagement)

National Technical Institute for the Deaf, 85

New Jersey Institute of Technology, 139

Overview: Case Study, Physics (OSC Physics), 143–145, 146–148

Portland State University, 191–192

Prewriting exercises, 93–95

Reflective teaching, 202; leading to effective learning, 154–155; making assumptions explicit, 18–19, 208 (*see also* Assumptions about learning and teaching; Individualizing instruction, framework for, what the teacher brings); related to assessment, 208–209; in supporting the success of individual students, 17–19, 208. *See also* Instructional problem solving; Teacher, as instructional problem solver

Rochester Institute of Technology, 71–72

San Diego State University, 173–174

Second teaching, 140, 141–143, 144–145, 148 (*see also* Individualizing instruction, within group settings)

Self-regulated learning, 155, 163. *See also*, Individualizing instruction, re-

About the Contributors

Anne C. Coon is professor of language and literature at the Rochester Institute of Technology. She earned her Ph.D. in English from the State University of New York, Buffalo. She has published and presented extensively on the intersection of literature and mathematics and the implications of technology for learning. She also is a published poet. Anne is the recipient of numerous awards and recognitions for outstanding teaching, in and out of the classroom.

Ronald Gautreau earned his Ph.D. in physics from Stevens Institute of Technology, Hoboken, New Jersey. He taught introductory physics courses for engineers for more than thirty years and he has presented that subject in the summer program of New Jersey Institute of Technology's Equal Opportunity Program for more than twenty-five years. His introductory physics telecourses were popular with college and high school students. In the early 1990s, he participated in New Jersey's Master Faculty Program and began his transformation from traditional physics instruction by listening to individual students. He developed an understanding of individual student learning and experimented with pedagogical variations that matched his students' learning needs. Ron began to specialize in teaching introductory physics to nontraditional physics learners with great success. Aside from publishing on physics education reform, Ron continued his research and publications on relativity and relativistic cosmology, uncovering flaws in the theoretical underpinnings that led to the notion of black holes. He was the recipient of the New Jersey Institute of Technology's teaching award and the Harlan Perlis Research Award. Ron died in the spring of 2000.

Ananda Gunawardena is senior lecturer in computer science at Carnegie-Mellon University. He earned his Ph.D. in mathematics from the Ohio University. Ananda has taught mathematics, computer science, and economics. His recent presentations and publications focus on the role of interactive technologies in teaching mathematics and computer sciences as applied in classroom and laboratory settings.

Randall Isaacson is assistant professor of educational psychology at Indiana University, South Bend (IUSB). He earned his Ph.D. in educational psychology from Michigan State University. Randy teaches courses in educational psychology, educational motivation, human relations and interpersonal communication, child and adolescent development, sport psychology, and field experience and student teaching. He is a founding board member of IUSB's University Center for Excellence in Teaching and has received many IUSB recognition awards for excellence in teaching. Randy has numerous presentations and publications on academic risk-taking, self-regulation and performance in college students, and the scholarship of teaching and learning.

Keith Kester is professor of chemistry at Colorado College. He earned his Ph.D. from Harvard University. Keith teaches courses in chemistry, computer science, general studies, and women's studies. Recent publications and presentations focus on teacher development, curriculum development in chemistry, and relationships between science and religion.

Lisa Novemsky is assistant professor of education in the School of Education at Brooklyn College (City University of New York). She earned her Ed.D. in science education from Rutgers University. Lisa is a charter member of the New Jersey Institute of Technology's Master Faculty Program and has many presentations and publications in science education and physics learning, technology in education, education for inclusion, women in science, and science, technology, and society. She teaches courses in science education and early childhood education.

Bunny Paine-Clemes is professor of humanities at the California Maritime Academy (a campus of the California State University System). She earned her Ph.D. in English from the University of Houston. In addition to teaching courses in creative writing, humanities, and psychology, Bunny serves as the campus assessment coordinator. She has taught in community colleges and given presentations on teaching techniques for unlocking creative writing.

Judith Patton is professor in university studies at Portland State University. Judy earned her master of liberal arts and sciences from Reed College. She has taught interdisciplinary freshman courses, family studies, and dance. Her recent presentations and publications focus on interdisciplinary curriculum development in general education and transformation of undergraduate education for urban student success.

Jeffrey E. Porter is an associate professor at the National Technical Institute for the Deaf, Rochester Institute of Technology. Jeff earned his Ph.D. in educational psychology from Washington University, St. Louis. He teaches courses in educational psychology for teachers in training, introduction to psychology, and assessment for classroom teachers. His recent presentations and publications focus on tutoring as a means for individualizing instruction within undergraduate education, the use of technology to support student learning, and alternative meanings of disability in higher education.

Carol Venable is professor of accountancy in the School of Accountancy at San Diego State University. She earned her Ph.D. from the University of Arizona in business administration and accounting. Carol teaches undergraduate courses in accounting information systems, auditing, federal income taxes, and reporting for accountants. Recent presentations and publications focus on developing critical thinking and communication skills within accounting education, and the application of technology to accounting education. Carol is a recent national award winner for Outstanding Application of Technology to Accounting Education.